**Understanding Infrastructure
Edge Computing**

Understanding Infrastructure Edge Computing

Concepts, Technologies and Considerations

Alex Marcham

Registered Office(s)
John Wiley & Sons, Inc., 111 River Street, Hoboken, NJ 07030, USA
John Wiley & Sons Ltd, The Atrium, Southern Gate, Chichester, West Sussex, PO19 8SQ, UK

Editorial Office
The Atrium, Southern Gate, Chichester, West Sussex, PO19 8SQ, UK

For details of our global editorial offices, customer services, and more information about Wiley products visit us at www.wiley.com.

Wiley also publishes its books in a variety of electronic formats and by print-on-demand. Some content that appears in standard print versions of this book may not be available in other formats.

Library of Congress Cataloging-in-Publication Data
Names: Marcham, Alex, author.
Title: Understanding infrastructure edge computing : concepts, technologies and considerations / Alex Marcham.
Description: Hoboken, NJ, USA : Wiley, 2021. | Includes bibliographical references and index.
Identifiers: LCCN 2020050691 (print) | LCCN 2020050692 (ebook) | ISBN 9781119763239 (hardback) | ISBN 9781119763246 (adobe pdf) | ISBN 9781119763253 (epub)
Subjects: LCSH: Edge computing.
Classification: LCC QA76.583 .M37 2021 (print) | LCC QA76.583 (ebook) | DDC 005.75/8–dc23
LC record available at https://lccn.loc.gov/2020050691
LC ebook record available at https://lccn.loc.gov/2020050692

Cover Design: Wiley
Cover Image: © Metamorworks/Shutterstock

Set in 10/13.5pt STIXTwoText by SPi Global, Pondicherry, India
Printed and bound by CPI Group (UK) Ltd, Croydon, CR0 4YY

C9781119763239_250321

To the Fun Police. Careful!

Contents

Preface

How to Use This Book

This book is intended to be read from start to finish in order for the reader to get the most benefit from all of the subject areas which it covers. However, for information on a specific topic, each of the chapters in this book can be read in a relatively standalone manner. There is crossover between chapters in many cases, for example, between a section on the physical redundancy of an edge data centre facility in one chapter and a section describing infrastructure edge computing network level resiliency in another, where if the reader has not read the prior section, some context may be lost.

I hope however you choose to read it that you enjoy reading this book as much as I did when writing it.

About This Book

As with any emerging area of technology, the information presented within this book represents a moment in time and the best practices available at that moment in time. The information here is represented to the best of the author's knowledge and does not favour one vendor over another.

Audience

This book was written for an audience of technologists, decision makers, and engineers in the fields of telecommunications, networking, data centres, and application development and operation who are interested in new emerging areas of technology, such as edge computing, fifth generation (5G), and distributed artificial intelligence (AI).

About the Author

Alex Marcham has been in the networking industry for over a decade working on wireless networks, enterprise networks, telecommunications, and edge computing. He created the terms infrastructure edge and device edge and was the primary author of the Open Glossary of Edge Computing, which is now a Linux Foundation project. When not at work, he can often be seen hiking somewhere remote.

Acknowledgements

This book would not have come to fruition were it not for the help of a few special people.

First, I would like to thank the friends whom I share each day with as we all do our best to keep each other moderately sane from one week to the next. I'll always do my best to listen and help you as you each do for me, and I wish you all the greatest happiness and success in life. That is, unless one of you says that my hair is rubbish again, in which case we will be forced to engage in a cage fight.

Second, thank you to my family. Although we may spend a lot of time apart, physical distance is no match for our combined love of badgers, elephants, and hummingbirds. That said, it is a lot easier to maintain a set of hummingbird feeders than it would be to provide for a load of badgers or a passing herd of elephants, but this is matched by the difficulty of photographing any hummingbird properly.

Third, thanks to the team at Wiley for their insight and support for this project from start to finish. The telepathic portion of this book will be available at a later date, so this will have to do for now.

Finally, thanks to everyone I have spoken to and learned from on the topics of engineering, writing, and life in the past three decades across the world. We are the sum of our choices and experiences.

1

Introduction

Few could have guessed the impact the internet would have on us all at its inception. Today, the internet and the services it provides are essential for billions of people across the world. It is a primary source of communication with friends, family, and our communities; it is the primary way in which we access many essential services, as well as the way that increasing numbers of us go to work, pursue our educational goals, and access sources of entertainment, all on demand.

We did not get to this point by accident. Although the current state of the internet could not have been fully foreseen decades ago, it is due to the continuous efforts of skilled and driven people from across many different disciplines that the modern internet is able to support us as it does today. The story of the internet is not one of a single grand original design; it is one of consistent iteration and ingenuity to adapt to new technical and business challenges which have emerged over the decades.

As they have in the past, new and emerging use cases are driving the evolution of internet and data centre technology. This is resulting in new generations of infrastructure which are reimagining how the internet that we all use on a daily basis should be designed, deployed, and operated as a whole.

Distributed artificial intelligence (AI) and machine learning (ML) are set to permanently reshape how many industries, from healthcare and retail to manufacturing and construction, operate due to their ability to enhance the decision-making process and automate difficult tasks with extraordinary speed and precision. City-scale internet of things (IoT) and cyber-physical systems provide machines the means to interact physically with our world in ways that have been impossible or impractical to achieve before, supported by fifth generation (5G) cellular network connectivity and new versions of cloud computing, which are able to support high-bandwidth, low-latency, and real-time use cases.

Understanding Infrastructure Edge Computing: Concepts, Technologies and Considerations,
First Edition. Alex Marcham.
© 2021 John Wiley & Sons Ltd. Published 2021 by John Wiley & Sons Ltd.

The key element underpinning all of these areas of advancement in both technology and business is infrastructure edge computing. It is one thing to demonstrate a use case in a laboratory environment where everything is a known variable; it is quite another to then operate a commercial service in the real world with all of the messy constraints that introduces, from cost to performance to timescales.

Edge computing is one of the most frequently mentioned emerging technologies, which many believe will make a significant impact on the landscapes of both technology and business during the decade of the 2020s. The concept seems simple: By moving compute resources as close as possible to their end users, theoretically the latency between a user and their application can be reduced, the cost of data transport can be minimised, and these two factors combined will make new use cases practical.

But what really is edge computing, beyond the hype, marketing material, and hyperbole that always accompany any major technological shift? With so many competing definitions of even the most basic elements of the technology, can we succinctly define concepts and terminology which allow us to have a consistent understanding of the challenges we are trying to solve together as an industry?

What are the key factors driving edge computing, and what must a solution provide in order to solve key technical and business challenges? How does edge computing really replace, compete with, or augment cloud computing? What is infrastructure edge computing, and does it stand alongside the traditional regional, national, and on-premises data centre, or does it seek to replace them entirely?

This book aims to answer all of these questions and provide the reader with a solid foundation of knowledge with which to understand how we got to this inflection point and how infrastructure edge computing is a vital component of the next-generation internet – an internet which enables suites of new key use cases that unlock untapped value globally across many different industries.

2

What Is Edge Computing?

2.1 Overview

Before delving into the details and technical underpinnings of infrastructure edge computing, it is necessary to understand some of the history, terminology, and key drivers behind its development, adoption, and usage. This chapter aims to detail some of these factors and provide the reader with a shared base of knowledge to build upon throughout the rest of this book, starting with terminology.

2.2 Defining the Terminology

One of the most challenging aspects of edge computing has been agreeing upon a set of terminology and using it consistently across the many industries to which edge computing is of interest. This is by no means a unique challenge when it comes to emerging technologies, but in the case of edge, it has contributed significantly to confusion between multiple groups and companies who have struggled to reconcile their individual definitions of edge computing so that ultimately a shared view of what the problem to be solved is, in addition to where it is and how to solve it, could emerge and be used.

Part of the challenge in defining edge computing is that by its very nature, the concept of an edge is contextual: An edge is at the boundary of something and often delineates the specific place where two things meet. These two things may be physical, as pieces of hardware; they may be logical, as pieces of software; or they may be more abstract, such as ownership, intent, or a business model.

Understanding Infrastructure Edge Computing: Concepts, Technologies and Considerations,
First Edition. Alex Marcham.
© 2021 John Wiley & Sons Ltd. Published 2021 by John Wiley & Sons Ltd.

Another part of the challenge has been attempting to compress the many dimensions across which a group or company may be concerned with edge computing into a small number of terms which are general enough and yet able to convey a specific meaning. Although it is appealing to create terms which describe a complex and specific set of dimensions as they relate to edge computing, this is a challenging path to create terminology which is general enough to use outside of that same group because the more dimensions a term or phrase aims to address, the less approachable it becomes.

The key to any set of terminology is consistency, and the way to achieve that even in highly technical discussions is to limit the scope of the concepts which the terminology aims to define. Once the key parameters of the definition are established, a neutral set of terminology can be created which then serves as the basis for additional layers of complexity to be added, promoting adoption and usage.

The Open Glossary of Edge Computing [1], a project arising out of the initial State of the Edge report [2] and co-authored by the author of this book, established a neutral and limited dimension set of terminology for edge computing which has seen adoption across the industry and aims to simplify the discussions around edge computing by using the physical location of infrastructure and devices to delineate which type of edge computing each is able to perform by using the last mile network as the line between them to create a clear point of separation. Additional dimensions such as ownership, a specific business model, or any other concern can then be layered on top of this physical definition.

Along with the State of the Edge itself, the Open Glossary of Edge Computing has been adopted by the Linux Foundation's LF Edge [3] group as an official project and continues to contribute to a shared set of terminology for edge computing to help facilitate clear discussion and shared understanding.

2.3   Where Is the Edge?

As previously described, an edge is itself a contextual entity. By itself, an edge cannot exist; it is the creation of two things at the point at which they interact. This somewhat floaty definition is one part of what has made establishing a concise and clear definition of edge computing difficult, especially when combined with the many different factors and dimensions that edge computing will influence.

This book will focus on the accepted definition from the Open Glossary of Edge Computing which uses the physical and role-based separation provided by using the last mile network as a line of demarcation between the infrastructure edge and device edge to provide separation and clarity.

2.3.1 A Tale of Many Edges

Although there are many potential edges, for the purposes of this book and to the most general definition of edge computing, the edge that is of the greatest importance is the last mile network.

The last mile network is the clearest point of physical separation between end user devices and the data centre infrastructure which supports them. In this context, the last mile network refers to the transmission medium and communications equipment which connects a user device to the network of a network operator who is providing wide area network (WAN) or metropolitan area network (MAN) service to one or more user devices, whether large or small, fixed position or mobile.

Examples of last mile networks include cellular networks, where the transmission medium is radio spectrum and the communications equipment used includes radio transceiver equipment, towers, and antennas. Wired networks such as those using cable, fibre, or digital subscriber line (DSL) are also examples of last mile networks which use a copper or fibre-based transmission medium. The specific type of last mile network used is irrelevant here for the terminology of edge computing.

This definition cannot capture all of the potential nuance which may exist; for example, in the case of an on-premises data centre which is physically located on the device side of the last mile network, the owner of that data centre may regard it as infrastructure rather than as a device itself. However, a different definition and accompanying set of terminology offering equal clarity without introducing unnecessary dimensions into the equation has not been established within the industry, and so this book will continue to use the infrastructure edge and device edge, separated by a last mile network.

Fundamentally, if everything can be recast as an example of edge computing, then nothing is truly an example of edge computing. It is similar to referring to a horse and cart as a car because both of them consist of a place to sit, four wheels, and an entity that pulls the cart forward. This is important to note with both the infrastructure edge and the device edge. In the case of the former, an existing data centre which exists a significant distance away from its end users should not be referred to as an example of edge computing. If, however, that same data centre is located within an acceptable distance from its end users and it satisfies their needs, an argument can be made for it to be so.

Similarly, if a device edge entity, such as a smartphone which already had significant local compute capabilities is now referred to as an edge computing device yet does not participate in any device-to-device ad hoc resource allocation and utilisation, this is a somewhat disingenuous application of the term edge computing. However, where there was once a dumb device or no device at all which is now being augmented or replaced with some local compute, storage, and network resources, this can be reasonably argued to be an example of device edge computing, even if limited in capability.

Although "edge washing" of this type is not unique to edge computing as similar processes occur for most technological changes for a period of time, due to the difficulties previously mentioned in the industry arriving at a single set of terminology around edge computing, this can be challenging to identify. This identification challenge can be addressed by using the framework described in the next section.

2.3.2 Infrastructure Edge

The infrastructure edge refers to the collection of edge data centre infrastructure which is located on the infrastructure side of the last mile network. These facilities typically take the form of micro-modular data centres (MMDCs) which are deployed as close as possible to the last mile network and, therefore, as close as possible to the users of that network who are located on the device edge. Throughout this book, these MMDCs will typically be referred to as infrastructure edge data centres (IEDCs), whereas their larger cousins will be referred to as regional or national data centres (RNDCs).

The primary aim of edge computing is to extend compute resources to locations where they are as close as possible to their end users in order to provide enhanced performance and improvements in economics related to large-scale data transport. The success of cloud computing in reshaping how compute resources are organised, allocated, and consumed over the past decade has driven the use of infrastructure edge computing as the primary method to achieve this goal; the infrastructure edge is where data centre facilities are located which support this usage model, unlike at the device edge.

Although it is typically deployed in a small number of large data centres today, the cloud itself is not a physical place. It is a logical entity which is able to utilise compute, storage, and network resources that are distributed across a variety of locations as long as those locations are capable of supporting the type of elastic resource allocation as their hyperscale data centre counterparts. The limited scale of an MMDC compared to a traditional hyperscale facility, where the MMDC represents only a small fraction of the total capacity of that larger facility, can be offset by the deployment of several MMDC facilities across an area with the allocation of only a physically local subset of users to each facility (see Figure 2.1).

2.3.3 Device Edge

The device edge refers to the collection of devices which are located on the device side of the last mile network. Common examples of these entities include smartphones, tablets, home computers, and game consoles; it also includes autonomous

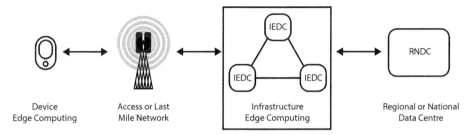

Figure 2.1 Infrastructure edge computing in context.

vehicles, industrial robotics systems, and devices that function as smart locks, water sensors, or connected thermostats or that can provide many other internet of things (IoT) functionalities. Whether or not a device is part of the device edge is not driven by the size, cost, or computational capabilities of that device but on which side of the last mile network that it operates. This functional division clarifies the basic architecture of an edge computing system and allows several more dimensions such as ownership, device capability, or other factors to be built on top.

These devices may communicate directly with the infrastructure edge using the last mile network or may use an intermediary device on the device edge such as a gateway to do so. An example of each type of device is a smartphone that has an integrated Long-Term Evolution (LTE) modem and so is able to communicate directly with the LTE last mile network itself, and a device which instead has only local range Wi-Fi network connectivity that is used to connect to a gateway which itself has last mile network access.

In comparison to infrastructure edge computing, many devices on the device edge are powered by batteries and subject to other power constraints due to their limited size or mobile nature. It would be possible to design cooperative processing scenarios using only device edge resources in which a device can utilise compute, storage, or network resources from neighbouring devices in an ad hoc fashion; however, for the vast majority of use cases and users, these approaches have proven to be unpopular at best with users not wishing to sacrifice their own limited battery power and processing resources to participate in such a scheme at a large scale outside of outliers such as Folding@home, a distributed computing project that is focused on using a network of mains powered computers, not mobile devices. Bearing this in mind, the need for access to dense compute resources in locations as close as possible to their users is provided to users at the device edge by the infrastructure edge (see Figure 2.2).

Although this book is primarily focused on infrastructure edge computing, topics related to device edge computing will be discussed as appropriate, especially as they relate to the interaction that exists between these two key halves of the edge computing ecosystem and their interoperation.

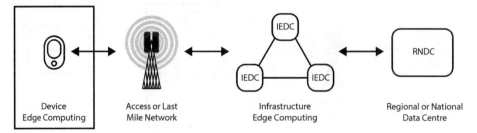

Figure 2.2 Device edge computing in context.

2.4 A Brief History

As with many technologies, upon close inspection, infrastructure edge computing represents an evolution more than the radical revolution that it may initially appear to be. This does not make it any less significant or impactful; it merely allows us to contextualise infrastructure edge computing within the broader trends which over time have driven much of the development of internet and data centre infrastructure since their inception. This progression lets us understand infrastructure edge computing not as the wild anomaly which it has been portrayed as in the past but as the clear progression of an ongoing theme in network design which has been present for decades and driven by the need to solve both key technical and business challenges using simple and proven principles.

2.4.1 Third Act of the Internet

One framework for understanding the technological progression which has brought us to the point of infrastructure edge computing is the three acts of the internet. This structure distils the evolution of the internet since its inception into three distinct phases, which culminate in the third act of the internet, a state which is driven by new use cases and enabled by infrastructure edge computing.

2.4.1.1 The First Act of the Internet

During the 1970s and 1980s, as the internet began to be available for academic and public use, the types of services it was able to support were basic compared to those which would emerge in the 1990s. Text-based applications such as bulletin board systems (BBS) and early examples of email represented some of the most complex use cases of the system. With no real-time element and a simple range of content, the level of centralisation was sufficient to support the small userbase.

It may seem obvious to us in hindsight that the internet would achieve the explosive growth that it has over its lifetime in terms of every possible characteristic from number of users to the volume of data that each individual user would transmit on a daily basis. However, it is a testament to the first principles of the design of the internet that its foundational protocols and technologies have, with the addition of more modern solutions where needed, been able to scale up over time as required.

2.4.1.2 The Second Act of the Internet

During the 1990s and 2000s, internet usage amongst consumers became mainstream as the types of applications and content which the internet supported grew exponentially. The combination of a rapidly growing userbase as millions of people began to connect to the internet for the first time using dial-up modem connectivity and other technologies such as cable or DSL and the addition of more types of content, as well as far more content being available online in general, began to strain the infrastructure of the internet and led to the development and deployment of the first physical infrastructure solutions, which were designed specifically to address these newly emerging issues.

The widespread advent of cloud computing during the 2010s further exacerbated this trend as new generations of data centre facilities were required globally. As more applications and data began to move from local on-premises facilities to remote data centres, the locations of these data centres became more important. Cloud providers began to separate their infrastructure on a per-country basis and, in the case of the United States or other large countries, then began to subdivide their presence within that country into smaller regions, as Amazon Web Services (AWS) has done with their US East and US West regions to optimise performance and the cost of data transportation.

2.4.1.3 The Third Act of the Internet

With the internet now firmly established as a constant in the lives of billions of people across the world who rely on it every day for essential services; connectivity to work, family, and friends; and their primary source of entertainment, the same pressures which drove the evolution from the first to the second act of the internet are mounting once more. More users – now including both humans and machines which will both be essential users of the internet – and a range of new use cases that demand real-time decision making are pushing the current generation of internet infrastructure beyond its original design intentions and capabilities from both a technical and business standpoint.

For these reasons, the 2020s are the first decade of the third act of the internet, a transformation of the network and data centre infrastructure which supports the internet on a global scale towards a new methodology of design, deployment, and operation which heavily relies on infrastructure edge computing to achieve its aims of improving performance, lowering operational costs, and enabling a new class of use cases which are impossible or impractical to support without this continued push towards new levels of network regionalisation and less reliance upon centralised infrastructure.

Now that the three acts of the internet have been established, it is worth considering additional detail in regard to network regionalisation and some early examples of this methodology being applied to the infrastructure of the internet in response to the emergence of the second act itself.

2.4.2 Network Regionalisation

The key trend which the three acts of the internet highlights is the increasing growth of network regionalisation that has occurred over the preceding decades in response to the need to support new use cases, reduce the opportunities for network congestion across the internet, and provide a measurable increase in performance to end users. From a network perspective, which is especially crucial when we are talking about the internet which is itself a global network of networks, generally the shortest path between the source and destination of data in transit is preferable for reasons of both optimal performance and lowest cost, all other characteristics being equal across the network.

This regionalisation of internet infrastructure where key pieces of the network and the data centre move outwards from centralised locations to be deployed on a distributed and regional level is not an accident. As the number of users and their individual usage of the network increased, it became urgent to minimise the length of the network path between the source and destination of traffic.

The Advanced Research Projects Agency Network (ARPANET), first established in 1969 [4], was the precursor to the modern internet. Although other projects existed across the world to develop technologies and standards around such transformative technologies as decentralised networks, packet switching, and resilient routing of data in transit to provide a network with the ability to withstand an attack on its infrastructure, the ARPANET was by far the most influential example.

Although considered to be a leading example of a decentralised network at its inception and during the 1970s and 1980s, by the 1990s the level of centralisation in the architecture of the ARPANET was being strained under the emergence of a large number of new internet users and applications. More regionalisation of internet infrastructure was required to address these challenges, and perhaps the most influential method of achieving this was positioning static content in caches which are placed strategically throughout the network, creating a shorter path between traffic source and destination.

2.4.3 CDNs and Early Examples

One of the best examples of network regionalisation to solve a specific use case as well as address the needs of network operators is the content delivery network (CDN) work done by Akamai Technologies in the late 1990s [5]. Although compared to today the internet and the world wide web it supports were still in their infancy, with both having gained mainstream acceptance only a few years previously, need for the regionalisation of key infrastructure was already beginning to show as the internet became known for distributing new multimedia content, such as images and early examples of hosted video, which began to strain its underlying networks. If left unaddressed, this strain would have limited the uptake of online services by both businesses and home users and ultimately prevented the adoption of the internet as the go-to location for businesses, essential services, shopping, and entertainment.

The importance of CDNs and of the practical proof point of the benefits of network regionalisation which they represent cannot be understated. By deploying a large number of distributed content caching nodes throughout the internet, CDNs have drastically reduced the level of centralised load placed on internet infrastructure on a regional, national, and global scale. Today, they are a fact of life for network operators; these static caches are widely deployed in many thousands of instances from a variety of providers such as CacheFly, Cloudflare, and Akamai, who reach agreements with network operators for their deployment and operation within both wired and wireless networks which provide last mile network connectivity. This regionalisation of static content, by moving the CDN nodes to locations closer to their end users, improves the user experience and saves network operators significant sums in the backhaul network capacity which would otherwise be needed to serve the demand for the content were it located farther away in an RNDC.

Where infrastructure edge computing diverges from the historical CDN deployment model is in its ability to support a range of use cases which rely on dense compute resources to operate, such as clusters of central processing units (CPUs), graphics processing units (GPUs), or other resources which enable infrastructure edge computing to provide services beyond the distribution of static content. Many CDN deployments do not require significant compute density, nor are many of the existing telecommunications sites where they are deployed (such as shelters at the bases of cellular towers, cable headend locations, or central office locations) which were originally designed to support low-density network switching equipment capable of supporting the difficult cooling and power delivery requirements which these dense resources impose. Additionally, in many cases infrastructure edge computing deployments bring additional network infrastructure to provide optimal paths for data transit between last mile networks and edge data centre locations and between edge data centres and RNDCs; typical CDN nodes in contrast will usually be deployed atop existing network operator infrastructure at aggregation points such as cable network headends.

It is worth mentioning here, however, that infrastructure edge computing and the CDN are not at all mutually exclusively concepts. Just as a CDN can operate from various locations across the network today by the deployment of server infrastructure in locations such as cable network headends, they are also able to operate from an IEDC. One or multiple CDNs are then able to use infrastructure edge computing facilities as deployment locations for CDN nodes to replace or augment their existing deployments which use the current infrastructure of the network operator.

Although CDNs in many ways pioneered the deployment methodology of placing numerous content caches throughout the internet to shorten the path between the source and destination of traffic, it is important to understand the distinction between a deployment methodology and a use case. The CDN is a use case which needed a deployment methodology that achieved network regionalisation in order to function. As infrastructure edge computing is deployed, CDNs can also be operated from these locations as well. This is an important point that will be revisited later on the subject of the cloud.

2.5 Why Edge Computing?

Now that we have established the terminology and some of the history behind the concept of edge computing, we can delve deeper into the specific factors which make this technology appealing for a wide range of use cases and users. We will return to many of these factors throughout this book, but this section will establish these factors and the basic reasoning behind their importance at the edge.

2.5.1 Latency

The time required for a single bit, packet, or frame of data to be successfully transmitted between its source and destination can be measured in extreme detail by a variety of mechanisms. Between the ports on a single Ethernet switch, nanosecond scale latencies can be achieved, though they are more frequently measured in microseconds. Between devices, microsecond or millisecond scale latencies are observed, and across a large-scale WAN, such as an access or last mile access network, hundreds of milliseconds of latency are commonly experienced, especially when the traffic destination is in a remote location relative to the source of the data, as is the case when a user located on the device edge seeks to use an application being hosted in a remote centralised data centre facility.

Latency is typically considered to be the primary performance benefit which edge computing and particularly infrastructure edge computing can provide to its end users, although other performance advantages exist such as the ability to avoid current hotspots of network congestion by reducing the length of the network path between a user and the data centre running their application of choice.

Beyond a certain point of acceptability, where the required data rate is provided by the network to the application for it to function as intended, increasing the bandwidth and therefore the maximum data rate that is provided to a user or application on the network for a real-time use case does not measurably increase their quality of experience (QoE). The primary drivers of increased user QoE are then latency, measured at its maximum, minimum, and average over a period of time, and the ability of the system to provide as close to deterministic performance as possible by avoiding congestion.

The physical distance between a user and the data centre providing their application or service is not the only factor which influences latency from the network perspective. The network topology that exists between the end user and the data centre is also of significant concern; to achieve the lowest latency, as direct a connection as possible is preferable rather than relying on many circuitous routes which introduces additional delay in data transport. In extreme cases, data may be sent away from its intended destination before taking a hairpin turn back on a return path to get there. This is referred to as a traffic trombone, with the path which the data takes resembling the shape of the instrument.

2.5.2 Data Gravity

Data gravity refers to the challenge of moving large amounts of data. To move data from where it was collected or generated to a location where it can be processed or stored requires energy which can be expressed both in terms of network and processing resources as well as financial cost, which can be prohibitive when dealing with a large amount of data that has real-time processing needs.

Additionally, many individual pieces of data that are collected or generated can, once processed, be considered noise as they do not significantly contribute to the insight which can be generated by the analysis of the data. Before processing occurs, however, it is difficult to know which pieces of data can be discarded as insignificant, and an individual device may not have all of the contextual information or the analytic processing power available to accurately make this judgement. This makes the use of infrastructure edge computing key as this processing can occur comparatively close to the source of the data before the resulting insight is sent back to a regional data centre for long-term data storage.

2.5.3 Data Velocity

Many pieces of data have a window of time in which they are most useful. If within that time period they cannot be processed and used to extract an actionable insight, the value of that data decreases exponentially. Examples of this type of data include many real-time applications; for example, in the scenario of an industrial robotics control system, instructing the system to perform an action such as orienting a robotic arm in a certain position to catch a piece of falling material is of limited use if the command reaches the arm too late to perform that action in a safe manner before the material falls.

Data velocity is the name given to this concept. If data for real-time applications can be processed and used to extract insight within the shortest possible span of time since its creation or collection, that data and the resulting insight are able to provide their highest possible value to their end user. This processing must occur at a point of aggregation in terms of both network topology and compute resources, such that the resulting data analysis has the full context of relevant events and the power to perform the analysis at an acceptable rate for the application and its users to prevent any issues.

2.5.4 Transport Cost

Particularly with emerging use cases such as distributed artificial intelligence (AI), the cost of transporting data from the device edge locations where it is generated to a data centre location where it can be processed in real time will present a growing challenge. This is not only a technical consideration where network operators must appropriately provision upstream bandwidth in the access and midhaul layers of the network, but there is also a significant operational expenditure (OPEX) and capital expenditure (CAPEX) burden on the network operator associated with over-provisioning long-haul network connectivity.

Infrastructure edge computing aims to address this challenge by moving the locations at which large amounts of data can undergo complex processing, for example, by distributed AI inferencing, to a set of locations which are positioned closer to the sources of this data than with today's centralised data centres. The shorter the distance over which the bulk of data must be transmitted, the lower the data transport cost can be for the network operator which allows any use case reliant on moving such large volumes of data to be more economical and thus more practical to deploy and operate.

2.5.5 Locality

The locality of a system describes both the physical and logical distances between key components of the system. In the context of infrastructure edge computing, the system we are most concerned with spans from a user located on the device edge to an application operating from an edge data centre at the infrastructure edge, a facility which itself is then connected to a regional data centre.

Locality is an important concept in system design. In many ways it is the summation of all of the previously described issues in this section; by addressing all of them, locality allows infrastructure edge computing to enable a new class of use case which generates large amounts of data and needs that data to be processed in a complex fashion in real time. This is the true driving factor of why the infrastructure edge computing model is needed; new use cases in addition to useful augmentations of existing use cases require the capabilities which it offers, and these use cases are valuable enough to make the design, deployment, and operation of infrastructure edge computing itself worthwhile.

2.6 Basic Edge Computing Operation

With an understanding of the basic terminology and history behind infrastructure edge computing, as well as the primary factors, beyond specific use cases, which are driving its design, deployment, and adoption, we can explore an example of how edge computing operates in practice. This example will describe how each of the primary factors are addressed by infrastructure edge computing, as well as how interoperation can occur between the device edge, infrastructure edge, and RNDCs to make a useful gradient of compute, storage, and network resources from end to end.

To begin, let's explore the operation of an application which needs only device edge computing to function. In this scenario, all of the compute and storage resources required are provided by a local device, in this example, a smartphone. Any data that is required is being generated locally and is not obtained from a remote location as the application operates, unlike if the application were reliant on the cloud. The application is entirely self-contained at the user's device, and so operates as follows in Figure 2.3:

In this case, the application is limited by the capabilities of the device itself. All of the resources that the application requires, such as to process data, display a complex 3D rendering to the user, or store data which results from the user's actions, must all be present on the local device and also available to the application. If this is not met, the application will either fail or its operation will be degraded, leaving the user with a suboptimal experience. The use of only device resources requires devices to be powerful enough to provide everything that is required by any application which the user may wish to use, which is especially detrimental to mobile devices which must be battery powered and so not capable of supporting dense amounts of compute and storage resources as may be needed.

The extent to which this is a drawback varies depending on the type of application and on the type of device in question. A lightweight application may operate exactly as intended on a device alone, whereas an application which introduces more of a

Figure 2.3 Self-contained application operating on device.

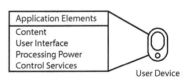

mismatch between the capabilities of the device and the requirements of the application, such as performing high-resolution real-time computer vision for facial recognition on a battery-powered mobile device, may either not operate at all or compromise the user experience, for example, by providing greatly reduced performance or poor battery life, to the extent that the application is unable to fulfil the needs of the user and so fails.

Next, we will add an RNDC to the same application. This addition opens up significant new functionality and opportunities for the application but also comes with its own set of drawbacks. The user's device is connected to the remote data centre using internet connectivity. The device connects to a last mile network, in this example a fourth generation (4G) LTE cellular network, and uses this connection to send and receive data to an application instance which is operating in the remote data centre. This application instance is now using a combination of device resources and data centre resources, most likely by utilising a public or private cloud service. Note, however, that the cloud is a not a physical place in and of itself; it is a logical service which uses physical data centre locations and the resources present inside them to provide those services to its users. This distinction will become increasingly important throughout this book as the infrastructure used by the cloud includes not only RNDCs but also IEDCs (see Figure 2.4).

In this case, the application is able to call on not just the local resources which are available at the device but also remote resources located within the remote data centre in order to perform its functions. These resources are primarily processing power and data storage, both of which are capable of adding additional capabilities and levels of performance to the application which the device alone is unable to support, and access to them often greatly enriches the user experience.

One difficulty with this case is that the RNDC is typically located a large distance away from the end user and their device. This imposes two challenges on the application: When the transmission of large amounts of data is required, that data is sent using long-distance network connectivity which, if all other characteristics of the network are equal, is costlier and is prone to introducing more opportunities for network congestion than the network connectivity which would be required for a shorter distance between a device and its serving data centre. The other challenge is latency: Should a real-time element of the application be required which

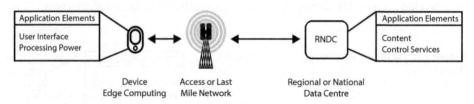

Figure 2.4 Application with access to remote data centre resources.

is not possible or practical to support using the local resources of the device, then the data centre must be physically located close enough to the device for the network connectivity between them to provide acceptable latency so that the user experience will not be degraded and the application will be able to function as intended. This is often challenging as a user may be many hundreds or thousands of miles away from the data centre, which is supporting their application, exacerbating these issues.

Finally, let's examine what this same use case looks like with the introduction of infrastructure edge computing. A single IEDC has been added to our previous topology, with its location being in between the user's device and the RNDC. In addition the IEDC is interconnected with the last mile network which the device is connected to, and is connected back to the RNDC. These two elements are crucial to ensure optimal network connectivity, and they will be explored further in the next chapter.

In this case, the application has access to three sets of resources in increasing degrees of the total potential resources available: the device itself, the IEDC, and the RNDC. As can be seen in Figure 2.5, these resources are physically located in a gradient from the device in the user's hand to a national data centre which may be thousands of miles away. The IEDC is optimally located no more than 15 miles away from the user to minimise latency while still being able to support the dense resources that are required by the application; in this way, the IEDC is able to support the needs of the application in the same way as an RNDC but from a physical location that is much closer to the end user. This blend of characteristics shows the power of the optimal infrastructure edge computing deployment, where an edge data centre can provide a low latency comparable to the device itself, with the back-end muscle of the larger scale data centre.

Although the IEDC is physically a fraction of the size of the RNDC, its resources are capable of providing similar capabilities for the users that are within its area of operations. This is a balance which is achieved by deploying many IEDCs in a given area, such as across a city, and determining the user population that surrounds each one of those facilities; this can be achieved by drawing a 15-mile radius around each

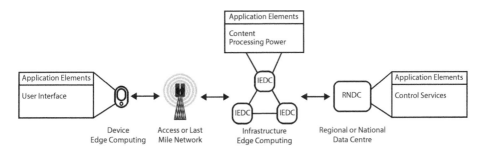

Figure 2.5 Application with access to infrastructure edge computing resources.

facility to maintain low latency. Should additional resources be required over time, additional IEDCs can be deployed, and the user population is then segmented again to prevent individual data centres from becoming heavily congested. This deployment and operation methodology allows infrastructure edge computing to scale over time beyond an initial deployment.

In many cases, the ideal set of resources does not exist in only one of these three locations. To make the best use of this gradient of resources from device to national data centre, an application and its operator should seek to optimise which functions are performed using which set of resources and take into account the individual characteristics of each of these sets. This is a complex issue which will be explored further in this book; do not worry too much about the minutiae of this right now.

As can be seen from this example, just as the use of the RNDC expanded the capabilities of applications which previously could rely on the resources available to them only on a user's device, the IEDC adds an additional layer of resources which augments the capabilities of both the device and the RNDC. This gradient of resources which spans from the device in a user's hands to an IEDC all the way to a national data centre which may be thousands of miles away, is the foundation of the next-generation internet, enabling new valuable classes of applications and use cases to be practical.

2.7 Summary

This chapter formed the basis of an introduction to edge computing, describing the key terminology and many of the core concepts which are driving the design, deployment, and operation specifically of infrastructure edge computing but also with coverage of device edge computing. The terminology and concepts described in this chapter will be used frequently throughout the rest of this book, so it may be useful to refer back to the key points of this chapter at a later date to refresh your memory.

In the next chapter, we will explore the foundations of network technology to give full context to the impact of infrastructure edge computing on these concepts and to then establish a clear baseline on which to build our understanding of how tomorrow's networks will differ from those we see today.

References

1 The Linux Foundation. Open glossary of edge computing [Internet]. 2019 [cited 2020 Sep 30]. Available from: https://www.lfedge.org/openglossary

2 The Linux Foundation. State of the edge [Internet]. 2019 [cited 2020 Sep 30]. Available from: https://www.stateoftheedge.com

3 The Linux Foundation. LF Edge [Internet]. 2020 [cited 2020 Sep 30]. Available from: https://www.lfedge.org

4 DARPA (Defense Advanced Research Projects Agency). ARPANET [Internet]. 2020 [cited 2020 Sep 30]. Available from: https://www.darpa.mil/about-us/timeline/arpanet

5 Akamai Technologies. Company history [Internet]. 2020 [cited 2020 Sep 30]. Available from: https://www.akamai.com/us/en/about/company-history.jsp

3

Introduction to Network Technology

3.1 Overview

To gain a fully contextualised understanding of the impact of infrastructure edge computing on our internet infrastructure, we must have a common understanding of the design and operation of the networks which are in use today from the grand scope of their overall architectural principles to the underlying protocols which make them work. This chapter will explore modern network design and operation, with the aim of establishing the reader with an understanding of the most relevant parts of the topic, which will be used throughout the rest of this book as further concepts are introduced.

3.2 Structure of the Internet

Although the internet may appear to be one single amorphous entity, this is not the case at all. The internet is a network of networks – a complex system of protocols, physical infrastructure, and many layers of agreements between network operators to work together for the mutual benefit of each party involved. A thorough analysis of every aspect of the structure of the internet is outside of the scope of this book, but a progression through the major stages of the parts of internet infrastructure which are most relevant to infrastructure edge computing and its main driving factors is warranted.

Although many of the major stages in the evolution of the internet have been described briefly in the previous chapter, the following sections will describe the implications of these changes for the design of the networks which, joined together, make up the internet as we know it in greater detail.

Understanding Infrastructure Edge Computing: Concepts, Technologies and Considerations,
First Edition. Alex Marcham.
© 2021 John Wiley & Sons Ltd. Published 2021 by John Wiley & Sons Ltd.

During this chapter, the term network endpoint, or endpoint, will be introduced. It refers to any entity on the network that is capable of sending and receiving data which is transmitted using the network. It is a generic term that encompasses any scale, capability, or role that an endpoint may have, from the tiniest embedded sensor for internet of things (IoT) to a room-sized supercomputer, as long as that entity can perform those functions, regardless of the speed at which it does so or its other uses.

3.2.1 1970s

Although telephone or telegram networks, as well as other attempts at computer networks, could be considered precursors to the modern internet, for the purposes of this section we will choose to use the Advanced Research Projects Agency Network (ARPANET) as designed at its inception in 1969 as our starting point. This focuses the discussion in this book on the parts of the internet which are deployed in the United States; however, this pattern has been observed across the internet infrastructure that exists in many other countries worldwide.

The ARPANET was an advanced design and implementation of cutting-edge network technologies that laid the foundation for the internet of today and tomorrow, despite how quaint it may look to some in the present day. It remains an excellent example of how even though over time the specific technologies used to achieve an aim may change as progress is made in their individual areas, solid design principles can still be used to ensure that any changes are in service of the original intention.

3.2.2 1990s

Throughout the 1990s, internet usage rapidly accelerated across a variety of dimensions. Not only did the number of internet users grow quickly, but so did the amount of data that they each sent and received due to a slew of new use cases and services which were accessible online. This pushed internet infrastructure to evolve across each of those same dimensions; coverage expanded, speeds increased across each part of the internet's constituent networks, and regionalisation accelerated.

As described in the previous chapter, the key theme that we can see developing between each of these stages in the architectural evolution of the internet is increasing regionalisation. Both network and server or data centre infrastructure have at this stage begun to push out closer to the locations of their end users, through a combination of expanding existing areas of internet service availability and the addition of new areas over time to capture the growing demand for new key online services.

3.2.3 2010s

The 2010s saw the widespread adoption of two significant use cases for internet infrastructure: cloud computing and streaming video services. Both of these have proved instrumental in how we design large-scale networks in the years since, driving both heavy, highly asymmetric use of downlink network bandwidth during the evenings as people turn to internet-provided alternatives to cable TV services for entertainment and large uploads of data for both transactional purposes as well as long-term storage during the day as more business applications shift from on-premises to cloud services.

Originally deployed during the 1990s, content delivery networks (CDNs) fully came to the fore during this period as a means to achieve several important aims. Moving stores of content closer to their intended users brought a number of key benefits to users, network operators, and content providers, ranging from the ability to provide a better user experience, reducing the growing strain on backhaul and midhaul network infrastructure, and helping to address concerns from network operators that content providers who send much more traffic than they receive were upsetting the established balance of interconnection.

3.2.4 2020s

During the 2020s, the trend of increasing network regionalisation will continue, enabled by the use of infrastructure edge computing. This operational and deployment methodology for moving small data centres and their associated network infrastructure out to increasingly local locations, often 15 miles or less from their end users, augments all of the other regionalisation methods employed from the 1990s through 2020. This methodology and set of technologies results in a densification of the network and data centre resources at the access layer of the network, the closest to their end users.

Infrastructure edge computing enables the architecture of the internet to progress from its origins in the ARPANET of a handful of comparatively centralised locations to a highly distributed architecture that pushes network and data centre infrastructure out into urban and rural areas, building on what began as a network with four initial hosts back in 1969 into a regionalised and densified internet that brings the capabilities of the data centre in terms of application operation, data storage, and network interconnection to potentially thousands of micro data centre locations across even a single country.

3.2.5 Change over Time

It may seem easy to look back at the design decisions made in previous architectural generations of the internet and scoff: If the benefits of network regionalisation are clear and the first steps along this path had already been taken, then why not build it out in this way from the beginning? Like all choices made during system design, there are many trade-offs which govern whether it is feasible both technically and economically to deploy a specific level or type of infrastructure at a given time. The choices made during a particular decade as highlighted previously must be appreciated within the time and context they were made in, without judging them by what we now know in the present.

Although these changes over time to the architecture of the internet in response to the needs of both its users and its operators are remarkable, it is important to note the level of difficulty that is inherent in making any change to a complex network system. The next section describes one of the methods used by the global network engineering community to minimise the impact of any changes on other parts of the system so that changes can often be made as and when they are ready, with no need to concurrently change other links or endpoints in the network to ensure correct operation.

3.3   The OSI Model

Any detailed discussion of network technology would be incomplete without a shared understanding of the Open Systems Interconnection (OSI) model [1]. This is an often used conceptual model which allows us to create highly interoperable, open, and scalable communication systems by categorising the technological functions required by the network into a stack of layers that are numbered from 1 to 7, each of which has a set of interfaces to communicate with its directly adjacent layers (see Table 3.1).

This model is very powerful, as by isolating a set of technological functions into a specific layer that has interfaces to talk to the layers it is directly adjacent to, changes to any one specific layer do not need to impact the operation of any other layer in the system, allowing asynchronous evolution of the entire stack of network technologies where one or more layers experience more rapid change than their neighbouring layers. An example of this can be seen with each new generation of Wi-Fi; significant advances in speed can be achieved by changing only layers 1 and 2, without any of the upper layers being aware of the change. Consider what the situation would be like if the entire network technology stack had to be remade to accommodate a change at any layer. The stack that would result would be highly inflexible as even an isolated change would require significant work. Over time, this would become a key barrier to keeping up with the edge of technological progress and prevent open contribution to the stack by other companies or individuals, limiting innovation.

Now that the reasoning behind the OSI model has been established, we will briefly describe the functionality of each layer as it is relevant to infrastructure edge computing, and the number of each layer will be used throughout this book to quickly refer to the concepts that they represent. In this example, we will be taking the perspective of a network endpoint receiving data that has been transmitted across the network, so

Table 3.1 OSI model layer numbers, names, and examples.

OSI layer number	OSI layer name	Example entity or protocol
1	Physical	Copper cabling
2	Data link	Ethernet
3	Network	IPv4
4	Transport	TCP
5	Session	NFS
6	Presentation	PNG
7	Application	HTTP

our progression will be from layer 1 through layer 7. When considering the process of sending data, this progress through the layers is reversed in order as data flows from layer 7 down to layer 1 to be transmitted across the physical network.

3.3.1 Layer 1

From a physical perspective, the first layer of the OSI model is at the bottom, layer 1. This layer is known as the physical layer and is responsible for encapsulating the functions of the network which are concerned with the physical transmission medium that is being used to send and receive data, whether that be radio frequency (RF), in the case of many wireless networks, copper cabling, fibre optic cabling, or another medium of choice. Although these three options are the most commonly used today, other options such as infrared (IR) light exist and are used in some specific use cases.

As well as the physical transmission medium itself, layer 1 includes the functions that are needed to encode and decode all data transmissions using that medium. For example, to send and receive data across copper cabling, an encoding scheme must be used to convert some digital application data into a sequence of physical electrical energy, which is then applied to the copper transmission medium, which carries those electrical signals to the remote end of the transmission medium where a corresponding decoding scheme reverses the process, turning these electrical signals back into the digital application data which they represented and passing this data up to layer 2 of the stack.

3.3.2 Layer 2

Layer 2 is known as the data link layer and is responsible for a few key functions of the network stack. One of these is medium access control (MAC), which is the process of determining the means by which a network endpoint may access the transmission medium to send data. In many networks, this is not as simple as merely transmitting immediately whenever layer 3 communicates to layer 2 that it has data to send. Consider a wireless network as an example: The radio spectrum used by these networks is a shared medium, where transmissions from one network endpoint are able to be received by many other network endpoints. If one endpoint were to transmit without checking to see if the "coast is clear" and transmitted at the same time as another endpoint, it is likely that both transmissions would be garbled, resulting in data being lost or being retransmitted. This is to be avoided wherever possible as it reduces the efficiency of the network considerably.

Protocols operating at layer 2 are also responsible for providing link local addressing, a form of network endpoint identification where endpoint interfaces are given locally unique identifiers that enable intranetwork communication but which are not intended to be used as globally unique; this means that they are not suitable for use between networks but can uniquely identify endpoints on the same network. Through various means such as broadcast and multicast data transmission, these link local addresses are often used to allow an endpoint to discover the globally unique addresses of the endpoints it needs to communicate with, or at least that of the next hop in the path to get there.

3.3.3 Layer 3

Referred to as the network layer, layer 3 is the only layer of the OSI model which is responsible for internetwork addressing, where network endpoints can be assigned globally unique addresses. This is crucial as without this function, endpoints that are located in other networks would not be reachable and the internet (as a network of networks) would not be able to exist as it does today.

The globally unique addresses which layer 3 provides are mapped on to the link local addresses that are used by protocols operating at layer 2 by a process that is specific to each of those lower layer protocols. This ensures that when data sent from an endpoint on an external network targeted for an endpoint on the local network enters the local network, it can be correctly forwarded using its link local address (such as a MAC address in the case of Ethernet) as if that traffic had originated on the local network to begin with. The external network endpoint is unaware of this process entirely.

3.3.4 Layer 4

Layer 4 is named the transport layer. This label may seem odd, but it is for good reason: Above the means to transcode digital data into physical signals at layer 1, the MAC functions and link local addressing provided by layer 2, and the globally unique endpoint addressing capabilities enabled by layer 3, there is a need for a group of functions which determine how to send and receive data on the network at a layer of abstraction, which enables them to perform tasks such as flow control and integrity checking of any data received without reliance upon any specific set of layer 1, 2, or 3 technologies. This transport layer is the bridge between the application at higher layers of the stack and the underlying network technologies below, whatever they may be.

Two popular examples of layer 4 protocols are the Transmission Control Protocol (TCP) and the User Datagram Protocol (UDP). The primary difference between these two is that despite the fact that both protocols operate at the transport layer, TCP provides a guarantee that any traffic sent across the network will be delivered to its destination complete and in the order that it was sent. Comparably, UDP provides no such guarantee; data sent using UDP does not create any layer 4 acknowledgement from its destination that it was or was not received correctly. If a piece of data were lost in transit across the network and the application were using TCP, the receiver of the data would notify the sender and a retransmission would be arranged, whereas with UDP, it would just be lost. Although this may seem like a large drawback, whether it is or not depends on the use case; for real-time applications such as video conferencing or Voice over Internet Protocol (VoIP) calls, it is beneficial to the user experience to allow a certain amount of lost data compared to incurring the delay of the sender having to retransmit any lost data, which can result in odd sound or video to an end user.

Although still very commonly used, the TCP and UDP protocols are not always the optimal choice. These protocols emerged in 1974 and 1980, respectively, and as such predate the applications that today generate the vast majority of traffic on the internet and its constituent networks, sometimes by several decades. Modern alternatives (such as the Stream Control Transmission Protocol [SCTP], which is designed to incorporate many of the desirable features of both TCP and UDP) are emerging and will see increasing use in the near future for use cases that require their additional capabilities such as native support for multihoming in the case of SCTP, where two endpoints may each have multiple globally unique addresses, allowing for the use of redundant network paths for added resiliency.

3.3.5 Layers 5, 6, and 7

These three layers are referred to as the session, presentation, and application layers, respectively. In practice their details are not encountered as much from the network perspective as they are by the inner workings of a specific application, which is why they are not going to be described in the same level of detail as the lower levels of the stack are in this chapter. As the functions at these layers are often handled within a single application at a single endpoint, the protocols at each of these upper layers as well as the interfaces between them tend to be less distinct than those at the lower layers where interoperation between endpoints from many sources is needed for the network to function.

As further degrees of interoperation between the network and the processing resources of the data centre both at the infrastructure edge and at the regional or national scale are used to support next generation use cases, the functions of these three upper layers of the OSI model will be increasingly used to provide that underlying network and data centre infrastructure with intelligence about the specific characteristics of the application in use, which will then be used to make nuanced decisions about how infrastructure resources can be allocated and used for optimal cost and user experience.

3.4 Ethernet

Ethernet is an example of a layer 2 protocol and is the most commonly used layer 2 protocol today. A basic understanding of some of the characteristics of Ethernet is useful in the context of infrastructure edge computing, as the protocol is so widely used both within the infrastructure edge data centre, as well as between them and between other facilities of both similar and larger scale.

Ethernet uses broadcast communication to perform network endpoint discovery. This means that when an Ethernet endpoint receives a frame with a destination MAC address and the endpoint does not have an existing entry in its switching table for that destination MAC address, a request is sent to all other Ethernet endpoints on that segment of the network, asking for the location of the endpoint which has that destination MAC address assigned to one of its interfaces. The protocol was designed in this way for implementation simplicity and low cost, both of which have helped Ethernet become established as the dominant layer 2 protocol today; but there is an equal drawback in regard to the inefficiency of this behaviour in a larger network, where the volume of broadcast traffic can be substantial enough to impact the performance of network endpoints and ultimately of the network.

The protocol is capable of supporting frame sizes between 64 and 1518 bytes as standard, and some equipment can be configured to support so-called jumbo frames of up to 9600 bytes. The latter are useful for some use cases which rely on these jumbo frames in order to lower the overhead of large numbers of Ethernet frame headers involved when carrying data, or for protocols such as those of storage area networks (SANs), which natively use data segmentation sizes closer to a jumbo frame.

The most common type of traffic encountered on a modern network today is an Ethernet frame that encapsulates an Internet Protocol version 4 (IPv4) or Internet Protocol version 6 (IPv6) packet, using TCP or UDP as its transport layer protocol, carrying some application data from a source endpoint to its destination endpoint.

This combination of protocols is used for a wide range of use cases and across almost every scale of network in common use today.

3.5 IPv4 and IPv6

Both IPv4 and IPv6 are examples of layer 3 protocols. They are the most commonly encountered layer 3 protocols, and as such, they provide a method for the end-to-end addressing of endpoints across the network using a globally unique address space. When each endpoint has a globally unique identifier, data can be addressed to a specific endpoint without ambiguity; this function allows data to be transmitted between endpoints which reside on different networks, even at a worldwide scale.

In the context of both the internet and infrastructure edge computing, both of the Internet Protocol (IP) versions, IPv4 and, to a growing extent, IPv6 are ubiquitous. Any application, endpoint, or piece of infrastructure must support these protocols; no real competitor currently exists and is unlikely to do so for some time due to the ubiquity of both IPv4 and IPv6, driving their integration into billions of devices and applications across the world. In addition, many of the issues with these protocols have been tempered by the industry using various means, so few see a pressing need to replace them.

IPv6 adoption, although behind its earlier cousin IPv4 as of today, is growing across the world and is expected to reach parity with and then exceed the amount of global internet traffic transmitted atop IPv6 compared to IPv4 as measured on a daily basis. One of the growth areas for IPv6 is expected to be the widespread deployment of city-scale IoT, where potentially millions of devices must be able to connect with remote applications operating in other networks, requiring these devices to have a globally unique IP address. This need combined with the global exhaustion of the IPv4 address space looks set to drive the future adoption of IPv6, although IPv4 address conservation mechanisms such as network address translation (NAT) remain in use and will continue to be for many years ahead.

3.6 Routing and Switching

Both routing and switching are vast topics, each with significant history and many unique intricacies. The focus of this book is not on either of these fields, but they are closely related to any discussion of network design and operation, and so this section will describe some of the key points related to routing and switching that are relevant to network design and operation for modern networks so that it can be referred to during later chapters as many of the same core principles apply to the new networks being designed, deployed, and operated to support infrastructure edge computing as well.

3.6.1 Routing

On the subject of routing, which is the process where a series of network endpoints use layer 3 information as well as other characteristics of the data in transit and of the network itself to deliver data from its source to its destination, there are two primary approaches to performing this process.

One approach is referred to as hop-by-hop routing. Using this routing methodology, the onus for directing data in transit on to the optimal path towards its destination is placed on each router (a term referring to an endpoint which makes a routing decision, based on layer 3 data and other knowledge of the network, in order to determine where to send data in transit) in the path. Each of these routers uses its own local knowledge of the state of the network to make its routing decisions.

Another approach is resource reservation. This approach aims to reserve a specific path through the network for data in transit. Although this approach may seem preferable (and is in some cases), historically it has been challenging to implement as the act of resource reservation across a network requires additional state to be maintained for each traffic flow at each network endpoint in the path from source to destination to ensure that the resource allocation is operating as expected. In cases where the entire network path between the source and destination is under the control of a single network operator, this methodology is more likely to be successful; a resource reservation scheme is easier to implement in this case as the network operator can be aware of all of the resources that are available on the path, compared to a path which involves multiple network operators who may not provide that level of transparency or may not wish to allocate available resources to the traffic.

Both of these approaches seek to achieve best path routing, where traffic is sent from its source to its destination using the combination of network endpoints and links, which results in the optimal balance of resource usage, cost, and performance. If both approaches have the same aim, why are there two approaches to begin with? First, the definition of what would make a particular path from source to destination the best path is not always as simple as the lowest number of hops or using the lowest latency links in the network; once factors such as cost are introduced, business logic and related considerations begin to influence the routing process, which is where resource reservation becomes more favourable in many cases. Second, there is a trade-off between the ability of a single system which oversees the network to identify and reserve specific paths in a manner that provides enhanced functionality or performance compared to a hop-by-hop routing approach. Across a large network such as the internet, it is not uncommon for traffic to pass through a number of networks, many of which use hop-by-hop routing alongside others which use resource reservation internally.

One consideration is when a router receives traffic for which it does not know a specific route on which to send the traffic to reach its destination. In this case, a router will typically have a default route configured. This is a catch-all route for destination networks that the router is unaware of, which often directs the traffic back to another router within the network in the hope that a route will be found for the traffic. The alternative is for the traffic to be dropped and a message be sent back to the source of the traffic indicating this. Should a situation arise where two routers are each other's default route, traffic will not bounce between them forever; both IPv4 and IPv6 feature a time to live (TTL) field in their packet headers, which will result in the traffic being discarded if it becomes stuck in such a routing loop for a considerable period of time, protecting the network against unnecessary congestion caused by routing misconfiguration or any temporary conditions.

3.6.2 Routing Protocols

The majority of network and internet routing is performed by using the hop-by-hop approach today. As this approach relies on each router using its own knowledge of the network in order to make any routing decisions, it stands to reason that each router must have a means by which to generate its own map of the network so that it can make the optimal routing decision for a given piece of data. Routing protocols are used to allow a router to generate this network map. Using a routing protocol, routers exchange information between themselves across the network including the state of their local links and the locations of any IP address ranges that they are aware of. These pieces of data, combined with cost metrics and best path calculations which the particular routing protocol in use provides, are then used by each router to generate its own picture of what the network looks like from its perspective. When each router in the network has generated this picture or map of what the network looks like, hop-by-hop routing can be performed with each router using this map to route data to its destination according to the best route of which it is aware using this information.

Routing protocols can be organised into two categories: Interior Gateway Protocols (IGPs), as well as Exterior Gateway Protocols (EGPs). The former is concerned with routing data in transit across the network using layer 3 information within a single network. In this context, a network is defined as the administrative domain of a single network operator, even if the networks within that domain consist of multiple segments of layer 3 devices. In comparison, EGP protocols provide the means to route data between the networks of different network operators. Whether a network is internal or external is typically not a major technical distinction; rather it is one of administration, as each of the network operators agree to establish what is referred to as a peering between their networks by means of their EGP of choice to route data between them. This is the combination of an agreement at the business level between two network operators to accept traffic from and send traffic to each other's networks as peers, as well as the establishment of a peering session using their agreed EGP.

Routing traffic through a network to its destination relies on an effective way of calculating the best path to that destination. There are many ways of determining what that best path is and which set of metrics should be used to characterise the desirability of each endpoint to endpoint connection which, combined, creates the network as a whole. Early examples of IGP protocols such as Routing Information Protocol (RIP) used a simple metric of hop count to determine the best path for traffic from its source to its destination. In this context, a hop was defined as a layer 3 endpoint, and the lower the number of hops on a network path, the faster it was assumed the path would be. In reality this simplistic metric does not capture the details of the network such as link speed, the use at that time of the links between endpoints, available endpoint routing capability, or other factors.

These limitations led the early routing protocols such as RIP to provide suboptimal routing decisions. This issue spurred the development of routing protocols which used more sophisticated measures of understanding the status of each link in the network and calculating the optimal path from source to destination for traffic. Edsger W. Dijkstra created the Shortest Path First (SPF) algorithm in 1956 [2]. This algorithm rapidly finds the shortest path between two given nodes in a graph, and its use in communications networks was studied since shortly after its inception to improve their efficiency.

Two examples of commonly used modern IGPs are Open Shortest Path First (OSPF) and Intermediate System to Intermediate System (IS-IS). Both of these protocols are used today on large-scale internal networks, and both use the SPF algorithm. The choice of which specific IGP to use on a network is a decision to be made based on the individual requirements of the specific network, which draws on a wide range of criteria that will not be fully described in this book; but for large-scale internal networks IS-IS is often preferred over OSPF. Regardless, both of these protocols perform the same function in the network and allow efficient routing to be performed that takes into account a more realistic and detailed view of the network topology than other preceding protocols were capable of, such as RIP.

As has been previously described, the internet is a network of networks and so as traffic is routed to its destination, it is likely to cross several different networks, each of which are operated by different entities. While an IGP provides the internal network of one of these network operator entities with information on the topology of the network, when the traffic must egress to an external network, an EGP is required. Much like how an IGP uses information from each router on an internal network to create a topological view of the network, such as the status of each router's interfaces and the many subnetworks that each router may be connected to, an EGP allows a router in one network to inform a router in another network of the destinations that are reachable through that network and various characteristics of paths that it can provide to peer networks to deliver traffic to those destinations.

Without an EGP, each internal network along the multi-network path between the source and the destination of a particular traffic flow would be flying blind. An EGP provides each network with an understanding of the paths available to it through external networks. With this information, each network can make an informed decision on which path to send traffic, optimising for performance, cost, additional services, or any key preference that the network operator has due to business need.

The most common EGP in use is the Border Gateway Protocol (BGP). The BGP was originally introduced to the internet in 1994 and has seen several iterations over time, resulting in the current version (Border Gateway Protocol version 4 (BGP4)), which forms the underpinning of the global IPv4 and IPv6 routing system the internet relies on to function. Although considerably older than many of the users of the internet today, BGP has proven to be a scalable protocol and a large part of the ongoing success of the modern internet.

One of the key aspects of BGP is its routing table. Although all routing protocols maintain a routing table of some type, which is a store of known destination networks and the metrics of the various paths which can be used to reach them that are known to that network endpoint, BGP is unique in that as it is the dominant EGP in use today, the size of the total routing table is orders of magnitude larger than that encountered by instances of IGPs, even compared to very large internal networks. Separate routing tables are maintained for IPv4 and IPv6, despite BGP being used for both protocols.

This is typically not an issue but has in some cases resulted in the BGP routing table exhausting the memory resources available in some routers. One technique to address this is route summarisation, where many more specific routes can be addressed as a single summary route, similar to how in a library all book titles starting with E can be used to represent all the books starting with Ea, Ex, or Es. During this section, the term subnetwork is used; this refers to a specific range of routable address space, such as books starting with Ex, to continue our library example, rather than everything titled E.

Another key concept in BGP is that of the autonomous system (AS). Each AS represents a single and unique administrative network domain that is owned and operated by a specific network operator, distinct from any other network domain. An AS is identified by a unique number which is assigned to it and which is used to differentiate one AS from another. Interoperation between networks using BGP uses these AS numbers for exactly that purpose, and people who spend a lot of time arranging internetwork connectivity will typically refer to external networks by their BGP AS numbers as well.

As BGP is used to route traffic between networks that are under the control of different operators, the protocol includes a set of capabilities to route traffic based not only on what is calculated to be the best path towards the destination in terms of performance (even though BGP's measurements of performance are not as advanced as those of an IGP in most cases) but also based on the explicit preference of both network operators. This means that any business agreements they have created in regard to the routing of each other's traffic can be implemented between their networks by BGP. The reasons for these arrangements are many, and they have helped spur the growth of the internet.

On each BGP router, the BGP protocol allows the configuration of the local preference and the multi exit discriminator (MED) values. Although both of these values are used to directly influence routing decisions, they operate from two different sides. As the sender of traffic, one BGP router may have a local preference value configured which instructs it to use a specific route to reach a destination, and concurrently the MED value configured on the receiver of traffic allows that router to indicate to the sender which path it would prefer to receive traffic on, which is entering its AS. Although the effect of the MED value can be overridden by any of its BGP peers, this feature allows a BGP AS to attempt to influence the paths that traffic inbound to the AS takes. BGP path selection is a detailed topic itself, but the concepts in this section will provide the required background for later sections in this book.

3.6.3 Routing Process

To contextualise all of the routing information presented so far in this chapter, let us use an end-to-end example of traffic being routed across multiple networks from its source to its destination (see Figure 3.1). In this example, traffic will flow from a source on the left of the diagram to a destination on the right.

In this example, traffic will need to be routed across two networks which are peering using BGP as their EGP. One network is using OSPF for its IGP, while the other will use IS-IS. The traffic is using IPv4, though the same concepts and flow seen in this example would apply to IPv6 traffic as well:

1) Traffic is generated by a device within the first network. Its destination is a server in the second network. The majority of internet use cases follow this general

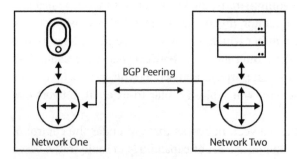

Figure 3.1   Routing process example.

structure; examples include a device accessing a video or a cloud service from a remote server across networks.

2) The device sends its traffic to its local gateway, which is a router. This router inspects the IP packet headers of the traffic from the device and deduces that its neighbouring router is the best route available to reach this destination. The information to inform this deduction was the result of the router querying its local routing table, which was generated by OSPF using information received from the local router and its neighbouring routers across the network.

3) The traffic is sent to that neighbouring router, which then inspects its own routing table and determines that the best route to the destination of that traffic is via an external network. This same router has established a BGP peering with that external network, and so it sends the traffic to its BGP peer. Although it is an external network, this process is identical from a routing perspective to how traffic was moved within the network, excepting the use of BGP.

4) Once the traffic has entered the second network, the router which received it repeats the process of looking up the optimal route to the destination of the traffic in its routing table. This routing table informs the router that the optimal path is through its neighbouring router within the network, and so it sends the traffic over its link to that router. Note that although this network uses IS-IS for its internal routing protocol, once the routing table is created by the routing protocol, the traffic routing process itself is identical on a hop-by-hop basis.

5) Finally, the last router receives the traffic and, upon inspecting its routing table, discovers that the subnetwork containing the destination of the traffic is directly attached to one of its local interfaces. The router sends the traffic over that link to its destination, and the process of routing traffic from source to destination is complete. Often traffic will be sent responding to the traffic which was sent; in this case, the same process is performed, from right to left.

Regardless of the size or number of networks between the source and destination of traffic, this is the routing process which takes place. Although different routing protocols differ in how they create their routing tables, how they pass information between each other to create them, and the criteria they use to determine the optimal route, this does not affect the general routing process as above.

3.6.3.1 Switching

Compared to routing, switching uses only layer 2 information in order to direct network traffic to its destination. In the example of Ethernet, as described previously, the Ethernet frame header itself features a pair of MAC addresses, which are the source and destination addresses of the traffic. This section will focus primarily on Ethernet as a data link layer protocol used to perform switching, just as the previous section focused on IPv4 and IPv6 as network layer protocols used to perform routing.

In this section, much as devices that perform routing on network traffic are referred to as routers, a device which performs switching on network traffic will be referred to as a switch. Although these terms are often used interchangeably in the networking industry, in this book routing refers only to the layer 3 process of directing traffic from its source to its destination and switching refers in turn only to the layer 2 process that is used to achieve this same end goal. As will be seen in an upcoming section, these two processes are typically used together to operate a modern network.

Switching is generally used on networks which are local in scope. This is due to both the nature and limitations of link layer endpoint addressing but also the operational characteristics of switching as a process. Unlike IP addresses, Ethernet MAC addresses are not assigned to endpoints or interfaces of endpoints by the network administrator whether manually or via automation. Instead Ethernet MAC addresses are assigned to an endpoint or endpoint interface at the factory where they are produced and are not intended to be changed during normal operation. This does not allow the network to be arranged in an hierarchical or summarised fashion as is possible using a layer 3 protocol such as IP and so makes organising and scaling the network more difficult due to a few key operational factors.

Much like the routing table described in the previous section, all switches maintain a switching table that operates in a similar fashion; once populated, it is a record of the local interfaces of that switch via which a particular destination MAC address can be reached. This table is then used by the switch to forward traffic to those destinations as it is received. Each switch makes a forwarding decision by using the contents of its switching table, much like the hop-by-hop routing process described earlier.

A key difference between routing and switching is in how the routing table and switching table are built. As previously described, a routing protocol exchanges information between routers across the network and in some cases even with external networks in order to create its routing table. However, in the case of switching there is no such protocol; the switching table is created over time by using flooding, learning, and forwarding. This is a simpler, albeit far less scalable method of determining where in the network a particular destination is located. When a switch receives traffic without a corresponding entry in its switching table, it floods a request for the destination of that traffic from all of its interfaces besides the one it received the traffic on. The switch then expects an endpoint within the network to reply that it knows or is the destination of the traffic; the interface that this reply is received on is marked in the switching table as the path to reach the destination, and the original traffic plus any subsequent traffic to the same destination is then sent using this interface.

Unlike routing, due to the comparatively simple methods by which the locations of endpoints are learnt when using switching, a switch does not have a sophisticated view of the cost of the paths which are available or of the overall network topology. Although protocols such as the Spanning Tree Protocol (STP) and other similar protocols provide some level of intelligence to a switching network, primarily to enhance network resiliency by eliminating broadcast loops or enabling the network to utilise multiple layer 2 paths without creating these loops, switching decisions are inherently simpler than those which are possible with routing and so require simpler networks.

Without the ability to summarise layer 2 addresses due to how they are randomly distributed across a network or networks because they are statically assigned in the factory to an endpoint, switching would not scale to a network the size of the internet. The size of the switching tables required and the impact of the flooding process on the network would quickly become untenable. However, layer 2 networks are valuable in their simplicity and speed for many use cases, and for them to be used in a variety of different ways, new capabilities have been added to them over time.

One of the most important concepts in this regard for layer 2 networks is the virtual local area network (VLAN). VLANs represent a simple example of network overlays, where the physical local area network (LAN) network itself is used to support a number of virtual networks which operate on top of it and are all logically distinct from one another despite utilising the same physical resources such as switches, endpoints, and links.

Network virtualisation is a key topic which will be referenced in later chapters, and VLANs provide us with a framework upon which we can build our understanding of this topic. Consider the following example of a single LAN which is connecting multiple endpoints by using a common set of physical resources. However, each of these endpoints is owned and is operated by a different department within the same company, each of whom has very strict requirements for who has access to their network and how their network operates. The network architecture team now has two choices:

1) Construct a separate physical network for each department at excessive cost and complexity.
2) Use a single physical network and logically split it into virtual networks for each department.

As you might imagine, the second option is far more attractive from a cost standpoint as long as the underlying physical network is capable of supporting the combined requirements of all of the logical or virtual networks used by each department. This is an example of network virtualisation making a single, common physical network capable of multi-tenant operation, rather than just single tenant. This is itself another key trend which will be returned to throughout later chapters, as it has enabled many telecoms networks and data centres to become increasingly economically viable worldwide. Without supporting multi-tenant operation, investing in these physical pieces of infrastructure is a greater challenge, and so the ability of the industry to provide ubiquitous services is greatly reduced.

For an example of how this works from a technical perspective, consider the following traffic flow:

1) An endpoint on VLAN 1 sends traffic to another endpoint on VLAN 1. That destination endpoint happens to be across the network, with traffic passing through a single switch.
2) As the switch receives the traffic, it recognises that it is from an endpoint that is assigned to VLAN 1. This may occur because the traffic was already tagged (using the VLAN tag field, which the 802.1Q standard by the Institute of Electrical and Electronics Engineers (IEEE) added to the standard Ethernet header), or it may occur because the switch has been configured to recognise that all endpoints on an interface are in a specific VLAN, and so when it receives standard untagged traffic, it tags them itself.
3) The switch consults its switching table, which as well as being a record of where destinations for traffic are located across the network is also a record of which interfaces and endpoints reside in which VLANs. This means that even if traffic arrives from an endpoint on VLAN 1 and the switch does not know the location of its destination, it will flood a request for that destination out of interfaces it knows are assigned to VLAN 1 only. This keeps each VLAN operating separately from one another. The switching table in this example does know the location of the destination, and so the traffic is sent out of the corresponding interface.
4) The destination endpoint receives the traffic, and no endpoints on any other VLAN were aware of what was sent or if anything was sent because each VLAN operates separately.

The trend of network virtualisation follows similar trends that have been seen at the server level in the past decade, where virtualisation tools such as virtual machines (VMs) and containers have been instrumental in allowing multiple applications or instances of operating systems (OSs) to operate in harmony alongside one another atop the same piece of physical server hardware. Much like in our VLAN example, these separate logical entities are unaware of each other despite operating on the same physical resources. This is vital as it allows entire companies who may be competitors to be capable of operating on the same physical infrastructure, as long as they are logically separated.

VLANs are a very common example of this trend as applied to networks, but they are far from the only example. Network virtualisation and isolation between users of the same physical underlying infrastructure can be achieved at layer 3 as well, using technologies such as virtual routing and forwarding (VRF). With VRF, a router operates with multiple instances of a routing table at the same time; these routing tables do not share routes, and so they operate in much the same way as VLANs do, with traffic being handled by each independent routing instance depending on the interface the traffic was received on, or other tagging criteria applied to that traffic to direct it to a specific table.

The ability of these and other technologies to enable a piece of physical infrastructure to support multiple users while concurrently isolating their activities from one another is, as briefly mentioned above, a key consideration; the ideal infrastructure edge computing system is itself multi-tenant and so requires this type of isolated multi-user operation at many levels throughout the entire system to be as attractive as possible economically to both its customers and its operator, spanning from the network infrastructure required to support it through to the distributed data centres themselves.

3.6.3.2 Network Boundaries

In the previous sections in this chapter describing the functions of layer 2 and layer 3 of the OSI model, intranetwork and internetwork network endpoint addressing were described, respectively. This leads to the question: How can we determine the boundaries of a network for the purpose of endpoint addressing? Where should switching end and routing begin to be used in a given network?

The majority of networks use a combination of both routing and switching at different locations to operate effectively. On a local network segment or subnetwork where a router connects directly or via a switch to endpoint devices such as PCs or printers, it may seem simpler to use switching and rely on layer 2 alone. However, a network architect or administrator may opt to use layer 3 across the entire network. In this case, switching is still used, as can be seen in the following example.

To describe how routing and switching are used together across the same network, we will return to the diagram we used previously for our routing process example earlier in this chapter. Segments of the network which operate only at layer 2 have been described in this section, as has the routing process, so this example will cover how layer 2 switching supports layer 3 routing operations (see Figure 3.2).

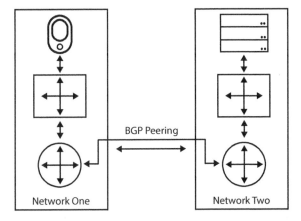

Figure 3.2 Routing and switching at a network boundary.

Returning to our description of the OSI model and its use of layers, this example shows that a single layer cannot operate in isolation and successfully pass information between endpoints across the network. This example of routing and switching being used together shows how layers 1 through 3 interoperate closely to achieve this goal and are supported in turn by other layers.

This process is repeated for each of the steps in the routing process that require traffic forwarding:

1) An endpoint (whether a router or not) determines where to forward received traffic to, based on that endpoint's knowledge of the network topology, as from its routing table.

2) Before the traffic can be sent, the layer 2 address of the next hop destination for the traffic must be determined. Remember that in the OSI model, as we send traffic we must traverse down the stack towards layer 1. We cannot simply skip layer 2 just because we are using layer 3 addressing as well in the network. Our IP packet at layer 3 will first be encapsulated in an Ethernet frame at layer 2, which needs a pair of source and destination MAC addresses. The source MAC address is that of the interface about to send the traffic on to its destination; but the destination MAC address may not be known yet.

3) The endpoint checks its switching table, also referred to as its Address Resolution Protocol (ARP) table in the case of IPv4. This table contains a list of MAC addresses that are matched with IP addresses. If an entry exists that matches the destination IP address of the traffic to a MAC address, that MAC address is then used as the destination MAC address of the Ethernet frame being created. If it is not known, the ARP protocol (or an equivalent process based on the specific layer 3 protocol in use) is invoked to discover that destination MAC address.

4) With the IP packet encapsulated in an Ethernet frame with both source and destination MAC addresses, the Ethernet frame is then ready to be transmitted to its destination. Where layer 2 switching occurs, only the layer 2 information contained in the frame is required; and when a device uses layer 3 information to perform routing, it decapsulates the Ethernet frame and then acts upon the layer 3 information of the IP packet within. When traffic must then be sent towards its next hop destination, this encapsulation process is repeated.

In this way, layer 2 and layer 3 technologies function together closely to transport traffic from its source to its destination across a network that may span from one end of the same building, or it may span the globe in the case of an application delivered across the internet. Regardless, the same basic processes are repeated to move traffic over the network irrespective of any physical distance.

The examples in this section are a key foundation for topics in later chapters, which will use network virtualisation and inter-layer interoperation to provide the flexibility and performance required to support next-generation infrastructure and applications. Although many of the characteristics of and use cases enabled by infrastructure edge computing are new, these same basic processes apply from a network infrastructure and operation perspective just as they do to the current networks of today.

3.7   LAN, MAN, and WAN

Modern networks exist at drastically varying sizes, and it is useful to categorise them into three main classes according to their scale. The three most commonly used terms to describe the scope or scale of a particular network are the local area network (LAN), metropolitan area network (MAN), and wide area network (WAN), in order of their increasing geographical size. Although there are no real hard and fast standards that dictate the size a specific network must be to qualify as a specific scale denoted by one of these terms, it is usually not difficult to come to an agreement on terms to use.

In many cases, there is an hierarchical relationship between these three grades of network scale. One LAN may be combined with many others in a metropolitan area and can be interconnected to form a MAN; and one or more MANs across multiple metropolitan areas may be interconnected to form a WAN. On the other hand, networks at any of these three scales could be created as single networks. This choice is driven by a combination of business and technical factors depending on the individual parties and technologies involved in a specific area and is not prescribed by the terms themselves.

To show each of these network types visually, consider the diagram in Figure 3.3, which shows two cities:

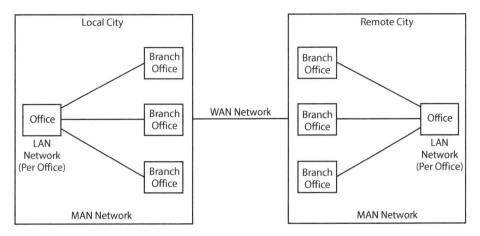

Figure 3.3   LAN, MAN, and WAN networks.

The diagram shows multiple LANs within a city, a single MAN covering all of that city, and a WAN that is connecting the two cities to each other despite them being 100 miles apart. Of course, a city may have hundreds or thousands of LANs, and there may be multiple MANs and also multiple WANS in that area or between areas; but this example serves to show the difference in scale between typical networks in each of these categories and how one may appear to nest within another from above.

There is also not necessarily any direct hierarchical relationship between these network categories at all. For example, depending on the network topology in a particular area, a LAN may just connect directly to a WAN. In another, it may need to connect to a MAN, which itself connects to a WAN. The specifics in this regard are location and implementation choices made by those network operators.

As well as a different physical scale, the purposes of each of these types of networks are different from one another. A LAN is typically used to connect endpoints within a single building or campus together or to other network resources, whereas a MAN is often used to connect multiple LANs to each other across an area such as a city. A WAN, then, is typically used to connect one network or endpoint to a network resource that is a significant distance away, hence its "wide area" naming.

3.8 Interconnection and Exchange

As mentioned previously, the internet is far more than the combination of physical infrastructure and logical protocols; it is a network of networks that are joined as much by agreements between their operators towards a mutual benefit as they are by anything else. This can be best seen in the way in which the networks of different operators interconnect and exchange data. This exchange of data between networks is essential; without it, endpoints of one network would not be capable of accessing resources or endpoints on another network, making the internet we know today useless.

The large-scale exchange of data between networks typically occurs inside an internet exchange (IX). Often, IXs are located within large data centres which terminate a high number of WANs inside the facility. The higher the number of networks aggregated into one location, the higher the theoretical value of that IX as a place for networks to exchange data. Chapter 7 focuses on this interconnection.

The physical locations of IXs are of considerable interest when thinking about infrastructure edge computing. Our previous example describes only the location of the IX itself, and not the locations of any of the endpoints which are ultimately sending and receiving the traffic. Consider the scenario, however, where these two endpoints are located close together but neither is near to an IX. In this example, each endpoint is connected to a different access network, and so for the data that they are sending each other to reach its destination, it must go all the way to the IX, be exchanged between their networks in that remote location, and then it will be sent all the way back to those endpoints.

Where the endpoints are using applications that rely on either very low latencies between endpoints or are sending a large amount of data, this is not an ideal network topology. For the former, latency is added between the source and destination of the traffic due to its need to traverse the IX before it can be delivered to its target endpoint, which would be minimised if a point of data exchange were available closer to those endpoints. For the latter, network resources are used between each of the endpoints and the IX to transfer the traffic, which some entity (even if it is not the users of each of the endpoints themselves directly) must pay for, with the possibility to introduce congestion as well.

These factors have led to the need for more distributed points of data exchange across the internet. Infrastructure edge computing addresses this challenge by the implementation of an edge exchange (EX) within infrastructure edge data centres. Conceptually, this idea is simple; a smaller-scale version of the functions performed by an IX can be implemented inside an infrastructure edge data centre to allow networks to exchange data at locations closer to the endpoints, which are generating the traffic in order to decrease latency and minimise the cost of data transportation. This topic will be explored in a later chapter in this book, but its existence is a useful primer for the reader at this point as well.

Many agreements to exchange data between networks are reciprocal. One network may agree to interconnect with another because each network would bring a roughly equivalent benefit to the other, in terms of accessible endpoints and resources as well as establishing a balance in terms of the volume of traffic that each sends and receives with the other network, creating an equilibrium.

However, this understanding has been tested in recent years by the widespread use of streaming video services and other networks which send orders of magnitude more traffic than they receive. These services can place significant strain on the networks which they interconnect with due to the sheer bandwidth use generated by the widespread adoption of these services. This has prompted some network operators to move such relationships away from traditional reciprocal agreements.

Other agreements are considered "pay to play" arrangements, where a network may agree to interconnect with another network only if that other network agrees to pay for them to do so. Future payments may then be organised on a usage basis or on some other means as agreed between the parties involved. Although unpopular with some, the idea of paying for interconnection is a viable option where one party requires an additional incentive to interconnect with another. Alternatively the interconnection may not occur, reducing the overall ability of the internet to grow over time.

On-ramps are an interesting part of network interconnection and exchange which have become more prominent over the past decade with the rise of cloud computing.

Although there is some variation in how the term is used, an on-ramp generally refers to a dedicated piece of network infrastructure which gives one or more parties direct access to the network of a cloud provider. Examples of these on-ramp services include Amazon Web Services (AWS) Direct Connect [3] and Microsoft Azure ExpressRoute [4]. As more applications operate from cloud instances, such services become increasingly important to minimise latency and the cost of data transportation long term.

3.9 Fronthaul, Backhaul, and Midhaul

Much like the term edge itself, fronthaul, backhaul, and midhaul are all contextual terms. Whether a particular segment of network connectivity fits into any of these three categories depends primarily on the context in which it is observed, specifically by the locations where the network connectivity begins and where it ends combined with the point of view of the person using the terms. Whenever these terms are used, it is worthwhile clarifying the context of the speaker so that the topology that is being described can be fully understood to help to minimise the chance of any resulting confusion.

In the context of infrastructure edge computing, we will use the infrastructure edge data centre as the starting point for our network connectivity when using these terms. This means that when we refer to fronthaul connectivity in this context, it is network connectivity between an infrastructure edge data centre and a piece of network infrastructure such as a telecoms tower or cable headend.

Midhaul in this context refers to the network infrastructure that is used to connect infrastructure edge data centres to one another across an area such as a city. This network is often an example of a MAN, as it connects network endpoints together across an area which is typically the size of a city. Building upon our use of LAN, MAN, and WAN in an earlier section, each infrastructure edge data centre can be considered a LAN in itself, and so the midhaul network infrastructure often does fit our description of a MAN as a network connecting many LANs distributed across a specific area.

Backhaul, when used in the context of infrastructure edge computing, refers to the range of network infrastructure which is used to connect an infrastructure edge data centre back to a piece of regional network or data centre infrastructure. An example of this is a WAN link, which is used to connect one or more infrastructure edge data centres to an IX in a neighbouring city. As such, this connectivity is typically a WAN although, depending on the distance required, it may alternatively be called a MAN.

The way in which we will use these terms throughout this book can be seen in the diagram in Figure 3.4. Terms denoting geographical network scale such as LAN, MAN, and WAN are overlaid as appropriate:

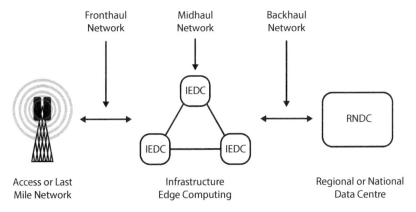

Figure 3.4 Fronthaul, backhaul, and midhaul networks.

3.10 Last Mile or Access Networks

When defining infrastructure edge computing in a previous chapter, the term last mile networks was used to denote the dividing line between the locations of the device edge and infrastructure edge to allow us to separate these two very different domains from one another. Last mile networks are key because they represent, for the majority of users and endpoints, the way that they connect to any of the network-accessible resources that they seek to use. That is why these networks are also referred to as the access layer, when we consider the internet as a network of networks; there must be a first layer of network infrastructure which the endpoint connects to. The connectivity between that first layer then shapes much of the performance and cost that will be achievable in the network overall.

Recalling our discussion in a previous section on network interconnection, we can see that last mile network interconnection is especially critical to fulfil the promises of infrastructure edge computing. Where one endpoint is connected to one network and the endpoint or resource they want to access is connected to another, even if that endpoint is located in a nearby infrastructure edge data centre, if interconnection between these networks must take place a significant distance away in an IX, then the lower latency and cost of data transportation offered by the infrastructure edge data centre will not provide any benefit, as all traffic will move through the IX before it reaches the edge data centre.

The diagram in Figure 3.5 illustrates this challenge. Where access networks are not interconnected at the infrastructure edge, the benefits of the infrastructure edge data centre then cannot be achieved:

A last mile network does not necessarily have to be a publicly accessible LTE network, cable network, or a similar entity; it may be a dedicated fibre connection for a single large entity such as a hospital to provide that entity with direct connectivity to

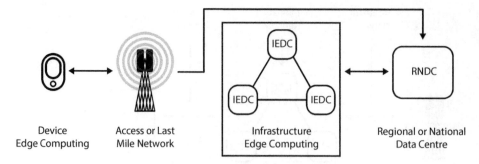

Figure 3.5 Last mile or access network interconnection failure.

resources which are of significant interest on the infrastructure edge. This network connectivity could be referred to, playing on the terminology used for the cloud on-ramp services briefly described in a previous section, as an edge on-ramp of sorts.

Infrastructure edge computing does not prescribe a specific type or scale of access network, and the ideal infrastructure edge computing deployment will be able to support multiple concurrent access networks of scales varying from a single intended user through to hundreds of thousands. How each type of access network can interconnect at the infrastructure edge data centre will be explored in a later chapter, but for the purposes of this section, just remember that the more networks the better.

3.11 Network Transport and Transit

Ideally, an infrastructure edge computing network, which we will define here as the combination of infrastructure edge computing data centres combined with their supporting network infrastructure within a specific area such as a city, will serve as much of the traffic entering it from interconnected access networks as possible. Serving the traffic in this context refers to the ability of these resources to respond satisfactorily to the needs of the traffic and not have to send that traffic to a destination that is off of the infrastructure edge computing network, such as a regional data centre via backhaul.

Network transport is the ability of a network to move data from one endpoint to another, such as from its source to its destination. This is the core functionality of all communications networks. It does not matter what scale the network is operating at in terms of geographical coverage or the number of endpoints; ultimately it is required to provide transport from one endpoint to another using however many endpoints or links between endpoints are required to achieve this single goal.

Network transit is the ability of a network to function as a bridge between two other networks. In the context of infrastructure edge computing, consider the diagram in Figure 3.6, which shows how the infrastructure edge computing network

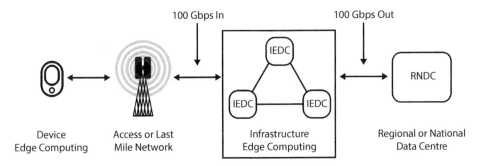

Figure 3.6 Infrastructure edge computing network providing transit services.

can provide transit services between an access network on the left and a backhaul network on the right. In this example, the infrastructure edge computing network is not serving any of the traffic which comes in from the access network and is instead simply passing it through to another destination, which is accessible via its own backhaul network.

A typical infrastructure edge computing network will aim to minimise the amount of network transit it provides; although it is essential that the infrastructure edge computing network is able to provide transit for traffic that the network itself is unable to serve, this capability should not be seen as the main use of the infrastructure edge computing network. Although it is beneficial to the operator of the network if as great a proportion of the access layer traffic flows through the infrastructure edge computing network as possible, because this provides the greatest opportunity to serve traffic using resources at the infrastructure edge, if the bulk of this traffic cannot be served by the infrastructure edge due to the tenants present or other factors, the network is just joining access back to backhaul. This does not utilise the full capability of the infrastructure edge computing network for applications.

Of course, the physical data centre and network infrastructure of the infrastructure edge computing network is not enough alone to satisfy traffic; first, the right networks must be interconnected at the infrastructure edge to enable traffic to be exchanged efficiently without transporting it all the way to the IX and back, and second, the resources that an endpoint is trying to access must also be located at the infrastructure edge. These resources may include streaming video services, cloud instances, or any other network accessible resources, including new use cases such as IoT command and control.

Data Centre Interconnect (DCI) typically refers to the physical network infrastructure that is used to connect one data centre to another, regardless of the scale of the two facilities, combined with a protocol set used to facilitate inter-data centre communication. This connectivity between facilities may be used to provide both transport and transit services; for example, in the context of several infrastructure edge data centres deployed within a single area such as a city, where a resource is not available in one data centre, it may be in another where that data centre is connected to directly or indirectly. In this case, the traffic can be sent to that serving data centre and can be served while still remaining on the same infrastructure edge computing network, providing some latency advantages.

Although in the ideal case traffic is served by the first infrastructure edge data centre that it enters, as long as the connectivity between infrastructure edge data centres is sufficient to provide a lower latency and cost of data transportation than sending the traffic back to another destination over a backhaul network, this process can still provide a better user experience than is otherwise possible.

Physically, the network connectivity between data centres regardless of the scale of these facilities is typically implemented using high-capacity fibre optic networks. These networks provide far greater capacity than any other currently used transmission medium and economically are capable of the lowest cost per bit of transmitted data by far when compared to alternative technologies such as copper or wireless networks. As data centre facilities are not physically moving, they do not require the mobility advantages of wireless technologies, and fibre exceeds the capacity possible in copper.

Additionally, many entities ranging from telecommunications network operators to municipalities have gone to considerable expense to lay fibre optic cabling throughout many urban and even some rural areas. Locations where this fibre happens to aggregate, such as at tower sites used for cellular networks, make ideal locations for infrastructure edge data centre deployments due to the ability to access existing fibre networks and minimise the expense of deploying the infrastructure edge itself.

3.12 Serve Transit Fail (STF) Metric

The ability of the infrastructure edge computing network to serve traffic is a key measure of its value, and so high targets, such as serving 75% of all traffic received from the access network, are common. Although these targets may seem high, the key to achieving them is defining a realistic scope and an understanding of real user needs; once the underlying infrastructure is established, this is typically a task for the tenants of the infrastructure edge computing network such as content providers. These entities must then optimise the software resources such as application instances or pieces of specific content present on the infrastructure edge network in order to maximise all the achievable benefits.

Three possibilities exist when an infrastructure edge computing network receives traffic. It can serve the traffic; it can transit the traffic to a destination which it believes can serve it; or it can drop the traffic, which is a failure. The latter may

occur where the infrastructure edge computing network has no route to any destination which it believes will be able to serve the traffic, and so the traffic is just
dropped instead. This is of course suboptimal and to be avoided wherever possible
by all parties. In an ideal scenario, the infrastructure edge computing network
performs measurably better than its centralised counterpart in terms of lower
latency and the reduced cost of data transportation and introduces as few cases of
lower performance as possible; where traffic cannot be served by the infrastructure
edge network itself, the network should not significantly decrease performance by
transiting that data to a destination such as to a regional data centre compared to
the alternatives.

There is a simple metric used to calculate the value of an infrastructure edge computing network in the form of serve transit fail (STF). It can be calculated as follows
over a given period of operations:

1) Compare statistics from the ingress (traffic that is entering the infrastructure
   edge network from any of its interconnected access networks) and egress (traffic
   exiting the infrastructure edge network that is transiting from those same access
   networks) data flows collected over a period of time such as a week or longer to
   provide a realistic view of network operations.
2) Calculate the proportion of ingress to egress traffic as described previously. In
   this example, we will use the following figures for this step, which have been
   chosen just for their simplicity. We can see that with these figures, 90% of the
   ingress traffic was either served or failed at the infrastructure edge network, and
   the remaining 10% was transited to another destination.
   a) Ingress traffic: 100 GB
   b) Egress traffic: 10 GB
3) At this stage, our infrastructure edge computing network has a very high STF of
   0.90. This is encouraging, although we do not have the full picture yet. Next, we
   must then subtract the impact of any failures to deliver traffic from this metric.
   Because in this example we are measuring traffic only in terms of size and not in
   terms of individual session requests, we must be able to coarsely estimate the
   impact of a failure by the amount of traffic that, if the failure had not occurred,
   would have been served in response to the failure either on or off edge.
   a) For this example, we will estimate that each failure would have generated on
      average 50 MB of traffic had it not failed. In a production network, this
      estimate would be generated based on the type of traffic observed across the
      network and, where possible, the specifics of the failures themselves; but this
      suffices for now.
   b) We can arrive at a rough estimate for this example of the number of failures
      by using a combination of Internet Control Message Protocol (ICMP) destina-
      tion unreachable messages, which are returned to an endpoint by an endpoint

within the infrastructure edge computing network, and by application-level error responses which indicate a particular missing resource or piece of content within the edge.

4) We then need to subtract the impact of these failures from the current STF metric. For the sake of simplicity in this example, we will continue to use the overall volume of traffic to do this. If we estimate that 100 failures occurred, each averaging 50 MB of traffic, this requires us to subtract 5 GB (100×50 MB) from our 0.90 STF, which in this example is equal to 90 GB. This leaves us with 0.85 (90 − 5 GB) for our STF. We could weight failures more heavily to reflect their impact on the user experience, but for this example we will leave them neutral.

5) The STF for the infrastructure edge computing network over the measurement time is 0.85. With this information, the network operator can tune the network as required over time.

There are multiple potential ways that the STF metric could be calculated. Numbers of application sessions could be used in place of traffic size measurements and estimates of the impact of failures; however, for the sake of simplicity, we will use the method described previously in this book. Other ways of calculating this and similar metrics to determine the real effectiveness of an infrastructure edge network are being explored across the industry, but the aim of all of them is the same: to determine whether a particular instance of infrastructure edge computing is helping or hindering the internet.

Consider the example of two infrastructure edge computing networks. One has achieved a high STF, and the other has not. With all other things being equal, the higher STF indicates a far more valuable and effective infrastructure edge computing network compared to one with a lower STF. For each of the networks of interest, the STF would be calculated as in the previous example, taking care to use the same method of calculation so that the comparison is as fair as possible. The metric figure is not tied to a specific scale of infrastructure edge computing network or a specific set of users or use cases; it provides a relatively neutral measure of the effectiveness of the network's ability to provide benefit.

The STF metric provides the infrastructure edge computing network operator with a useful figure by which to judge the effectiveness of the overall system. It is reasonable that a minimum acceptable STF then be used to determine whether a specific infrastructure edge computing implementation is worthwhile or if it needs to be improved to reach an acceptable level of effectiveness. The realistic STF metric for a specific infrastructure edge network deployment will vary depending on its users, the types of applications they are using, and the maturity of the deployment with the acceptable metric increasing over time. Table 3.2 indicates an example of this STF metric progression:

Table 3.2 Example minimum acceptable and desired average STF metrics.

Maturity of deployment	Minimum acceptable STF	Desired average STF
0–6 months	0.10	0.15
6–12 months	0.20	0.30
12–18 months	0.30	0.50
18–24 months	0.40	0.75

However, like any such metric, STF makes a few key assumptions which should be verified for each infrastructure edge computing deployment before it is used to compare two or more deployments:

1) Traffic served by the infrastructure edge computing network is served in a way that provides a better user experience, or a lower cost of data transportation, than is possible otherwise.
2) Failures have a definite impact on the user experience and are not the result of tangential requests or unwanted traffic generated by unimportant actions or entities such as malware.
3) The transit function provided by the infrastructure edge computing network is better or as good as but not significantly worse than other options available between access to backhaul.

Another key assumption of the basic STF metric is that the value of an infrastructure edge computing network can be fairly ascertained by using traffic volume or session count as a representation of the network's value. In some cases, the value of the infrastructure edge computing network is primarily that it enables a specific new use case, and in this scenario, it is appropriate to use a weighted STF metric that is oriented towards traffic for that specific use case, representing it overproportionally.

The STF metric will be used later in this book during use case and infrastructure edge computing network deployment examples, with specifically tuned variants of the metric used where required.

3.13 Summary

This chapter outlined many of the key topics around network technology, so far as they relate to infrastructure edge computing, with the aim of providing the reader with a foundation from which to build upon other network-related topics throughout the rest of this book. The terminology and concepts described in this chapter will be used frequently throughout this book in many chapters.

One key topic that was introduced was the STF metric. This metric allows an infrastructure edge network operator to understand the effectiveness of their network and, therefore, its real value. Although this metric could have been described in a separate chapter, it is primarily a metric that describes an infrastructure edge computing network and so it was included here rather than not.

In the next chapter, we will explore data centre technology in order to provide the context to fully understand the impact of infrastructure edge computing on data centre technology, operations, and other related topics. These topics will be explored in later chapters, using the next chapter as a base.

References

1 ISO/IEC. ISO/IEC standard 7498-1:1994 [Internet]. 1994 [cited 2020 Sep 30] Available from: http://standards.iso.org/ittf/PubliclyAvailableStandards/ s020269_ISO_IEC_7498-1_1994(E).zip

2 Richards, H. Edsger Wybe Dijkstra [Internet]. 2019 [cited 2020 Sep 30]. Available from: https://amturing.acm.org/award_winners/dijkstra_1053701.cfm

3 Amazon Web Services. AWS Direct Connect [Internet]. 2020 [Cited 2020 Sep 30]. Available from: https://aws.amazon.com/directconnect

4 Microsoft Azure. Azure ExpressRoute [Internet]. 2020 [cited 2020 Sep 30]. Available from: https://azure.microsoft.com/en-us/services/expressroute

4

Introduction to Data Centre Technology

4.1 Overview

To understand the implications of infrastructure edge computing on the data centre, we must first have a baseline of understanding across a few key areas of data centre design and operation as they exist today. This chapter will describe the basics of data centre technology and highlight many of the considerations surrounding it such as deployment and operational concerns, which will contrast with the description of these and other related factors during later chapters in this book, which will focus on the infrastructure edge data centre itself and its own unique requirements and considerations.

Data centre technology is a complex and multifaceted topic which cannot be covered extensively in just one chapter. Therefore, the aim of this chapter is to establish a baseline of knowledge which the reader can use to best understand the infrastructure edge data centre and its unique characteristics.

4.2 Physical Size and Design

Today, the average data centre is physically large. Although estimates vary across the industry and change over time as more facilities are deployed globally, a commonly quoted figure today is that the average data centre occupies around 100 000 square feet. The largest, however, scale up past several million square feet; The Citadel Campus [1] is a data centre facility in Reno, Nevada, in the US, which is gigantic at 7.2 million square feet, and there are many others worldwide, each above 1 million.

Understanding Infrastructure Edge Computing: Concepts, Technologies and Considerations,
First Edition. Alex Marcham.
© 2021 John Wiley & Sons Ltd. Published 2021 by John Wiley & Sons Ltd.

One of the key aspects of infrastructure edge computing is its interoperation with large data centre facilities. There may be one, multiple, or no data centre facilities on the scale of tens or hundreds of thousands of square feet within the same area, such as a city, as an infrastructure edge computing network. This concept will be explored further in later chapters, but it is useful to consider here too.

Because of the size of many data centre facilities, they are referred to in this book as being regional or national data centre (RNDC) facilities. This is to contrast their scale and the user population which they can serve effectively with that of the much smaller scale and user population which can be served from an infrastructure edge data centre facility. Although there may be a significant size difference between multiple regional or national scale data centre facilities, what matters most for the context of this book is their scale and their location compared to an infrastructure edge data centre facility.

Externally, there may be no obvious indication that a building is home to one of these data centres. In areas such as New York and Chicago, for example, data centres are often reusing historic buildings that are a part of a standard city block and look like almost any other when viewed from the outside.

Many data centres today are bespoke. Many of these facilities were built or retrofitted as one-offs of a sort and have since been bought by larger data centre operators who have made some elements common between all of their facilities, but not all of them due to the diminishing returns of doing so.

Within a data centre, customer equipment is deployed within racks. These racks come in a range of shapes and sizes, but the general standard used today in the data centre is the 19-in. rack. The size of 19-in. rack space is measured in rack units (RUs), which are defined as 1.75 in. high and 19 in. wide. These figures are the size of the customer equipment the rack can support, and so the rack itself will be a few inches taller and wider than that to support the equipment inside. A standard full-size data centre rack is 42 RU, although shorter racks may be used in some instances such as telecom rooms.

Most data centres today are designed to accommodate many rows of full-size 19-in. racks, each of which are full of customer equipment. Equipment which is deployed in a data centre facility is often described as being colocated in a data centre facility, as it is sharing the facility with others. This is also why the various services such as power, space, and cooling that are provided by a data centre operator in order to support a customer's equipment being deployed in a data centre facility are described as data centre colocation services, even if their exact specifics vary between facilities.

4.3 Cooling and Power Efficiency

As data centres are capable of supporting such large volumes of equipment, it is vital that they are able to effectively cool that equipment to prevent it from overheating and, in some circumstances, even heat the air entering the equipment so that it can continue to operate properly regardless of the external environment, such as whether the data centre is deployed in Chicago during a winter.

There are various ways to measure the power and cooling efficiency of a data centre facility. One measure which is frequently used is power usage effectiveness (PUE). The PUE is a measure of the overhead which the data centre facility incurs when delivering power to a customer's equipment, which is deployed within the data centre. To calculate the PUE, the total power which is consumed by the data centre facility is determined; next, the total power which is consumed by the customer equipment across the data centre facility is determined and then subtracted from the facility power figure. The result then tells us the overhead which all of the operational systems of the facility are requiring, such as the air conditioning system, as well as any other active noncustomer equipment.

For example, a PUE of 1.5 represents a 50% overhead. This means that where customer equipment requires 1 kW of power, the total amount of power consumed by the facility to provide this power to that customer equipment will be 1.5 kW. When all other factors are equal, a lower PUE is better as less electrical power is consumed, which means less expense must be passed on to the customer. Data centre facilities in hotter climates will often have worse PUEs than those in cooler climates, and it can be challenging to accurately compare two facilities using their PUE figure as this can be gamed. These figures are also difficult to compare between regional and national or infrastructure edge data centre facilities, the latter of which may be able to achieve a lower PUE score, depending on design.

Power and water usage is a key consideration in a data centre's design, deployment, and operation. Where water is required for the data centre facility's cooling system, access to this natural resource is key and will heavily influence the location of the data centre. The access to water is beginning to be seen as a key issue in the context of data centre deployment and operation. Especially in areas such as the southwestern United States, which may naturally be home to more arid landscapes compared to other locations, data centre designs which do not require large amounts of external water are the preferable option to avoid unnecessary impact on the local ecosystem. Despite their temperature, these areas are often attractive for data centre deployment due to the lower cost of land or power when compared to more temperate areas, both of which make a significant difference to their costs.

A positive trend in data centre design and operation has been the use of renewable energy by many of the large data centre operators in recent years. Whether these facilities are directly utilising real renewable power to replace fossil fuels, or they are participating in carbon credit schemes which can be used to offset the impact of any fossil fuels used, these efforts are positive for the environment. Combined with investment in sustainable energy and facility designs, they hold significant promise for data centres to be able to substantially reduce their environmental impact in the years ahead.

4.4 Airflow Design

According to the 2020 AFCOM State of the Data Centre report [2], the average rack density within the data centre increased from 7.2 kW in 2019 to 8.2 kW. As this trend of increasing rack densification continues, consider that a data centre may have hundreds to thousands of racks, each of which has to be cooled to an acceptable operating temperature constantly in order to maintain their uptime.

With such large amounts of heat to remove from possibly thousands of racks within a single data centre facility, the airflow system to use in a facility is an important topic during its design as it has an ongoing impact on the operational efficiency, cost, and maintenance of the data centre facility.

There are a few key factors to consider with any data centre cooling and airflow system design:

1) Cooling capacity
   a) The ability of a large air conditioning unit to ingest hot air and expel cold air cooled to a specific temperature is a bounding factor on the ability of the data centre itself to cool customer equipment to a suitable operating temperature. Data centres will utilise several large air conditioning units to perform this function and will typically have backup units arranged to take over in the event of any failure or maintenance.
2) Airflow rate and balance
   a) This cooling capacity, however, cannot be fully realised if the airflow throughout the data centre facility is not sufficient or is unbalanced. Insufficient airflow will result in hot air remaining around customer equipment rather than being moved through the cooling system, and unbalanced airflow will result in backpressure, which can cause hot air to be recirculated back through customer equipment, raising its temperature.
3) Localised cooling effectiveness
   a) There is a difference between being able to cool the central point of a room down to a desired temperature and being able to ensure that the air being drawn into all of the customer equipment racks dispersed around that room is at that temperature. To be most effective, the cooling system must be able to cool the customer racks, not just the centre point of the room, to the desired temperature and maintain it there.

There are many detailed considerations for cooling and airflow system design inside a modern data centre including various types of slab or raised flooring and different means of bringing air in and out of the data centre facility and its air conditioning system, which this section cannot cover. However, it is generally accepted that the use of containment in these facilities results in an effective cooling solution and which is currently the preferred way to design data centre cooling and airflow systems.

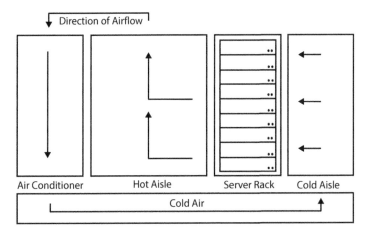

Figure 4.1 Hot and cold air containment cooling system example.

The concept behind these containment-based solutions is that by isolating the hot and cold airflows within the data centre cooling system from one another, the efficiency of the system is improved because cold air is not being unnecessarily mixed with hot air, which will raise its temperature and reduce its cooling capability. These systems also allow the data centre operator to precisely control and direct airflow to the locations where customer equipment is located such that they avoid being required to cool unused space within the facility. In this way, the cooling system has less air that it must cool, allowing the efficiency and effectiveness of a cooling system to be significantly improved (see Figure 4.1).

Chapter 6 includes a description of other airflow design and cooling system considerations which are relevant to the infrastructure edge data centre. Many of these considerations also apply to the large regional or national scale data centre as well, just as the considerations described in this section and the principle of hot and cold air containment applies to any infrastructure edge data centre facility.

4.5 Power Distribution

The type of power delivered to a specific rack of customer equipment may vary across the facility depending on the needs of the customer and their equipment. Although most equipment in the US will operate on single phase 120 V AC power, some equipment, for example, which is designed to be able to operate inside telecoms network structures, which historically supplied −48 V DC power, will typically lead to the customer requesting the same type of power within the data centre to operate.

For the data centre facility itself, is likely that multiple power connections are supplied, which each are capable of supporting hundreds of kilowatts of power, such as heavy duty three phase power from a specifically provisioned electrical sub-station, which can accommodate the energy needs of the data centre facility. This is a factor which is considered early on in the design and deployment of the site because an inability to provide adequate electrical power to meet the demands of the facility as it grows over time in scale and density will result in a smaller revenue opportunity for the operator.

A typical data centre operator is able to provide almost any combination of electrical power to the customer equipment in a given rack either by utilising a standard power feed or supplying power conditioning equipment which can convert between AC and DC power, for example, as requested.

4.6 Redundancy and Resiliency

Within a data centre, there are many ways to increase the uptime of a data centre facility above its basic level. In many traditional data centre facilities, this is achieved through the combination of very stringent operational controls and the use of heavily redundant components to support high uptime.

Redundancy is defined as having one or more backup components or entire systems for operational systems within the data centre, with the aim of being able to switch over to a backup should there be a failure of the original component or system. An example is a data centre featuring redundant cooling systems; should the compressor in an air cooling system fail, if a redundant cooling system is available, that system can then take over for the original one until it is repaired and able to operate.

In comparison, resiliency refers to the ability of a system or an operations team to recover from any failures which are experienced and to adapt operations to accommodate any failures. Resiliency can utilise redundant components and systems, but simply having that redundancy does not ensure that resilient operation will occur. Consider in the example of a redundant cooling system used previously what would happen if a manual switchover were required between the cooling systems but, when a failure occurred, the switchover was not activated. In this case, even though there exists a redundant system which could absorb the impact of the failure of the original cooling system, resiliency has not been achieved because the redundant system is not used after a failure of the original has occurred.

As the redundancy and resiliency provided by a data centre facility is such a key consideration for the customers who may deploy their equipment in that location, there are various ways for the customer to compare multiple data centre facilities in this regard. The Uptime Institute maintains classifications against which data centre facilities can be certified, ranging from Tier I to Tier IV. These classifications denote several key elements of physical redundancy and resiliency including the use of multiple redundant power feeds, the level of concurrent maintainability of the infrastructure, and the type of cooling system redundancy which is available. As will be seen in a later chapter, the challenges of physical space inside many infrastructure edge computing data centres make achieving the same levels of physical redundancy on a per-site basis as is possible in a traditional larger data centre facility difficult. This leads to the need to implement greater levels of software-based multi-site reliability measures to preserve application or service uptime even if a specific infrastructure edge data centre were to experience physical failures beyond their capability to handle physically.

The Uptime Institute [3] has for many years been the industry standard for measuring and comparing the level of redundancy and resiliency present at a data centre facility. The reader is advised to read the Institute's documentation for the specifics of each tier, but a brief summary is provided in Table 4.1.

One important note is that the maximum level of redundancy is not always the optimal solution for a data centre, or for the customers of that facility. Each level of redundancy increases the cost of that facility, which ultimately must be passed on to its customers and limits the physical spaces in which that data centre can be located. As the customer of a data centre, it is sensible to determine the real minimal level of redundancy that is acceptable for your equipment and then establish whether any software resiliency measures make sense for your application before deciding on a specific facility.

Utilising multiple data centres is also a viable route to providing redundant and resilient data centre infrastructure which is capable of supporting mission critical applications. However, this approach requires an additional level of software intelligence which is not typically supplied by a data centre operator to its customers,

Table 4.1 Uptime Institute tiers (numbers, names, and brief characteristics).

Uptime institute tier	Tier name	Tier characteristics
I	Basic capacity	Single component path without fault tolerance
II	Redundant capacity components	N + 1 component paths without fault tolerance
III	Concurrently maintainable	Concurrently maintainable with active and backup distribution paths and all previous
IV	Fault tolerance	Multiple active paths with multiple component paths, compartmentalisation of faults, and fault tolerance in addition to all previous protections

or for those customers to develop and implement their own application level measurements of potential service uptime issues and orchestration capabilities in order for an application to operate resiliently across multiple physical data centres. Issues related to the use of multiple data centre facilities are explored further in Chapters 10 and 11 across all data centre sizes.

A key consideration when choosing a data centre is the service level agreement (SLA) which the data centre operator is able to provide to the customer. This agreement defines the level of uptime that the customer can expect from the data centre facility and details any remediation capabilities that the customer has should this level of uptime be breached, including financial compensation.

Both to avoid penalties from breaching their SLA and to maintain their market reputation as a very reliable location for customer equipment, data centre operators are keen to avoid any failures that impact the uptime of their customer's equipment and services. There are many ways to measure if any issues have occurred, but a common method is if an interruption in power occurred which was severe enough for it to be detected by customer equipment, then a failure has occurred, as power continuity is an expected part of data centre colocation services and the customer should not be expected to supply, and may not be able to deploy, their own battery backup systems. The same principle can be applied to network connectivity, although there is more allowance for issues here.

Uptime itself can be split into two main categories: physical and virtual uptime. Virtual uptime is in many ways a superset of physical uptime. For example, should all of the physical resources which support a software service fail, the virtual uptime of that service will also suffer. However, if only one of those physical resources fail and the software service is able to accommodate this failure through migrating to another set of physical resources, its virtual uptime may still be maintained.

Traditionally data centre operators have focused on physical uptime and left it to the customer to maintain their virtual uptime. There are many methods that workloads may use to maintain uptime in the event of the failure of a single site, which include the operation of duplicate workloads across different data centre facilities which are interconnected such that one application instance can take over for another in the event of a failure. The design and operation of these resiliency measures is reliant on the underlying infrastructure provided by the data centre and network operators in use, but the higher level capabilities are typically provided by a cloud provider or by a user themselves.

Although data centre operators must be careful not to overcommit to levels of redundancy and resiliency that they cannot provide, these factors are key considerations for their customers, and they will often drive a purchase decision when choosing between any two data centre operators.

4.7 Environmental Control

Within the data centre, the data centre operator must maintain certain environmental parameters to ensure that customer equipment deployed within the data centre is able to operate effectively.

The data centre is a controlled environment, which means that parameters other than temperature must be managed such that they allow customer equipment and personnel to function efficiently.

The scale of a regional or national scale data centre and the amount of customer equipment which these facilities can contain make environmental control especially important. If a facility were to fail due to a flaw in an environmental control, the number of customers whose equipment and services would be taken offline for a period of time until the failure can be resolved is potentially very large.

Examples of environmental parameters which must be controlled are vibration and shock, humidity, particulates in the air which circulate through customer equipment and the cooling system, and the use of a suitable fire suppression system. For the latter, as the RNDC is in most cases constantly hosting onsite personnel, a fire suppression system which is safe for use with humans in the vicinity is more important than for a smaller facility which often operates unmanned.

Each of these environmental parameters are described further in Chapter 6 within the context of an infrastructure edge data centre. Regardless of the scale or topological position of a data centre, the issues and solutions relevant to these environmental parameters are common and include actions such as the dehumidification of air brought into the facility and the heating of the facility to prevent condensation forming around electrical or electronic equipment, and the filtering of that air for any excessive particulate matter which could obstruct airflow over time in any part of the airflow system.

4.8 Data Centre Network Design

Over the past two decades, data centre network design has been the focus of a significant amount of effort as the usage patterns seen in these networks have changed. The growth of cloud services and the widespread growth of applications operating in the data centre have resulted in traditional north to south traffic patterns, where a user device makes a request to a server in the data centre and the request is sent up to the server and back, being replaced with more east to west traffic, where many entities within the data centre must communicate with each other in order to support new services. An example of this type of network traffic is an application workload which utilises several different service components in order to function, all of which are distributed around the data centre facility.

Like many of the individual topics described in this book, data centre network design is a complex and evolving area of technology, design, and operation which cannot be extensively described in a single section or a single chapter, but the information presented here should allow the reader to understand some of the implications of design choices and how they can impact any data centre.

Traditional data centre networks were designed with the north to south traffic flow in mind. Traffic passed through three primary layers, from access to aggregation and finally to core. This approach made sense before significant east to west traffic was generated, and each hierarchical layer was a point of aggregation for those below it. For example, as its name suggests, the aggregation switch for a particular network segment aggregated the traffic from all of its connected switches that are at the access layer. This aggregation layer switch handled control plane and user plane operations for those access layer switches which it connected to, resulting in the need to upgrade the aggregation layer over time as the traffic load grew, even if traffic was often just between access layer devices (see Figure 4.2).

At the same time as the need for east to west traffic flows has grown, the need for north to south traffic has not diminished. The need for a data centre network which can then provide both axes of connectivity efficiently has brought about what are now referred to as data centre network fabrics, which utilise new network topologies. An example of a commonly used network topology is the leaf and spine, which is also referred to as a Clos network topology after its noted inventor Charles Clos.

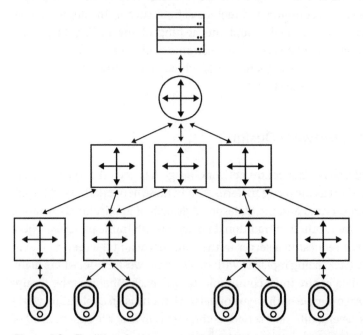

Figure 4.2 Traditional access, aggregation, and core layer network topology.

The term network fabric is often misused. Like many emerging technology terms, it has been used to describe both new solutions which embody the true meaning of the phrase but it has also been used to describe existing solutions or examples of basic network connectivity which do not achieve what a network fabric is intended to provide, which is a network topology where all network endpoints are connected to all other network endpoints while pushing functionality to the edges of that network.

In this leaf and spine, or Clos, topology, network functionality except the interconnection of network endpoints is distributed out to the edges of the network fabric. This results in a scalable architecture where additional endpoints can be added to the fabric without significantly increasing the difficulty of operating the control plane of the network. For a modern data centre network, consider each of the leaves in the system to be a top of rack (ToR) switch, which a customer will deploy within their rack of equipment and which is responsible for connecting that rack of equipment to the network (see Figure 4.3).

The growth over time of a Clos-based network is consistent because its architecture allows it to scale out over time. Additional network capacity and a greater number of endpoints can be added by the use of additional leaves, with the need to scale up the spines within the network not occurring at the same frequency as the need to scale up the aggregation switches in a traditional tiered network that utilises a scale up architecture where those switches are the bottleneck. This makes a network fabric optimal for a data centre which has the need to constantly add new endpoints over time in order to sustain the growth of its customer base as more equipment is added to the facility over many years.

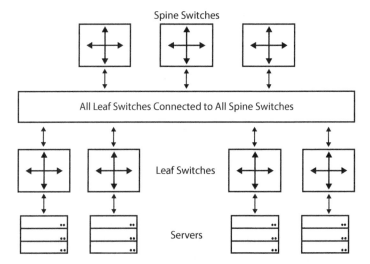

Figure 4.3 Leaf and spine, or Clos, network topology.

Depending on the specific needs of the data centre operator and their customers, the network will need to support a wide range of network virtualisation services. For example, even if a Clos network which utilises layer 3 is deployed, some applications such as a virtual machine (VM) migration between servers have traditionally expected a layer 2 adjacency between their source and destination network endpoints. The data centre operator may then have to deploy an Ethernet virtual private network (EVPN) that allows layer 2 network segments to be connected when they are separated by a layer 3 network. A configuration such as this can become complex and require the use of other protocols such as Border Gateway Protocol (BGP) for control plane functionality and virtual extensible local area network (VXLAN) for encapsulation in order to function. This type of virtualised layer 2 network atop a routed network underlay is now common and can be seen across many data centre facilities due to technology maturity and support.

Interconnection, as described further in Chapter 7, typically occurs within a data centre and so has a significant impact on data centre network design and the physical layout of the data centre facility. The data centre operator may offer customers the use of its public Internet Protocol (IP) address space for connectivity to external networks, but customers of a significant size are likely to use their own for this purpose.

From a protocol perspective, modern data centre networks utilise Ethernet and IP as their primary protocols for 2 and 3 of the Open Systems Interconnection (OSI) model. These protocols are typically used due to their widespread adoption elsewhere across the networks, which the data centre must interoperate with, and by the customer equipment to be deployed there rather than any specific beneficial capability inherent to those protocols themselves. From a routing protocol perspective, many data centre operators will choose to use iBGP, the Internal Gateway Protocol (IGP) variant of BGP, due to its capability to handle very large scale networks. Although other IGPs may be used as an External Gateway Protocol (EGP), BGP is used to allow interoperation with the external networks with which the data centre operator must peer in order to provide network connectivity.

Many data centres are, over time, part of a larger campus spanning an area such as a city where the multiple data centres operated in that area by one data centre operator are connected together so that they can be treated as a single abstracted facility. The term used to describe the network that connects these data centre facilities together is Data Centre Interconnection (DCI), which consists of redundant and high capacity fibre network connectivity between multiple data centre facilities that are in the same or adjacent areas. At large scales these networks begin to resemble infrastructure edge computing networks as their aim, key underlying principles, and technologies are really the same. These infrastructure edge computing networks are described in further detail throughout Chapter 5, both intra- and inter-area.

Additionally, it is important for a data centre operator to provide their customers with the option of an out of band (OOB) network connection so that the customer can maintain management access to their equipment in the event of a misconfiguration or another issue which causes connectivity using the main operational network to break. This is expected by the majority of operational customers.

4.9   Information Technology (IT) Equipment Capacity

The total IT equipment capacity of a given data centre is a combination of the power capacity of the facility, the physical space available within the facility, and the ability of the facility to remove heat so that the IT equipment can operate at an acceptable temperature indefinitely under any normal operating conditions. This IT equipment capacity can be broken down in terms of per rack, per floor, or per facility depending on the level of granularity that is required, but the typically quoted numbers are on a per rack and per facility basis to customers of the facility, plus the available physical space.

The capability of the data centre network is another factor which may constrain the total equipment capacity of the facility, although it is typically not mentioned in the context of capacity. If network resources are heavily oversubscribed, it may not be practical for the data centre operator to bring more customer equipment into the facility as this equipment would not be able to operate at the expected level of performance. This factor is worth exploring further in highly populated facilities.

Rack density is an interesting factor in IT equipment capacity within the data centre, which will be described further in Chapter 9. With all other things being equal, a data centre facility which is able to support a higher density of customer equipment per rack is preferable because this allows for a greater amount of customer equipment within the same number of physical racks. To achieve this, the data centre operator must be capable of removing the additional heat from each rack, not just from the room, and providing the airflow that is needed by all the deployed customer equipment.

The data centre operator may offer a standard range of rack densities but may also still be able to accommodate requests for extraordinary rack density for appropriate customers. Such racks may even feature specially adapted hardware which can support water cooling or other technologies.

One question which may come to mind is who deploys equipment within a data centre facility and why? Are these locations the preserve of only the largest hyperscale cloud providers such as Amazon Web Services (AWS), Microsoft, Google, or IBM, many of whom will also deploy their own large data centres? Although companies like these are often customers of large data centre facilities, they are far from the only ones. Many enterprises and other organisations deploy large volumes of equipment in data centre facilities which they do not own or operate, and data centres operated by a neutral host third party such as Digital Realty or Equinix are appealing locations for this equipment as they can offer data centre colocation services as well as function as large interconnection hubs, described in Chapter 7.

When it comes to the need for increased equipment capacity in a data centre facility, both scale up and scale out approaches are applicable in many cases. For the former, the facility which is being used by a data centre may be capable of supporting additional equipment by either adjusting the space which is currently being used, purchasing additional space in the case of a data centre that occupies a certain number of floors within a building where other floors are otherwise occupied, or where possible physically building additions on to the structure itself such as new floors or wings.

4.10 Data Centre Operation

As a large and complex facility where numerous technical disciplines are required to work together at scale and support mission-critical customers and applications, the way in which a data centre is operated has significant effects on its technical and commercial viability. Unlike an infrastructure edge data centre, a RNDC facility typically has onsite staff at all times for purposes of maintenance and security. This leads a traditional data centre facility to rely less on a model of facility automation than an infrastructure edge data centre, although many RNDC facilities will also employ automation for security and for configuration changes.

One key consideration is whether a data centre facility operates as single or multi-tenant. Much like the network infrastructure described in the previous chapter, which can become more economical for the operator when the same underlying physical infrastructure is shared across several users, each of which are unable to influence the operations of any other, this same concept applies to the data centre. This factor makes many data centre facilities multi-tenant, and the operators of these data centre facilities are usually also not deploying equipment that competes with their customers.

If a data centre operates as multi-tenant, it may operate as a neutral host facility. This term has a few connotations; it implies not just neutrality in terms of who the data centre accepts as a customer as long as those customers abide by its terms and conditions but also neutrality in regard to networks which may be present in that facility for interconnection purposes. Even when a facility is a neutral host location, the data centre operator always retains the right to enforce their own usage policies.

There are a few considerations for data centre operation which have a significant impact on a facility.

4.10.1 Notification

Today, many data centres are not wholly transparent in how they operate; should a system fail that does not impact the operation of customer equipment because another system is able to remediate the issue by functioning as a backup, the user will not typically be aware that this has occurred. Most of the time this is acceptable; it is up to the data centre operations team to ensure that any systems that provide redundancy and resiliency are operating successfully to avoid any impact on customer uptime. However, a problem may emerge where the equipment serving the customer has all failed and then, for example, the customer's equipment is on its final backup power source which is itself about to expire. In this scenario, the customer has little if any time to take action to maintain uptime whereas if they had been notified earlier, this may not have been the case and the user may have been able to move a workload to another location that is not experiencing issues or enact a safe shut-off.

Discussions about the type and frequency of this type of notification are a fierce topic of debate amongst data centre operations teams. Part of the problem is psychological; if your competitors provide only emergency warnings, customers may think your facilities are experiencing more issues simply because you choose to notify them about nonemergency issues to allow them take earlier corrective action if necessary, even though this does not truly reflect the real health of the facility.

4.10.2 Security

Due to the wide range of data and applications which may exist in any particular data centre facility, not to mention the cost of just the facility and the customer equipment operating within it, security is a key consideration in terms of data centre operation as well as throughout the design of a facility.

In a traditional large data centre facility, onsite manned security is typically employed alongside a range of technical security measures such as video surveillance, mantraps, and access control cards in order to maintain the security of the facility. A key consideration is not just who is allowed in the building itself but into which parts of the building they are allowed; a customer should be able to access only their own equipment or any necessary common space within the data centre so that any damage to or sabotage of another customer's equipment can be prevented by the facility operator.

4.10.3 Equipment Deployment

When deploying equipment in a data centre facility, a customer often has the option of installing it themselves or having this service performed by the data centre operations team at the facility as a remote or smart hands service.

With these services, the customer equipment is deployed under the direction of the customer using written instructions or over the phone, without the customer having to enter the data centre facility themselves. These services are often referred to as smart or remote hands, and a typical RNDC will have onsite personnel who perform them.

4.10.4 Service Offerings

Although many of the basic services provided by a data centre in terms of data centre colocation may appear common between different data centre operators, there are many ways that these operators are able to differentiate themselves from one another in order to establish a preferred position within the market. This is especially true once interconnection is integrated into a data centre facility and the data centre operator can begin offering different interconnection services.

Differentiation between data centre operators is becoming an increasingly pressing issue for these organisations as they seek to separate themselves from their competitors and establish unique and valuable positions in the market. In many ways, the number and scale of the data centre facilities which a data centre operator has in their portfolio is a differentiator against their competitors. In many cases this is true, but the value of the data centre has shifted over time such that network services such as interconnection are highly valuable for the operator as well as for their customers.

As this trend continues, many data centre operators will seek to define their own interconnection offerings within the market which offer something unique compared to their competitors, such as interconnection with nearby infrastructure edge computing networks or to large cloud providers. The extent to which a data centre operator offers these services impacts the operation of the data centre facility by determining how many and what type of personnel must be present as well as the duties and capabilities of those personnel in regard to the data centre and its customer equipment.

4.10.5 Managed Colocation

One way to distinguish the service offerings of data centre operators is the level of managed services that they provide to their customers. Some data centre operators offer a barebones service where customers must deploy their own equipment and are responsible for all major aspects of its ongoing operation. Others, however, will offer comparatively sophisticated managed colocation services that perform deployment and maintenance tasks for the customer. These services are often attractive to those key customers who do not have the personnel required to perform these tasks for themselves.

4.11   Data Centre Deployment

The deployment of a data centre is a costly endeavour, with costs typically measured in millions of dollars. Construction and other related activities to bring a site identified for data centre deployment all the way to a functioning facility which is capable of accepting customer equipment often takes several years and represents a major part of the development road map for a data centre operator.

4.11.1   Deployment Costing

When costing the deployment of a data centre, there are numerous metrics used in the industry to determine the overall expense which will be required. Two popular metrics for this purpose are the cost per square foot of the facility and the cost per megawatt of customer equipment that can be supported in that facility. Each of these metrics vary widely based on the location of the data centre, the local conditions concerning weather and temperature, as well as the cost of electrical power and water, and the ability of the data centre design to support high-performance cooling of equipment.

4.11.2   Brownfield and Greenfield Sites

There are two primary categories of data centre construction, known as brownfield and greenfield.

Brownfield data centre deployments utilise some piece of existing infrastructure, often a physical building, of which major parts are then retrofitted to accommodate the requirements of operating as a data centre. In the example of retrofitting an existing building, for example, the potential costs include designing and deploying a new high-performance cooling system, raised flooring, running many miles of fibre optic cabling throughout the facility as well as to external network connectivity points, the addition of physical and logical security systems, fire suppression systems, and other key requirements for modern data centre operation that an existing building such as a former shopping centre may not already include. Permitting may also be a challenge in areas such as New York City.

In comparison, greenfield sites are able to start from scratch without using significant parts of any existing infrastructure that the entity deploying the data centre does not want to use. An existing site which hosts a building may be used, but the building may be demolished and a new one built in its place; or an undeveloped piece of land may be chosen and building work may start from scratch. This approach allows a purpose-built facility to be utilised from the beginning rather than having to retrofit an existing structure to be a suitable site for a modern data centre. Greenfield deployment is often preferable, but sites may be challenging to acquire in desirable locations versus brownfield.

When comparing these two deployment models, one is not definitively better than the other, and the choice between them is typically driven by the available locations to support a data centre and the cost of its deployment and operation over time. For example, although it may often be cheaper to complete a greenfield deployment, there may be no greenfield sites close enough to key points of fibre aggregation to make that option cheaper or more desirable compared to a brownfield location.

4.11.3 Other Factors

Tax incentives are also a significant driver of many data centre deployments. Several countries and regions within countries have made themselves more attractive than their neighbours to those who are deploying large-scale data centres and, as a result, have become data centre hubs. To compound this, there is often an element of gravity that accompanies data centre deployments; where one is deployed, others will then often spring up over time as the usage of the original deployment grows since significant network traffic is already being routed towards a successful data centre and many customers are likely to have deployed their own equipment in that facility and may look to expand.

4.12 Summary

This chapter described a foundation of knowledge about the data centre which will be built upon throughout subsequent chapters. The design, deployment, and operation of a modern data centre is tremendously complex, and one chapter cannot capture all of their intricacies. However, the reader should now have a baseline which will allow the unique characteristics of the infrastructure edge computing model, including its infrastructure edge data centre facilities, to be fully understood.

In the next chapter, we will explore the design, deployment, and operation of infrastructure edge computing networks including their topologies, transmission medium, and other considerations.

References

1 Switch. The Citadel Campus [Internet]. 2020 [cited 2020 Sep 30]. Available from: https://www.switch.com/the-citadel
2 AFCOM. State of the data center report. 2020. Available from: https://www.afcom.com
3 Uptime Institute. Data center certification [Internet]. 2020 [cited 2020 Sep 30]. Available from: https://uptimeinstitute.com/tier-certification

5

Infrastructure Edge Computing Networks

5.1 Overview

Building on our foundation of understanding of network technology from previous chapters, in this chapter we will explore more elements of network architecture and operation related specifically to infrastructure edge computing. One of the most important aspects described in this chapter are the network topologies which can be used to connect multiple infrastructure edge data centre facilities to one another within the same and adjacent areas. The choice of network topology is crucial for the infrastructure edge computing network as it significantly alters the ability of the network to scale to additional facilities over time, as well as playing a key role in determining its overall coverage area.

5.2 Network Connectivity and Coverage Area

The most important factor of infrastructure edge network design is ensuring the network is able to interconnect with the most desirable access networks in locations which allow infrastructure edge data centre facilities to provide new and unique value. This means that the network infrastructure must in many cases extend from an infrastructure edge data centre facility to a location where the operator of the last mile or access network has exposed an interconnection capability, as described for several types of access networks in Chapter 7. Without the capability to support access or last mile network interconnection, the infrastructure edge computing network does not provide value.

Understanding Infrastructure Edge Computing: Concepts, Technologies and Considerations,
First Edition. Alex Marcham.
© 2021 John Wiley & Sons Ltd. Published 2021 by John Wiley & Sons Ltd.

Connectivity with backhaul networks is also essential, though it is typically easier to arrange when compared to last mile or access networks. However, the infrastructure edge computing network must also be present in locations where it can interconnect with these networks to achieve this interconnection. Regardless of the type of external network, this typically takes the form of an infrastructure edge data centre facility being deployed at or near to such a location before some network infrastructure, typically a comparatively short length of fibre, is then run between them.

These two factors have been listed before interconnecting the infrastructure edge data centre facilities themselves because if interconnection to external networks is not achieved, the entire infrastructure edge computing network is not capable of meeting its performance or cost targets.

The coverage area of an infrastructure edge computing network ultimately determines where an infrastructure edge data centre facility can be deployed. Unless it is connected to the network, the facility is essentially useless unless it is connected to one large customer facility using an access or last mile network and that customer will use the facility to its full capacity. Such situations are very rare and should not be relied upon as a useful alternative when considering a new deployment area.

Additionally the coverage area of an infrastructure edge computing network should be considered to be the area in which it can provide its specified level of performance between the user and the edge data centre facility. Because infrastructure edge computing networks perform Data Centre Interconnection (DCI) and provide some locations where interconnection can be achieved, and do not provide the means to connect an end user's devices directly to the infrastructure edge computing network as this must be done using an access or last mile network, the coverage area should really be considered as the coverage area of any access or last mile networks which the infrastructure edge computing network can interconnect with and achieve the required performance characteristics such as under 30 ms of latency for a user.

Every metre of network infrastructure which must be deployed has a cost to the infrastructure edge computing network operator. These costs vary greatly depending on the location, the owner of any existing infrastructure who may lease its use to the infrastructure edge network operator, the scale of the infrastructure that is required in terms of both distance and throughput, and the regulations related to its deployment and maintenance and so must be considered carefully to maintain costs.

5.3 Network Topology

The physical topology of the network interconnecting infrastructure edge data centre facilities in an area shapes the overall redundancy and resiliency of their network connectivity. In this section, the term endpoint refers to an individual infrastructure edge data centre facility, and interconnection is used to refer to both the physical and logical means by which data centre facilities are connected to one another such that they can exchange data and user applications can operate between facilities.

There are five main network topologies which matter for infrastructure edge computing networks:

1) Full mesh
   a) In a full mesh network topology, each network endpoint maintains a direct physical connection to every other network endpoint. Although this network topology offers the maximum number of redundant network paths, the cost is a dramatic increase in cost and complexity for each additional network endpoint that is added to the network. This makes a full mesh difficult to scale over time as the network grows.
2) Partial mesh
   a) As its name suggests, a partial mesh is not a full mesh. In a partial mesh network, only some of the network endpoints maintain direct physical connections to their peers within the network. This results in a topology which, while it is less physically redundant than a full mesh, is far more scalable and cost-effective for deployment.
3) Hub and spoke
   a) Also referred to as a star topology, in a hub and spoke network, there is one central endpoint which maintains physical connectivity to each of the other endpoints in the network. The distributed endpoints do not typically have direct connectivity to each other and instead must send traffic through the central endpoint to communicate.
4) Ring
   a) In a ring topology, network traffic flows between endpoints in the network, circling around the ring until it is able to arrive at its destination. If a link in the network is broken, traffic is able to then take the opposite route around the ring to maintain operation. Rings can be robustly designed and have been used well for many years.
5) Tree
   a) A tree topology creates a structure which looks like the roots extending down into the soil from the trunk of a tree. Flowing down from one central point, there may be multiple other smaller roots, each of which have their own endpoints and locations of aggregation, which get smaller in scale the further they extend from their origin.

All of these network topologies can be seen in a simplified form in the diagram below. Note that for the sake of simplicity, only a relatively small number of links and endpoints are shown in the diagram in Figure 5.1.

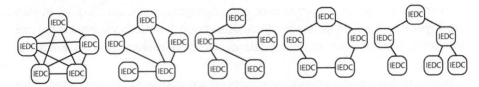

Figure 5.1 Full mesh, partial mesh, hub and spoke, ring, and tree network topologies.

Each of these network topologies has significant impact on the operation, redundancy, and resiliency of the resulting infrastructure edge computing network. The following sections will explore each of these topologies and their key characteristics so that we can choose the optimal network topology. The integration of any regional or national data centre (RNDC) facilities into these edge data centre network topologies is also described, as this is a key element in designing the required backhaul connectivity.

5.3.1 Full Mesh

Although a full mesh offers the highest level of network link redundancy, it is challenging to actually implement in an infrastructure edge computing network due to all of the cost inherent in deploying and maintaining the long distance network connectivity between the infrastructure edge data centre facilities. With every infrastructure edge data centre facility maintaining a network path to each and every other data centre in the network, the cost of the network connectivity required is massive and the cost increases greatly with each individual endpoint that is then added to the network over time.

In an ideal world, an infrastructure edge computing network would always be able to utilise a full mesh topology in order to provide the greatest number of redundant paths to protect against the failure of any one or multiple links within the network. Unfortunately, this is not the case, and so the infrastructure edge computing network operator, outside of small fixed size networks which totally require the redundancy level of a full mesh network, must instead utilise another network topology.

5.3.2 Partial Mesh

The partial mesh topology is easier to deploy than a full mesh due to the smaller number of network links it requires. For an infrastructure edge computing network, it is sensible to design a partial mesh such that any one infrastructure edge data centre facility maintains two or more connections to any two other data centres within the topology. This allows one link to fail and for the facility to remain online, even if its network traffic must thereafter take a different path through the network until the first path can be repaired and represents a good balance between infrastructure cost and reliability.

A regional or national scale data centre can function as part of a mesh network topology and may maintain direct network connectivity to one or more infrastructure edge data centres. This is also true for any of the other network topologies as well; if the entity deploying and operating the edge data centres is the same as or has a partnership with the operator of a nearby RNDC, that larger facility can function as a node in the infrastructure edge network as well.

Partial mesh network topologies are a robust and cost-effective choice for an infrastructure edge computing network of almost any scale as long as the cost of network infrastructure is considered.

5.3.3   Hub and Spoke

As there is no direct connectivity between endpoints which are located at each of the spokes, all of the traffic in the network must pass through the hub data centre facility. This is very different to the mesh topologies that were described previously, where multiple routes exist due to the presence of many redundant paths through the network between endpoints, and it requires the hub location to be capable of supporting enough physical redundancy to not disrupt the network due to its failure.

The central point of failure in a hub and spoke network is the hub. If the infrastructure edge data centre acting as the hub in the network topology were to fail, the entire network would become inoperable until the failure is corrected and network connectivity is restored. Endpoints on the end of individual spokes would not be able to communicate with one another as their connectivity is all directed to and from the hub by the network topology. For the majority of use cases, and efficiency of the overall infrastructure edge computing network, this is not ideal and wastes a lot of resources.

Additionally, the hub location must be capable of handing off the traffic from the network. This means that the hub location data centre facility must have direct interconnection with the peer networks to which network traffic is being sent to avoid an inefficient tromboning network path.

This type of centralised topology may make sense where a single operator is responsible for both the RNDC and the infrastructure edge data centre facilities in an area. Where an existing large scale data centre facility is present, infrastructure edge data centres may be added as spokes in order to extend the coverage area of the data centres operated by that operator. This topology is anchored by the enhanced level of physical redundancy which is often present at that larger data centre facility, but this redundancy does not provide additional network link protection.

However, the fragility of the hub and spoke topology makes it undesirable for an infrastructure edge network. A single network link can go down and cut off one or more edge data centre facilities until it is fixed, which does not allow the network to operate in a resilient fashion, even for maintenance.

5.3.4 Ring

Ring topologies have been used for many years in a wide range of use cases. As long as the routing protocols in use by the network are able to accurately detect the failure of the ring in one direction and reroute network traffic accordingly, some degree of failure, though not to the extent of a full or partial mesh, can be remediated without it inflicting significant damage on customer service uptime.

Expanding a ring topology network over time can be challenging. As new data centre facilities are added with their supporting network infrastructure, the resulting topology can begin to resemble a partial mesh instead of the original ring. Whether or not this is a problem depends on whether the infrastructure edge computing network operator wishes to stick to the ring model or can migrate.

5.3.5 Tree

Tree topologies, in the context of infrastructure edge computing, are a useful way to utilise facilities which are part of any network topology such as a partial mesh or a ring to extend the infrastructure edge computing network out from those facilities. They should not be used as the main topology for interconnecting the primary, larger infrastructure edge data centre facilities as if used in this way, the tree topology begins to resemble a hub and spoke with its same limitations in terms of redundancy.

By having one or more small tree topologies extending from one of the larger infrastructure edge data centre facilities in the network, smaller size category facilities can be added to the network in somewhat of a modular fashion over time without the need to rearchitect the main segments of the network. For example, a network with five size category 4 edge data centre facilities can add one or more size category 1 edge data centre facilities to each of those larger facilities without altering the main ring or partial mesh network which is interconnecting them. This can be a significant benefit for the infrastructure edge computing network operator as it reduces the cost of adding the new facility.

5.3.6 Optimal Topology

For many large-scale infrastructure edge computing networks, those utilising multiple larger edge data centre facilities, each of which have the potential either at the time of deployment or over time to support a number of smaller infrastructure edge data centre facilities, the optimal topology is a partial mesh with the capability to extend outwards from each edge data centre facility by using a series of distributed tree topologies. This allows the network to begin from a base which balances the cost of network infrastructure with redundancy and to scale out over time to support a large number of edge data centre facilities of multiple size categories, each addressing its own use cases (see Figure 5.2).

In the case of a smaller infrastructure edge computing network, the cost of network infrastructure may be harder to justify and so a simpler ring topology will often be sufficient to support the needs of the infrastructure edge computing network and its customers within that area at acceptable cost.

5.3.7 Inter-area Connectivity

An infrastructure edge computing network operator who is operating across multiple areas such as two different cities located a significant distance apart may seek to interconnect their networks in those areas together. This can be done either directly, utilising a typical point of interconnection such as a RNDC, or directly, by building or leasing network infrastructure which physically interconnects those networks across a long distance. The former option will be a significantly less expensive option, but there may be performance and network control losses that the infrastructure edge computing network operator does not wish to incur. Ultimately the value obtained from interconnecting multiple networks in this way must be repaid in terms of the use cases which it enables, and it is challenging to see many examples of these low latency use cases.

Figure 5.2 Partial mesh with distributed trees network topology.

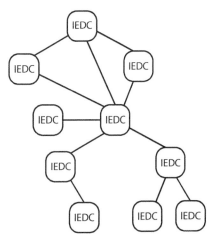

5.4   Transmission Medium

As with any network, the specific transmission medium used for the infrastructure edge computing network is of key importance as this determines the availability, cost, and performance of any of the resulting network infrastructure. For all these networks, there is one primary choice, which is fibre.

5.4.1   Fibre

Fibre network connectivity is the primary choice for any DCI use case due to its ability to support hundreds of gigabits or even terabits of data per second with the appropriate optical networking equipment at both ends of the connection. This is the primary means by which any modern long distance networks are designed, deployed, and operated; and as infrastructure edge computing networks may span significant distances even within one single area, fibre is the optimal choice.

There are many different options in terms of the number of fibre strands and the data encoding technology to utilise on fibre networks, as well as a choice of laser wavelengths and different ways for signals to be multiplexed utilising frequency, time, or spatial multiplexing techniques. The choice of which specific technologies to use is a question whose answer is dependent upon the existing and new network infrastructure being utilised as well as whether the infrastructure edge computing network operator will light all of the fibre themselves, which is the usual choice in order to be able to optimise the network for performance, cost, and control versus utilising a third party lit service.

Typically, higher throughput fibre network connectivity requires a greater number of strands, as well as potentially a higher number of connections to terminate, or the use of more advanced signalling technologies to accurately encode and decode network traffic as it is transmitted across a network. This is a key constantly evolving area of technology which requires keen attention from an operator.

5.4.2   Copper

In some areas, copper network infrastructure, primarily coaxial cable such as that used for cable television and cable internet services may be available either between infrastructure edge data centre facilities or between those facilities and customer locations. This infrastructure is limited compared to fibre when it comes to its achievable throughput and its maximum distance which makes it undesirable for DCI use cases, and it is not likely to be seen directly in an infrastructure edge data centre facility as the operators of these networks are likely to terminate any copper network infrastructure downstream before aggregating that data back onto fibre network links.

Although not preferable to fibre due to bandwidth and connection termination complications, if copper network infrastructure is the only option available, it may be used on a temporary basis.

5.4.3 Wireless

Wireless network connectivity is prevalent at the access layer due to the widespread deployment of cellular networks, Wi-Fi networks, Bluetooth, LoRaWAN, and many other access or last mile networks which are widely used and operated across the world. This has led some to consider using it for DCI.

However, wireless network connectivity is generally not suitable for fronthaul, midhaul, or backhaul network connectivity in an infrastructure edge computing network for several reasons, including:

1) Lack of bandwidth. Even when using high throughput millimetre wave connectivity, the capacity of any wireless network connection is insufficient for an infrastructure edge data centre of any size category above size category 1. These small and often mobile facilities can make effective use of wireless network technology where it is required, such as in the case of a mobile data centre attached to a truck. Even in these cases the facility will still be likely to retain wired fibre network connectivity for rapid data offloads.

2) Deployment challenges. Wireless networks which are designed to operate in a point-to-point topology with data being transmitted in as straight a line as possible between two points are not easily deployable in environments which do not present a clear line of sight between each end of that link. Due to the prevalence of buildings in urban locations which are taller than the infrastructure edge data centre when deployed at ground level, this is a considerable challenge. In some cases smaller size infrastructure edge data centres may be deployed on rooftops or near to towers which could support a clear line of sight, but combined with the other factors in this list, this is still not very preferable.

3) Urban spectrum availability. Many infrastructure edge computing networks will be deployed in urban locations. These environments often present challenge conditions for spectrum usage due to the number of wireless networks which are operating within the area. Unlicensed or lightly licenced spectrum presents a challenge in this regard, and licenced spectrum is too expensive and limited to make sense for use as any data centre backhaul links.

Cellular network connectivity, such as fourth generation (4G) Long-Term Evolution (LTE), in an infrastructure edge data centre facility, however, is useful as an available out of band (OOB) management measure should the primary data network go down. This will be used by infrastructure edge computing network operators themselves to monitor all of their facilities in the event of a sustained failure, as well as by individual customers within these facilities.

5.5   Scaling and Tiered Network Architecture

Much like any other network architecture and design activity, it is important that the foundation being laid for the infrastructure edge computing network is capable of supporting the projected future needs of the customers of that site as well as those of the network operator themselves.

Part of this activity is dependent on the topology which is chosen, and part of it is determined by the amount of network infrastructure that is deployed both at infrastructure edge data centre facilities and between them. Although a scalable network topology helps, it can be hamstrung if the network infrastructure used to support it is inadequate. Consider the example of a network which is utilising fibre network cabling pathways which impose limitations on the number of strands or the number of network links which can enter one particular data centre facility. These factors limit the ability of the network to scale over time due to a lack of upfront investment or poor infrastructure planning.

The ability to scale an infrastructure edge computing network also depends on the network that exists within each infrastructure edge data centre facility. These networks are described further in Chapters 4 and 6, and essentially if these networks are not capable of supporting the throughput of the inter-facility networks, then they will be constraining the total achievable system performance.

Viewed at a macro level, the network architecture between multiple infrastructure edge data centre facilities looks different from the network topology within a data centre, such as a Clos topology. A key element to infrastructure edge computing network design is an understanding of how to utilise multiple size categories of infrastructure edge data centre arranged in tiers to balance the needs of the users of these facilities in terms of performance and reliability with the end cost to the operator.

Within an infrastructure edge computing network, not all data centre facilities may be near the same scale or perform the same roles within the system; an hierarchical relationship can be useful between infrastructure edge data centres within an area such as a city as facilities of very different scales can be used to provide different functionality and support different use cases. For example, even a single size category 2 edge data centre facility may support several size category 1 facilities in the area due to their role in the network as leaf or spoke nodes versus the local hub role of the larger facility. To utilise the benefits of this tiering approach, the infrastructure edge computing network operator has to understand the traffic which may be generated or pass through each facility and all the workloads which may be operating from them. This and the physical locations of the facilities will determine if one or more facilities can be part of a distributed tree from a larger facility in the network or not.

Consider the example of our partial mesh with distributed trees from an earlier section. With this network architecture, it is possible to scale the network considerably over time both in terms of the need to add additional larger aggregating infrastructure edge data centre facilities to the network and the need to add smaller size category facilities or large customer facilities to the nearest of the aggregating facilities across the network. This is achieved by the use of tiered architecture, but it is only applied where it makes sense; between the largest size categories of edge data centres, there should be a flat network architecture wherever possible to promote a scale out approach, but when smaller size category facilities are anchored to a larger facility as part of a distributed tree, the type of hierarchical and tiered network design which the distributed trees enable also allows for scaling.

In this way, multiple network topologies can be combined across macro and micro perspectives to allow the infrastructure edge computing network operator to expand the network over time while preventing the need to spend exorbitant sums on network connectivity which may not be required.

5.6   Other Considerations

The security of the network infrastructure used to interconnect infrastructure edge data centres is a key consideration as if this infrastructure presents a flaw in the security of the system, it will be very difficult to detect and resolve in many cases while also exposing high value user applications or data to unauthorised access, capture, or disruptions to network availability. There are no specific security measures which are unique to the infrastructure edge computing network. Chapter 12 covers many security considerations for the operation of the infrastructure edge computing network as a whole, and Chapter 6 describes other security considerations for the design and operation of its facilities.

Quality of service (QoS) is another key consideration for any network infrastructure, especially that infrastructure which is intended to be multi-tenant. A multi-tenant network is typically oversubscribed according to a ratio determined by the network operator. The standard rule of thumb for residential network operators used to be 10 : 1, meaning that 10 users were assigned to a single link which any one of those users would effectively fully utilise if their access were not controlled. Infrastructure edge computing networks with their task of providing DCI, however, are different, and the cost of a customer's traffic being lost on the network due to congestion can be considerable. It may not be worthwhile attempting to save money by oversubscribing the network if the customer base for the infrastructure edge computing network is mission critical, such as public safety agencies or clouds.

5.7 Summary

This chapter examined key factors for the design, deployment, and operation of the infrastructure edge computing network. Specific emphasis was paid to the role of the network itself and whether particular network topologies were optimal in the context of infrastructure edge computing. Also, various forms of network transmission medium were considered with fibre network connectivity being preferable to copper and wireless networks. Combining network topologies according to an understanding of the hierarchical and tiered nature of the infrastructure edge data centre facilities, their customers, and their application workloads also allows for more efficient network topologies.

In the next chapter, we will explore the infrastructure edge data centre and its unique aspects.

6

Infrastructure Edge Data Centres

6.1 Overview

This chapter will focus on the infrastructure edge data centre facility and its unique characteristics. There are several discrete size categories of these facilities, each of which is useful for a specific set of deployment scenarios and use cases. Each of these is detailed in this chapter along with the scale of a typical deployment and their various key operational and design considerations to help create an understanding for the reader of how an infrastructure edge data centre is similar to and how it diverges from a regional or national data centre (RNDC). Additionally, redundancy and resiliency scenarios are described for the infrastructure edge data centre facility across several operational parameters.

6.2 Physical Size and Design

A key consideration for infrastructure edge data centres due to the number of individual sites which are required to create a meaningful deployment is the consistency of each infrastructure edge data centre facility. Design, deployment, and operational consistency across a large number of data centre facilities enables the infrastructure edge computing network operator to establish highly repeatable processes across each of these areas, allowing the overall system to be economical in comparison to the approach where each infrastructure edge data centre is treated as a unique and bespoke entity.

Understanding Infrastructure Edge Computing: Concepts, Technologies and Considerations,
First Edition. Alex Marcham.
© 2021 John Wiley & Sons Ltd. Published 2021 by John Wiley & Sons Ltd.

6.2.1 Defining an Infrastructure Edge Data Centre

Whether or not a specific data centre facility is an infrastructure edge data centre depends on, more so than anything else, its physical location and topological location within the network. These factors, combined with the physical scale of the data centre facility, will determine whether it is an edge data centre, a term which in this book refers only to the infrastructure edge data centre. Although terms such as regional edge are sometimes used in the industry, in some cases they refer to a regional data centre facility, which offers a regional point of network interconnection, or are a result of attempts to rebrand large regional or national scale data centre facilities as being examples of edge computing.

As described in Chapter 1, the infrastructure edge is located directly adjacent to the access or last mile network. By extension, an infrastructure edge data centre then is a data centre facility which is deployed in that location. That facility is the closest point, physically and topologically, to the end user who is connected to the access or last mile network, where interconnection of these networks can occur and data centre services can be supported. The vast majority of the data centre facilities which meet these requirements will be the types of facilities described in this chapter. However, in some cases, a RNDC also meets these requirements. In those cases, such a facility must be classed as an infrastructure edge data centre as well as it can fulfil the functionality and performance of an infrastructure edge data centre facility for end users within the same radius of the facility as in the case of a smaller infrastructure edge data centre facility a fraction of its size.

In this chapter and throughout this book, to avoid introducing confusion, we will refer to the smaller data centre facilities described in this chapter as infrastructure edge data centres. We will refer to a larger data centre as a RNDC facility, regardless of whether it is located in such a way that it meets the infrastructure edge data centre requirements described above or not.

6.2.2 Size Categories

Infrastructure edge data centres can be designed at various different scales depending on the needs of a particular market or deployment scenario. Much like large traditional data centre facilities, which may vary anywhere from tens of thousands of square feet through to several million, the difference in size between infrastructure edge data centres may be by orders of magnitude between the largest and smallest of these facilities. Some are even designed for mobile use and unorthodox deployment.

Although all infrastructure edge data centres may be considered micro data centres in comparison to larger traditional facilities, this single term does not cover the variation of sizes which may need to be deployed in an infrastructure

Table 6.1 Infrastructure edge data centre facility size categories and example roles.

Size category number	Typical kW capacity	Estimated size (W × H × D)	Number in example city	Example role
1	<1 kW	<2' × 2' × 1'	10	Network termination
2	1–10 kW	5' × 5' × 5'	20	Network functions
3	10–50 kW	10' × 8' × 10'	5	Network aggregation
4	50–100 kW	10' × 8' × 15'	3	Low latency workloads
5	100–200 kW	10' × 8' × 25'	2	Low latency workloads
6	200–250 kW	15' × 8' × 25'	1	Regional edge hub

edge computing network. Table 6.1 describes the size ranges for infrastructure edge data centres, measured by the customer equipment they are capable of supporting in kilowatts, and the roles they fulfil as part of the infrastructure edge computing network:

As described later in this chapter, some infrastructure edge data centres may be deployed as fully self-contained units designed for outdoor deployment whereas others use retrofitting of an existing structure. This factor does not change the size category that any particular infrastructure edge data centre belongs to, although it does significantly impact many other characteristics of the facility such as the heating and cooling system, the cost of deployment, and the available fire suppression system. Each of these categories of infrastructure edge data centre can be deployed as a self-contained system or within an existing structure, depending on the specific location and its current buildings.

Modularity is a key consideration when designing and deploying infrastructure edge data centres. It makes significant business sense to obtain the necessary permitting to deploy multiple facilities in a specific area but then to be able to deploy them in a modular fashion within the size of area which has already been permitted. The permitting process can often take significant time and resources by the infrastructure edge computing network operator and so may incur delays or additional expense.

This can be accomplished by two main approaches: scale up or scale out. Where sufficient land is available within the permitted space, another infrastructure edge data centre may be deployed to augment the capabilities of the existing facility. In other cases, the footprint available under the permit is fixed, but there may be sufficient headroom in height. In this case, a modular design that allows infrastructure edge data centre facilities to be stacked can be of significant value and allow the capabilities present at a location to be expanded significantly over any alternative approaches.

In many cases, however, the height of the deployed infrastructure may not support this approach, and the infrastructure edge computing network operator will be required to acquire any additional permits needed to deploy additional edge data centre facilities on nearby land. An operator may also choose to utilise this geographically dispersed deployment approach to increase its footprint while remaining close enough to the original facility deployment location to support low latency use cases.

Each size category of infrastructure edge data centre has its own unique set of considerations and use cases to which it is best suited. There is no one size fits all solution; although categories nearer to the middle of the list tend to cover more use cases than those at the extremes, each category of size fills a unique role within an infrastructure edge computing network. In a particular city example, there may not be a need for infrastructure edge data centres of one or more size categories. Other locations will, however, see multiples of each size category of infrastructure edge data centre used.

As the size of an infrastructure edge data centre decreases, the cost and difficulty of its deployment also falls. This is due to the lower cost of a physically smaller data centre when compared to a larger data centre, and the increased number of pieces of real estate where a smaller facility can be placed.

6.2.2.1 Size Category 1 (<1 kW)

This size category represents the smallest infrastructure edge data centres. Physically this category of infrastructure edge data centres can take many unique forms. Because of their size, these facilities can be deployed in a range of different ways across many locations as long as their need for network connectivity and power is fulfilled, which opens up several unique possibilities for the use of these facilities in unorthodox and resource-constrained roles. Consider the following example scenarios:

1) Lamp post/light pole deployment
    a) Lamp posts, traffic lights, and other similar pieces of street furniture can often be interesting deployment locations for the smallest infrastructure edge data centres. These locations typically provide access to power and the ability to mount the edge data centre facility at sufficient height to protect against common vandalism issues. Additionally, these locations are often home to network connectivity equipment as cities utilise them for purposes such as traffic cameras and communication networks for use by either the public or by agencies such as law enforcement or government.
2) In-rack deployment
    a) A self-contained data centre incorporating all of the compute and network capability required in order to function as a very small scale hub facility can be deployed in a housing that fits into a standard 19-in. rack at 6 rack unit (RU) high. This in-rack form factor can be utilised in locations where there is

either a permanent or temporary rack set up at a location for use cases such as internet of things (IoT) device data aggregation or the termination of network connectivity. These facilities are distinct from device side servers, despite their physical similarity, due to their key functional role as infrastructure facilities.

3) In-vehicle deployment

   a) Distinct from the compute resources hosted by an autonomous vehicle for its own use to support navigation and propulsion, a vehicle may host compute resources which are for use by other devices in the role of a travelling small-scale data centre. Example use cases include a mobile operations centre for first responders, where the compute and network resources required for establishing communications and determining the risk at the scene are located on board the vehicle to avoid issues.

Although many of these form factors are small enough for it to seem odd to refer to them as data centre facilities, we will continue to use this term to avoid introducing additional confusion because regardless of their size, topologically they reside on the infrastructure edge side of the last mile or access network and so they should be treated as a piece of infrastructure rather than as a device. Where one of these data centre facilities is used for network termination, this does not change as topologically the facility is fulfilling the same role as a larger facility would for this specific use case.

To illustrate an example form factor as well as the topological location of a size category 1 edge data centre facility, the diagram in Figure 6.1 illustrates a deployment of such a facility at a traffic light. The use case for this facility is as a network termination point for private law enforcement networks, as well as a location to

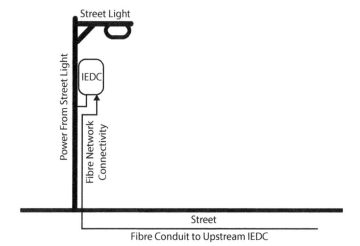

Figure 6.1 Example deployment of size category 1 infrastructure edge data centre.

aggregate traffic cameras for connectivity back to a larger infrastructure edge data centre which is operating a distributed AI application workload, providing computer vision capability:

Topologically, due to their size and deployment cost, this category of infrastructure edge data centres is best used for the distributed termination of network connections spread at comparatively remote locations which can connect back onto the infrastructure edge computing network. The equipment which these facilities would be able to support is minimal and best suited to a specific purpose and not used for other use cases which can be served from larger sized infrastructure edge data centres that are located an acceptable distance away and so are still able to support the latency required.

An exception to this rule of thumb is where these edge data centre facilities are deployed in support of use cases which cannot assume that backhaul network connectivity is available. An example of a use case where this is particularly important is a vehicle mounted size category 1 infrastructure edge data centre which is designed to provide processing support for first responders or other emergency personnel who must be able to arrive at the scene of an incident of unknown scale and severity and rely only on their local resources until other resources, such as fibre or wireless network connectivity to the area, have been re-established. In this case, up to 1 kW of equipment may be deployed in the data centre facility to support the processing and network functions required for this vital use case.

In this scenario, the utility of size category 1 infrastructure edge data centres can be seen. Wireless network connectivity can be provided from the edge data centre facility itself using either licenced spectrum for use by first responders and government agencies or unlicenced spectrum depending on which is available in the deployment location. This network connectivity allows the team on the ground to communicate with local and remote resources and to perform tasks such as launching a reconnaissance drone from the vehicle, which collects video data of a disaster area. This data is then processed by graphics processing unit (GPU) and central processing unit (CPU) resources in the vehicle mounted data centre facility for machine learning (ML) inferencing. When public network connectivity is re-established, the edge data centre can interconnect between its private network and one or more public networks in order to send this data to relevant agencies.

This and other scenarios show that although there may be a physical similarity between this smallest size category of infrastructure edge data centres and customer equipment, which is considered to be devices, the role which they play topologically is very different. The unique capabilities of this small size category of infrastructure edge data centre enable infrastructure edge computing to address a range of use cases which would otherwise rely on non-optimal solutions using device edge systems or have reliance on RNDC facilities, which both introduce new challenges.

Interconnection between last mile or access networks and the wider infrastructure edge computing network can be established at these facilities; however, the speed and number of interfaces that are supported would need to be matched appropriately to the size of the equipment that will fit inside the infrastructure edge data centre so that a speed mismatch is not created and issues are avoided.

In terms of operation and maintenance, these edge data centre facilities will not support the same type of access that is provided to a typical data centre facility due to their physical size and use of unorthodox deployment locations. However, key security measures such as cameras and remotely controlled door or enclosure locks can still be used and be centrally managed to maintain security.

6.2.2.2   Size Category 2 (1–10 kW)

As the second smallest category of infrastructure edge data centres, this size category is best suited to network termination and the operation of network functions, whether they are virtualised or to be performed using dedicated hardware. Facilities in this size category are small enough to support several kilowatts of processing power and network equipment but are not large enough to warrant multi-tenant operation in the majority of cases. This balance of physical size and equipment capacity is the key to these facilities being well suited to the case of extending the infrastructure edge computing network out to locations which are near to key pieces of network infrastructure operated by many other network operators, such as the nationwide operators of wired and wireless access networks.

Unlike the preceding size category, size category 2 facilities are not capable of mobile operation and are not capable of the types of unorthodox deployment scenarios that a size category 1 edge data centre facility can support. However, despite this, there are likely to be larger numbers of this size category of edge data centres across an example area such as a city than any other due to the need for the infrastructure edge computing network to be interconnected with as many access or last mile networks as is possible across every area in which the infrastructure edge computing network operates. By capturing the traffic from these networks as close as possible to its source and maintaining a reliable and performant network connection back to the closest larger size category infrastructure edge data centre, size category 2 facilities are then able to funnel as much of the access or last mile network's traffic through the infrastructure edge computing network as possible, providing the most opportunity for the traffic to be served by customer equipment located in edge data centre facilities.

Although facilities of this size category could be used by customer equipment to support applications beyond network functions, in the majority of cases, these applications are better served by operating from a larger infrastructure edge data centre. The number of individual customers which, due to the size of the size category 2 facility, could be present within the facility is very limited, and an edge exchange (EX) is not likely to be deployed in these locations because its value is driven by larger numbers of customers. Additionally the use of these facilities for purposes other than network functions may be possible topologically depending on the types of access or last mile networks which connect to the facility and the type of network functions processing, which is performed in the edge data centre facility. Cellular networks in particular may be organised such that the core network interfaces, which are responsible for exposing their customer traffic as standard routable Internet Protocol (IP) traffic, are not exposed inside size category 2 edge data centre facilities to reduce the number of instances of a distributed core.

However, despite them representing in many ways a departure from the traditional data centre model in terms of their size, operational utility, and potential deployment locations, size category 2 data centres are one of the most vital scales of infrastructure edge data centre, precisely due to the benefits of these unique characteristics. Many infrastructure edge computing network operators are likely to reach a point where they have initially deployed larger edge data centre facilities and must then expand their footprint out to more geographically distributed locations in order to capture the traffic from access or last mile networks as close as possible to its source. Size category 2 edge data centres offer a way to achieve this by drastically shrinking the cost and time required for deployment when compared to a larger edge data centre facility combined with their ability to support the type of network function processing, which many networks, including common variants of fifth generation (5G) and fourth generation (4G), will require in order to achieve the performance and cost base needed to meet their own business goals.

Consider an example scenario where a small number of much larger size category edge data centre facilities have been deployed to create an infrastructure edge data centre network. However, these facilities are not located close enough to key pieces of network infrastructure which are spread out across the wider area for them to make sense as points of interconnection for these access or last mile networks. In some cases this decision is driven by performance, such as in 5G and 4G networks where many network functions must be performed within a specific time window and thus a specific latency budget. In other cases, the cost of the fibre connectivity from the access or last mile network to the larger size infrastructure edge data centres can be prohibitive for those network operators. By deploying size category 2 facilities out from the larger facilities, these needs can then be addressed.

As previously described, due to their size, facilities in this size category are likely to be operated as single tenant data centres. This may mean that only equipment that is owned and operated by the infrastructure edge computing network operator is present at the facility, or that some equipment owned and operated by a customer in addition to that equipment is present. In cases where such a facility is used only for network extension, the former model is most likely, with the latter model being predominant where network function processing also occurs in these data centre facilities.

Some edge data centre facilities in this size category will utilise passive cooling for their customer equipment, depending on their environment and on the power utilisation of the equipment that is deployed inside. This is another decision which will be driven by the use case for the facility as the network hardware required for an interconnection with an access or last mile network consumes a fraction of the power required by network function processing for wireless networks, for example. The majority of these facilities will utilise active air cooling in a similar way to much larger facilities.

The operation and maintenance of this size category of edge data centre facilities is closer to that of a larger data centre facility than the preceding size category. As size category 2 facilities utilise fixed deployment locations and are physically much larger than size category 1 facilities, they are capable of being treated as smaller versions of larger data centre facilities in terms of their site security and access technologies for customers and personnel who may need to physically visit one of these sites.

6.2.2.3 Size Category 3 (10–50 kW)

At this category of infrastructure edge data centres, the traditional multi-tenant data centre model where a range of applications and services can operate from the same facility becomes more viable. Especially towards the larger end of this size category, there is sufficient space both physically and in terms of the customer equipment as measured in kilowatts that the facility can support, which makes the operation of an EX in the facility practical as well. Although in many cases the infrastructure edge computing network operator will want to deploy EX functionality in larger data centre facilities that are topologically better suited for aggregation and the deployment of a larger number of individual customers, some areas may not support the deployment of size category 4 and above facilities due to their expected end user density, and so a size category 3 facility represents a useful minimum EX.

Size category 3 facilities straddle a key line between single and multi-tenant operation, which makes them flexible, while at the same time introducing a series of decisions which have to be made by the infrastructure edge computing network operator to ensure that the right capabilities are present at such a facility to serve its intended purpose. This is the size category which will make the most sense for many brownfield edge data centre deployments, and topologically they allow an operator to establish a fully featured footprint in key rural areas which do not warrant a larger edge data centre.

For example, consider the following facilities, all of which fit within this size category but which vary considerably in their operating model, functional capabilities, and topological location in a network:

1) 15 kW single tenant facility, no EX
   a) Size category 3 data centre facilities at this smaller end of the scale are in many ways not significantly different from the preceding size category, but with the difference that a size category 3 edge data centre facility may, particularly when it is deployed as a brownfield development, be expected to expand over time. Such a facility may initially use only one part of an existing structure with the operator, then have the option to retrofit additional parts of the structure to expand the facility over time.

2) 40 kW multi-tenant facility, no EX
   a) An edge data centre facility of this scale may be deployed at this size initially or, as previously described, be the result of an evolution over time from a smaller initial deployment due to customer or infrastructure edge computing network operator requirements. As the available customer equipment space within the facility grows, the usefulness of supporting a multi-tenant operating model becomes apparent. In these cases, the number and types of customers and application workloads which are present within the facility along with the overall topology of the infrastructure edge computing network will determine whether an EX is present in this facility.

3) 50 kW multi-tenant facility, with EX
   a) At its largest and most functionally rich extent, a size category 3 infrastructure edge data centre facility can function as an important regional hub where customers are colocated, and the presence of an EX allows data to be exchanged locally between their equipment and between any other networks which are present in the facility. Building on the previous example, an EX could be added over time to this facility as the number of unique customers and the total volume of traffic in the facility grows or may be present from the start depending on the facility priorities of the operator.

These examples show the utility of this size category of infrastructure edge data centre. Their ability to support an evolution of scale and functionality over time, combined with their size, making for an excellent lighter cost deployment option for the support of infrastructure edge computing networks in rural areas, means that this size category of facilities has a unique niche below its larger cousins.

Consider an example of the evolution of a rural infrastructure edge computing network over time. At the core of this part of the network is a size category 3 data centre facility, which begins as a small regional hub for the support of a single anchor customer. This facility is then expanded over time by the infrastructure edge computing network operator to accommodate multi-tenant operation, and finally the network infrastructure required to support EX functionality is added, making the facility a hub for data exchange between multiple networks across that region, to the benefit of the operator.

Although facilities of this size category may not be what many people think of first when it comes to infrastructure edge computing, as these examples have shown, they are uniquely flexible and able to support parts of the network which would otherwise require a larger, more expensive facility which, as edge data centre facilities above this size category are most likely to be self-contained, would also not allow the operator to grow that facility over time from a small initial footprint inside a building.

6.2.2.4 Size Category 4 (50–100 kW)

Above size category 3, the infrastructure edge data centre begins to look more like a traditional and large data centre facility inside while retaining a comparatively compact external form factor. These facilities are what most people tend to think of for an infrastructure edge data centre precisely due to them straddling those two lines. Size category 4 is also the smallest size category where most of the edge data centre facilities it represents will be self-contained units which are manufactured in a remote location and are then delivered to their deployment location by a truck onto a foundation.

This size category, alongside size category 5, is expected to provide most of the infrastructure edge data centre capacity as measured in kilowatts. It is not likely to be the most numerous, however, as smaller size category form factors can be deployed in a greater number of locations. Notable for the number of expected edge data centre facilities is size category 2 due to the utility for the operator of the network extension and network function processing use cases that those facilities are suited for.

Size category 4 represents the first size category where an EX is present across all facilities of this size. This is a product of both the physical size of these facilities and their customer equipment capacity, as measured in kilowatts, combined with their ideal topological role which, in an infrastructure edge network, places them hierarchically above potentially tens or hundreds of smaller sized edge data centre facilities, each of which may be bringing traffic to the infrastructure edge network from different access or last mile networks, which can then be interconnected to one another at the EX present within the size category 4 facility. Where a size category 4 facility exists in an area, they will typically be the smallest edge data centres in that area which operate an EX due to these factors.

Unlike size category 3, the capacity and major functionality of a size category 4 and higher edge data centre facility is typically set at the time of its design and deployment. As these are likely to be self-contained facilities which are manufactured ahead of their deployment time, there is little benefit to limiting the user equipment capacity of network capabilities of the facility in order to increase them at a later date based on customer demand. As the unit is self-contained, the physical space that the edge data centre facility will require is set, regardless of the level of network functionality or other capabilities which the operator chooses to deploy in that facility, and the cooling system must be already capable of handling the heat generated by the maximum amount of customer equipment, which is expected to be deployed in the facility over time. This does make facilities of this size and above less flexible than smaller facilities, but the payoff for that cost is a larger capacity per facility and likely a significantly higher supported density of customer equipment due to cooling integration.

Due to their self-contained physical design and significant customer equipment capacity near to the higher end of the size category, facilities of size category 4 are often ideal flag planting locations for an infrastructure edge network operator who is establishing their initial footprint in an urban or a semi urban area. They provide an effective combination of capacity, deployment opportunities, and functionality, which makes them suitable anchors for an initial infrastructure edge network design.

Consider the example of an infrastructure edge computing network operator ana-lysing a new area into which they are looking to expand their network. The operator has no existing infrastructure in the area, and they believe that the expected density of end users will bring significant customer and network partner interest to new infrastructure edge data centre facilities distributed across the area. There is not an existing RNDC facility within an acceptable latency or data transport cost envelope for this area, and so EX capabilities are required for the operator to be able to offer an effective solution to a wide variety of use cases, many of which require a data exchange.

The combination of physical size and customer equipment capacity makes edge data centre facilities of size category 4 attractive, not just to infrastructure edge net-work operators but also to RNDC operators who may regard smaller edge data cen-tre facilities as outside of their typical view of a data centre and larger edge data facilities as nearing limits in size, which may place them in competition with that operator's existing data centre facilities. As such, this size category is at the interest-ing scale and level of key functionality to be not too little or too much data centre, but just enough in order for them to make sense to a wide variety of organisations who may either want to deploy these new facilities themselves or partner with other operators who are deploying them.

6.2.2.5 Size Category 5 (100–200 kW)

Facilities in this size category function well as sub-regional hub locations for the infrastructure edge computing network. They have sufficient capacity to support a comparatively large number of users and customers, and due to their size relative to smaller facilities, they make logical aggregation sites for the infrastructure edge computing network. Additionally, they retain all EX network functionality.

Size category 5 edge data centre facilities are most similar to those in size category 4. They are most likely to be self-contained units which are manufactured offsite and then transported to a new site for deployment, and the types of customers and general use cases supported using the size and the functional capabilities of a size category 5 data centre facility are very similar to those of category 4.

However, where they differ is in per-site scale. A large size category 5 data centre can support up to 200 kW of customer equipment, which is twice the size of the largest size category 4 facility. This is a substantial increase which requires additional physical space for the rack infrastructure to support the additional customer equipment, in addition to any cabling, accessible space, and other needs of the operator for this equipment. The cooling system will also need to be larger than that of smaller infrastructure edge data centres due to its need to remove more heat from and maintain all of the required environmental characteristics of the larger edge data centre facility space of this category.

Many of the infrastructure edge data centre facilities which are currently deployed fit into this size category. Much like facilities belonging to size category 4, those belonging to size category 5 are an ideal scale for an infrastructure edge computing network operator to deploy in an urban or a semi urban area to expand their network's operational footprint. These infrastructure edge data centre facilities incorporate significant space and cooling capability for customer equipment as well as the EX capabilities required to facilitate low latency applications and to limit the cost of data transport.

Whether or not size category 5 edge data centres are used to form their own aggregation layer that sits hierarchically above those facilities that are size category 4 is often dependent on the presence of a size category 6 facility in the area. Where one of these larger facilities is present, size categories 4 and 5 will typically be mixed together at the same hierarchical layer. However, when a size category 5 data centre is the largest facility in the network in that area, it is likely to be in its own higher layer.

Consider the example scenario where an infrastructure edge computing network operator has begun deploying infrastructure edge data centre facilities of various size categories. The customer and end user demand has grown to the point where there is very significant interest in additional edge data centre capacity in the area, but there is not a large number of available sites which are suitable for their deployment and which would be economical for the operator to develop to a deployable state.

The operator can make effective use of any locations which have been identified, and which are also suitable for the deployment of size category 5 edge data centre facilities, by deploying these units in a distributed fashion around the area. In this example, three size category 5 facilities can each add a significant amount of customer equipment capacity to the infrastructure edge computing network in that area, with the total contribution of all three facilities combined easily exceeding half of a Megawatt (MW).

Additionally, over time, if the operator is unable to identify any additional deployment sites but still must address the customer and end user demand for additional capacity across the network, in the locations where size category 4 edge data centre facilities are currently deployed, it may be possible to replace these facilities one by one with their larger cousins while repurposing the smaller facilities elsewhere. Although this approach is not as easy as the brownfield deployment scenario which was discussed for size category 3 facilities, it is a potential option where the size of each site permits it.

6.2.2.6 Size Category 6 (200–250 kW)

As the largest category of infrastructure edge data centres, this category includes those which are best suited to an aggregation role behind other infrastructure edge data centres. This size category will be the least frequently deployed due to their aggregation role, but they form an important and scalable layer between other infrastructure edge data centres and the nearest RNDC. This is especially true in areas which do not have an existing base of RNDC infrastructure, as in these locations transiting traffic back to the nearest data centre is likely to incur significant cost and latency penalties for the infrastructure edge computing network.

One or more size category 6 infrastructure edge data centre facilities can function as key aggregation points for a larger number of size category 4 and 5 facilities. The number of size category 6 facilities which would be required ultimately depends on the serve transit fail (STF) metric, which the network is able to achieve at each layer of the infrastructure edge computing network. This metric will determine the level of traffic which could be expected to pass from the lower layers of the network to the size category 6 facilities and, therefore, the locations and numbers of these facilities which would then be required.

The diagram in Figure 6.2 shows this concept. An example network is illustrated with three primary layers of infrastructure edge data centre facilities. The STF, which is contributed by each layer, is shown next to each layer, with the total STF for the network noted at the bottom. Depending on the customer equipment which is deployed at each layer of the network and the type of application workloads it is intended to perform, a size category 6 layer in the network with even a small number of data centre facilities can significantly contribute to the STF metric. The value of this potential metric increase is a decision to be made by the infrastructure edge computing network operator as to whether they will pay to deploy and operate these additional edge data centre facilities in order to improve efficiency.

Above this size category, it becomes difficult to distinguish between existing data centre facilities and those which are being deployed as part of an infrastructure

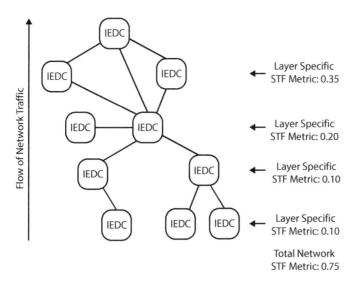

Figure 6.2 Tiered infrastructure edge computing network with example STF metrics.

edge computing network. The size limitation of this category can be overcome if needed by adding multiple edge data centre facilities in an area, but when single facility data centre capacity begins to approach an equipment capacity of nearly half a MW, its deployment flexibility reduces considerably and its ability to be located in the physical and topological locations, which are required to operate as an infrastructure edge facility, is made more difficult. Where larger infrastructure edge data centre facilities are created, they should be considered part of this size category and are likely to be outliers from other data centre facilities.

6.2.2.7 Size Category Interoperation

An infrastructure edge computing network operator is most valuable if they are able to deploy and operate all of the size categories of edge facilities required to support their target customers and use cases. To address the largest possible number of customers and use cases, an operator would need to be able to deploy and operate all size categories of edge data centre facilities across a given area.

In some cases, the operator will want to deploy only specific infrastructure edge data centre sizes. Consider the example of an infrastructure edge computing network operator who has invested in the design and development of their own proprietary facilities, with significant interoperation and functionality between the hardware, software, and operation of these facilities at size category 4. This is a highly versatile category due to its physical size and network capabilities, and the operator may choose to make the most use of this single size category rather than spend additional time and resources to develop or acquire edge data centre facilities across any of the other size categories.

For infrastructure edge network operators who must be limited to a pair of size categories, there are a few combinations which provide a useful combination together. Three of the most promising are:

1) Size categories 1 and 3
   a) By combining the smallest size category of edge data centre facility, which is well suited to a variety of mobile and unorthodox deployments, with the smallest size category that is suitable for multi-tenant operation and which may incorporate an EX, this pair of size categories allows an infrastructure edge computing network to be established in an area with the lightest footprint on a per-site basis. This type of network may be deployed by a dedicated infrastructure edge computing network operator, or by an organisation such as a law enforcement agency who requires the capabilities of a distributed network of mobile edge data centres combined with a local facility at which traffic can be exchanged with partner networks and equipment.
2) Size categories 2 and 4
   a) This pair of size categories represents the most versatile combination as it is able to address a high number of use cases and customers with the greatest chance at being consistent to deploy and operate over a large number of facilities. Both of these size categories avoid the bespoke and use case specific nature of size category 1 facilities while still providing enough deployment flexibility to adapt to a wide range of uses, including network function processing for highly distributed network infrastructure.
3) Size categories 2 and 6
   a) Similarly to the previous combination of size categories, combining size categories 2 and 6 provides the operator with the ability to support a large number of use cases but uses a larger edge data centre facility as the aggregation point. This combination is interesting for more rural areas, where it may be sufficient to bring large numbers of size category 2 facilities back to one size category 6 facility, which then functions as a regional hub due to its size and ability to support many customers and an EX.

The number of different size categories described in this section raises the question of which size category will see the most immediate deployment or will be the first to be typically deployed in an area such as a city or a rural town. This question can be answered by organising the size categories into pairs, with each successive pair being likely to be deployed later than the pair which precedes it:

1) Size categories 4 and 5
   a) These two size categories represent infrastructure edge data centre facilities which are of sufficient size to incorporate all of the expected capabilities of an edge data centre such as an EX but which are easier to deploy than a

larger facility and able to support more customers per site than each smaller size category. This makes these size categories ideal for initial deployment in an area as smaller size categories, of particular note being size category 2, can then be connected back to these facilities once they are themselves deployed at a later date to further utilise these facilities.

2) Size categories 2 and 3
   a) The combination of these two size categories allows an infrastructure edge network to address a more geographically distributed set of use cases than the combination preceding it, without introducing the complexities inherent in the unorthodox and single tenant deployment and operation model used for size category 1 facilities. In these two size categories, there is the potential for the operator to support several key use cases for network functions and deploy the smallest footprint where a multi-tenant facility incorporating all of the functionality of an EX will typically make sense.

3) Size categories 1 and 6
   a) Although both of these size categories provide the infrastructure edge computing network operator with the capability to support additional customers and use cases, they are not as versatile as the preceding size categories, and so they will typically be deployed last, outside of a specific customer need. In the case of size category 1, the most likely scenario is that these facilities are deployed only ever at the request of a specific customer due to their specialised nature and ability for unorthodox or even mobile deployment. For size category 6 facilities, their physical size makes them a more challenging proposition for deployment compared to smaller facilities, and so the most likely scenario is these facilities will see deployment as an additional layer of aggregation topologically above an existing layer of size category 4 and 5 facilities.

Note that these size category timings apply primarily to an infrastructure edge network operator who is building out their initial network footprint and wants to maintain a balance between the versatility of their infrastructure and its likely appeal to a wide range of potential customers. In specific cases where the operator is designing their infrastructure in an area based on the needs they have identified for a customer, the resulting market design should instead prioritise the size categories of edge data centre facilities that best serve the requirements of that customer instead.

To see the scale of each size category of infrastructure edge data centre in context, the diagram in Figure 6.3 shows each of them in sequence using their estimated physical sizes. Although these are estimates and the specific size of an infrastructure edge data centre will vary based on several design choices made by the infrastructure edge computing network operator, this comparison serves to illustrate the difference in scale between the size categories without product specifics.

Figure 6.3 Example scale comparison of infrastructure edge data centre size categories (W×D).

Table 6.2 Typical EXP and network capabilities of infrastructure edge data centres.

Size category number	EXP function	Customer equipment	Fronthaul termination	Direct connectivity to backhaul network
1	No	Yes or prefab	Yes	No
2	No	Yes	Yes	No
3	Maybe	Yes	Maybe	Maybe
4	Yes	Yes	Maybe	Maybe
5	Yes	Yes	Unlikely	Yes
6	Yes	Yes	Unlikely	Yes

The network capabilities of each size category of infrastructure edge data centre shape the role that each of these types of facility are best suited for as part of the network. Table 6.2 indicates if a particular size category of facility will be an edge exchange point (EXP), fronthaul termination, or backhaul connectivity:

Where multiple size categories of infrastructure edge data centre are deployed, there will typically be an hierarchical and functional relationship between them, shown visually by the diagram in Figure 6.4:

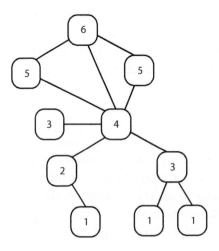

Figure 6.4 Topological hierarchy between size categories of infrastructure edge data centre.

Figure 6.5 Physical hierarchy between size categories of infrastructure edge data centre.

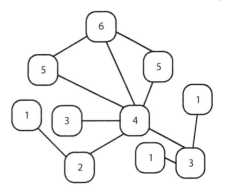

In this way, higher numbered size categories of infrastructure edge data centres can often function as aggregation points for lower numbered size categories. This is a simplistic topological view based on the order of these facilities from smallest to largest; in a practical deployment when viewed from above, the locations of different size categories of facilities are likely to overlap in order to fill in any gaps for specific use cases. Facilities belonging to the smallest two size categories are likely in a real world deployment to be dotted across the map, both far away from other infrastructure edge data centres and between them in order to terminate networks and provide network function processing.

An example of this physical view is shown in the diagram in Figure 6.5. Although some parts of the network when viewed in this way are in the same place as in the topological view from the previous diagram, others have moved in order to allow nearby network infrastructure or other use cases to be served.

Note that the network connectivity shown in these diagrams follows that of Table 6.2. All of the smaller infrastructure edge data centre facilities, as they do not have any direct connectivity to the backhaul network, must pass their traffic through a larger infrastructure edge data centre before it can be passed on to a RNDC. In cases where there are only these smaller size category edge data centre facilities deployed in an area, they will then connect directly to the backhaul network; but where other infrastructure edge facilities are available, it is useful to funnel their traffic back through facilities which contain an EX in order to support low latency use cases.

As shown in Table 6.2, not all infrastructure edge data centres will incorporate an EX. This is due to their size, which then drives the single tenant operating model, which is the most likely model at these facilities. It only makes sense for the infrastructure edge computing network operator to offer EX capabilities at edge data centre facilities which are large enough to support many different users, which may be true in a size category 3 facility but will definitely be across the larger size categories.

Although it is assumed in this book that the same infrastructure edge computing network operator is responsible for all of the edge data centre facilities in an area, there is no requirement for this to be the case at all. It is entirely feasible that some operators will focus in an area on the smallest of the size categories, especially with the specialised nature of many size category 1 deployments and use cases, while other operators deploy size categories 4 to 6 edge data centre facilities, which offer a more traditional data centre colocation model which may better suit their business goals and skills.

6.3   Heating and Cooling

An infrastructure edge data centre, regardless of its potentially unorthodox deployment location, remains a data centre facility, and as such, its ability to properly maintain a standard environment which allows its own operational equipment as well as customer equipment is vital to its success.

As these facilities are often capable of supporting significant rack densities for customer equipment while being physically compact, the cooling system is of primary importance to the operation of an edge data centre facility and therefore to the entire infrastructure edge computing network. In these facilities, the principles of heating and cooling remain the same as in larger RNDC facilities, but the physical size limitations of infrastructure edge data centres introduce new challenges.

Water cooling has been used for many years in applications which must remove significant amounts of heat from electronics systems. Compared to air, water is a more efficient medium to transfer and thus move heat away from where it is being generated to a location where the water can be cooled, typically by funnelling hot water through a radiator which uses blown air or other advanced cooling mechanisms to cool the liquid down as it passes through. Once the water is sufficiently cool, a loop physically transports it back to the source of heat in the system by the aid of a pump, and the cycle continues. In this way the temperature of an entity generating heat, such as the CPU sockets of a high performance server, can often be reduced to many degrees lower than is possible utilising a standard air cooling approach. The name water cooling is somewhat of a misnomer, however; in many cases the operators of these cooling systems are understandably uneasy at the prospect of pumping large volumes of electrically conductive fluid along rubber tubing in very close proximity to sensitive electronics. This has led to the use of non-electrically conductive fluids which are designed, should a leak ever occur onto electronic equipment, not to cause any damage or any short circuits.

Although air cooling, and to a lesser extent water cooling, are the most frequently encountered types of cooling system for infrastructure edge data centre facilities, there are other options which will see adoption in specialised deployments over time. All of these technologies require modification to the customer equipment, which will be deployed in the facility and are more expensive or more complex than water cooling, which limits their operational applicability in small, unmanned, and geographically distributed facilities until the total cost and operational maturity of these technologies improves. It is worth noting developments in this area though, as they may allow for rack density growth over time. Some of these advanced cooling technologies, which are promising for the edge data centre, include:

1) Phase change cooling
   a) Phase change cooling is another technology which has seen use in the design and operation of high performance electronics systems such as supercomputers. This process works by manipulating the properties of coolants changing back and forth between liquid and gas states in a similar way to normal household refrigeration or air conditioning systems. These systems are often complex to design and can be difficult to operate at large scale, but they are capable of lowering the operating temperature of electronic components significantly when compared to air cooling.
2) Liquid nitrogen cooling
   a) Liquid nitrogen, which is capable of cooling electronics to temperatures well below freezing, has been used for years by hobbyists and in specialised deployments to be able to cool electronic systems which generate massive amounts of heat. Today the most interesting example of liquid nitrogen cooling is perhaps in its applicability to the cooling of quantum computers, which currently need to be operated at close to absolute zero to work. Some systems for these computers use liquid helium instead.
3) Advanced passive cooling
   a) For size category 1 infrastructure edge data centres, some physical form factors of these facilities to support their deployment in unorthodox locations will require the customer equipment which is present in the facility to operate with passive cooling only. In a passive cooling system, an internal or external fan cannot be relied upon to move hot air away from the electronic components which are generating heat. Solutions to this problem include copper heat pipes which make direct contact to those heat generating components, such as CPUs and GPUs, and then transport the heat that is generated to a heatsink, which uses its large surface area to dissipate the heat. These systems make use of the high thermal conductivity of copper, and some systems will also fill these copper pipes with an appropriate coolant. The heatsink is then typically the entire metal housing of the infrastructure edge data centre itself.

The downside of these more exotic cooling technologies is they often require a customer to deploy equipment that is modified to support them. Although this may allow for superior performance, the customer may either be operating at a small scale and so the cost of modifying the equipment is in itself prohibitive, or they may be operating at such a large scale (as in the case of a hyperscale cloud provider) that any changes to the consistency of their operations are not tenable due to their need to have a single reproducible set of hardware and software that they are able to deploy anywhere.

This factor means that high-efficiency air cooling which does not require direct customer equipment modification remains the preferred choice for the majority of infrastructure edge data centres. The interesting exception to this is an entity such as a cloud provider which has the capability to deploy their own hardware as well as to deploy and operate their own infrastructure edge data centres, and who therefore may seek to deploy both at such a scale that this type of hardware modification yields a large enough benefit to make it worthwhile, whether in terms of an achievable rack density, utility usage requirements, or the overall physical size of the infrastructure edge data centre facility itself.

However, water cooling systems can be designed in two primary ways: one which requires the water cooling loop to make physical contact with the heat generating components, which has the same need for customer equipment modification as the other non-air cooling technologies which were described earlier; and another design where a water cooling loop can be deployed for an entire self-contained facility and be deployed at the rack infrastructure level. Although the former is common, well understood, and operationally proven, the latter may offer an interesting middle ground for the infrastructure edge data centre of size categories 4 and above if it can be effectively commercialised.

Ultimately, as a customer of an infrastructure edge data centre, the specific cooling technology that is used is of little real consequence so long as it meets the requirements of your operational model such as maintaining a target temperature and matching your tolerance for equipment modification. Where more exotic cooling technologies are being used in an infrastructure edge data centre facility which you are considering for equipment deployment, it is worth discussing the operational record of that cooling system with the edge data centre facility operator to determine any serious concerns.

In regard to heating, edge data centre facilities which are operating in areas where the external air temperature drops below freezing due to seasonal variations will typically include a heating element which is connected to the air flow of the cooling system. This heating element is then activated by a temperature control system, which maintains the operating temperature of the facility at any given point in time between the defined minimum as well as the maximum temperatures to avoid issues.

This heating capability of the cooling system is not only vital for the maintenance of a consistent and hospitable operating temperature, but it also plays a role in maintaining the operational efficiency of the facility itself. Areas such as Chicago are famous for their cold winters, and these temperatures, if left unchecked, can negatively impact the operation of the operational systems inside the facility. A good example of this is a battery backup system, which is sensitive to extremes of temperature and should be kept within a specific operating temperature range to ensure its safe operation as well as its long-term capacity, which can suffer if the temperature of the facility is allowed to cycle between seasonal extremes. Cooling systems may also cycle on and off if the internal temperature of the site is allowed to fluctuate, which some systems are not designed to handle, and so damage may occur.

Although it is not as often considered as the need to maintain a consistent operational temperature for the facility's operational systems and the customer equipment which is deployed there, it is also important to consider the personnel who may visit the site, whether they are employees of the edge data centre operator or of a customer of that facility. Excessively hot or cold temperatures within a facility may make it difficult or dangerous for personnel to perform their tasks. However, the range of operational temperatures for an edge data centre facility will typically not create these issues.

6.4 Airflow Design

The majority of infrastructure edge data centres will use air cooling systems. This is driven by several factors which make air cooling ultimately more practical than many of the other cooling technologies described in the previous section, despite the advanced cooling capabilities of those other systems:

1) Minimal equipment modification
   a) The ability for a customer to deploy their equipment without any need for physical modification is a very significant operational benefit for the customer as well as the infrastructure edge computing network operator. In both cases this capability to use standard customer equipment eliminates a potential source of cost and complexity in deploying equipment in the edge data centre facility, making these facilities more attractive to their customers while allowing the edge data centre operator to easily accommodate existing standard equipment, which may then need to be altered only in terms of configuration or equipment selection in order to achieve a densified rack.
2) Adequate equipment cooling capability
   a) Air cooling systems are capable of providing adequate cooling capacity for the vast majority of customer equipment configurations which are likely to be deployed in an infrastructure edge data centre facility. Even as the density of customer equipment in the average rack continues to increase due to the deployment of hardware such as GPU clusters for ML inferencing use cases, carefully designed air cooling appears to offer enough headroom to maintain

safe operational temperatures even as these types of deployments begin to cluster over time in infrastructure edge data centres.

3) Known operational and design limitations

   a) As air cooling systems have been used successfully at very large and very small scale across regional and national data centres, as well as in other cooling systems for the majority of active cooling systems which are used for electronic components, their operational and design limitations are well understood by a large number of cooling system engineers and other operational personnel. These factors can contribute in a significant way to removing risk from the design and operation of the data centre by limiting the number of unknowns which are introduced compared to other systems.

As is often seen in the success of technologies and their adoption in the market, air cooling is a good example of what may not technically be the best performing technology continuing to be the most widely used. It can be argued that the primary purpose of a cooling system is to cool equipment to be within a safe range of operating temperatures. In this regard, a phase change cooling system, for example, is able to alter the temperature of heat generating components more effectively than an equivalent air cooling system can. However, this capability is only one piece of the puzzle, because as was mentioned earlier, the operational or design challenges of this technology limit its use today.

Even when the decision to use air cooling has been reached for an infrastructure edge data centre, there are many subsequent design decisions which shape the overall structure of the resulting data centre significantly. These decisions will determine how the facility is oriented, the amount of space for customer equipment, a range of operating temperatures and heat densities for both the facility and on a per-rack basis, and other factors such as the external sound generated from the facility too.

As in any high performance cooling system, an air cooling system for an infrastructure edge data centre must be designed to achieve optimal airflow and heat exchange. The former ensures that enough air is circulating across heat generating components in the system, whereas the latter is responsible for cooling that air once it reaches a point of heat exchange such as a radiator or the outside air. If the airflow in the system is insufficient, it will be unable to move all of the hot air that is required in order to maintain the operating temperature of the customer equipment, and if the heat exchange ability is insufficient, warm air will be recirculated back across the equipment, which may then cause a continual rise in equipment temperature over time, leading to equipment failure.

This includes making sure that any cooling fans on customer equipment are oriented such that they are not fighting the rest of the system by pulling in air where it is being pushed out, or vice versa. In some cases this can severely impede the operation of the system as well as the ability of the system to adequately cool specific customer equipment. Issues like this are typically detected at the time of equipment deployment and can be arranged by mounting equipment and routing cabling as needed.

6.4.1 Traditional Designs

Some infrastructure edge data centres will use a traditional hot and cold aisle-based airflow design. There are several advantages to this approach; this cooling model is well understood for both the manufacture and operation of these facilities, which may help to lower upfront and recurring costs.

1) Proven designs
   a) As previously described for regional and national scale data centre facilities, the use of hot and cold aisle-based airflow systems is widespread. This allows these designs to be readily adapted to the smaller physical spaces available in infrastructure edge data centre facilities. Although this process will require design and development in order to be successful, it is likely to be easier than creating a more esoteric system due to the experience that is available in the industry with these cooling systems.
2) Operational simplicity
   a) Due to their widespread usage, data centre operations teams are used to the issues which may develop with hot and cold aisle-based cooling systems over time. In the case of an infrastructure edge computing network operator who is responsible for potentially hundreds of geographically distributed data centre locations, this key to ensuring that the number of personnel visits required to each site in order to resolve issues and perform preventative maintenance can be reduced and easily quantified.
3) Facility risk limitation
   a) Due to the two prior factors, the infrastructure edge computing network operator can remove risk that is associated with the development and the operation of the cooling system which may otherwise exist with the use of other designs. This has a significant benefit to the operator in terms of both site deployment and operation, as the cost to the operator of unforeseen issues can be substantial especially if an issue becomes visible to a customer, such as the failure of the cooling system being the cause of customer equipment failure by operating at an elevated temperature.

These designs will be seen in larger edge data centre facilities, from the largest end of size category 3 through size category 6. Internally such large edge data centre facilities are capable of supporting a physical layout which accommodates an aisle-based design whereas smaller facilities are often not. In addition, edge data centre facilities in these larger size categories must be capable of allowing people such as operator personnel or customer staff inside the facility for maintenance or the deployment of their equipment. Using an aisle-based design presents a more familiar and standard environment to customers in particular. Although this effect may be only temporary as customers would be likely to acclimatise to more esoteric layouts over time, this factor does help ease any concerns which a customer may have about the edge data centre facility caused by their first impression feeling odd.

Consider the example of a hot and cold aisle airflow design for a size category 4 infrastructure edge data centre facility. Although it is on a smaller scale, this design, when viewed from above, closely resembles that which can be used in a regional or national scale data centre facility, and so in a comparison between the two systems, the infrastructure edge data centre facility implementation resembles a miniature version with a reduced number of racks and aisle space, but with a somewhat oversized cooling system in order to achieve the rack densities which will be prevalent in the facility.

In the smaller size categories of infrastructure edge data centre facilities, notably size category 2 and the smaller end of size category 3, it is likely that a simpler push and pull air cooling system will be used. Especially for smaller edge data centre facilities, the air intake component of the system may be provided by the cooling fans, which are already part of the customer equipment itself. However, these fans are likely to be augmented by one or more intake fans on the facility itself in order for the operator to ensure that sufficient airflow occurs through the cooling system to maintain acceptable operating temperatures regardless of the cooling fans on any customer equipment that is deployed.

Consider a simple airflow design for an infrastructure edge data centre facility of size category 2. In this model, air is drawn into the front of the facility by a bank of fans. At the rear of the facility, there is a matching bank of fans which pulls the air through the facility and expels it by pushing it through a fine grille located on the rear of the facility. At the front of the facility, the air which is pulled in is cooler than the hot air, which is collecting around the heatsinks of the equipment, and so when the cool air passes over those heatsinks, most of that hot air is removed and expelled. This process repeats constantly in order to maintain the required temperature of the customer equipment. As the cooling system in this example does not have a refrigeration unit, it is not suitable for densified rack configurations or in a fully self-contained data centre facility which cannot draw in external air. This is a very simplistic example and in reality even small facilities will tend to utilise air conditioning.

This type of simple cooling system is also likely to generate high amounts of external noise if it were scaled up to support high density rack configurations. The addition of air conditioning equipment in the edge data centre facility would reduce this and improve the cooling capability of the system but would also introduce an increase in design, deployment, and operational cost for the facility. As the size of an edge data centre facility increases beyond this point, the types of cooling systems that are common in RNDC facilities using hot or cold aisle containment are likely.

The use of underfloor venting may also present a challenge for infrastructure edge data centres that are using hot and cold aisle airflow designs. Some regional or national scale data centre facilities use raised flooring which, due to the height requirements present in some deployment locations, may be an issue for an infrastructure edge data centre. This is to say that even if the general type of system, such as a hot and cold aisle-based cooling system, can be applied to an infrastructure edge facility, it may still require adaptation based on the unique requirements of the edge data centre model itself.

6.4.2 Non-traditional Designs

The physical size constraints of infrastructure edge data centre facilities in categories 1 through 4 are drivers for non-traditional cooling system designs, which range anywhere from passive cooling as can be used extensively in size category 1 facilities all the way to advanced airflow designs which still use air cooling but do so in a way which may be more optimally designed for an edge data centre facility, such as using a central exhaust fan to remove heat from customer equipment which is located in an arc or a circle around the fan to draw air upward and out of the top of the facility. However, as has been described in the previous section, these more esoteric cooling systems bring with them their own challenges, especially in terms of operational complexity and customer familiarity, which can be more important to an infrastructure edge computing network operator than their cooling efficiency.

There is an overlap between the size categories described in this section and those in the preceding section. This is because even though there are certain size ranges of facilities which make a specific type of cooling system preferable, it is ultimately the choice of the infrastructure edge computing network operator as to what level of design, deployment, and operational complexity they are able and willing to accept. The larger end of size category 3 and the smaller end of size category 4 make the most sense as the breakpoint between traditional and non-traditional data centre airflow and cooling systems, but the exact boundary chosen depends on the specific operator configurations of this density, which is a key deployment scenario for many edge facilities over time.

There are several considerations to take into account when designing an air cooling system for use in an infrastructure edge data centre, which can create additional complexity compared to the systems which are used for regional or national scale data centre facilities. Three of the most important are:

1) Greater rack density
   a) To make the most effective use of the limited physical space that is available within the infrastructure edge data centre facility, densified rack infrastructure is needed. This benefits customers, who are then able to serve more end users and application workloads from their presence at the infrastructure edge. It also benefits the facility operator who is then able to fit more unique customers and application workloads into their edge data centre facilities, which increases the value of their EX services. Additionally, the deployment of hardware accelerated distributed artificial intelligence (AI) use cases is a key driver for infrastructure edge computing and requires high rack densification.

2) Uneven loading between racks
   a) When a data centre is unevenly loaded, the heat output of each rack is not the same as its neighbours. Although some variation of heat output between racks is expected as a matter of normal operation, when there is a significant difference in this regard between racks, it can result in the data centre facility cooling system having difficulty in maintaining an acceptable temperature across each of those racks. Not all cooling systems are able to handle large (such as an order of magnitude) differences in heat output between racks and may then pass warm air from one rack to its neighbours.

3) External sound requirements
   a) Many infrastructure edge data centre facilities will be deployed in locations which impose environmental regulations on how the facility will be designed and operated. These regulations often include a requirement for the noise generated by the facility as measured from a prescribed distance away, typically 15 ft, and measured to be some acceptable level of noise. It is difficult to provide greater specificity at this level as these regulations vary considerably by region. For example, in some areas it is OK for such facilities to match the sound output of a home air conditioning unit, which is anywhere from 25 to 55 dB. In some areas such as Los Angeles, however, the rule can be relative, stating that facility noise cannot be more than 5 dB louder than a level of ambient noise which has been measured in the same area at a specific time of day. The size, speed, and position of fans in particular can greatly impact this for a facility, with lower noise levels being achievable in many cases by increasing the height from the ground of any fans at the facility and also directing them away from the ground.

Uneven loading can also be exacerbated due to the small physical spaces available in infrastructure edge data centres. In a larger RNDC, the spread of rack loading often evens out when an area of the facility is looked at on a larger scale and matched against its cooling system capability. In an infrastructure edge data centre, however, the disparity between the small number of racks present in the facility in terms of their heat output may be such that the cooling system easily becomes unbalanced and the operational efficiency of the system suffers substantially as a result.

Consider an infrastructure edge data centre which has four full size racks, each of which are filled by customer equipment. One rack is loaded at 35 kW, while the others are loaded at 5 kW. The cooling system is capable of handling 50 kW within normal operating conditions and with a safe operational margin. However, its airflow design assumes that 50 kW is distributed evenly across all of the racks within the facility, with each rack being populated at 12.5 kW. The unbalanced heat output across all four racks may cause the cooling system to operate inefficiently, similar to placing hot food on one shelf of a refrigerator. The extent to which this is an issue will depend on the cooling capability of the facility, however; ideally the cooling system will not be operating this close to its limitations and the infrastructure edge computing network operator will be responsible for managing how the heat generating components are distributed across the data centre facility in order to prevent this issue.

This issue does, however, raise a point of consideration for the operator. The expected rack density and the physical locations of a customer's racks are important factors for the operator to be able to avoid localised overloading of the cooling and power delivery systems of their edge data centres in particular. There are three key ways of dealing with this issue, both of which may be used together:

1) Operator control of customer equipment placement
    a) For the infrastructure edge computing network operator, the ideal situation is that the operator retains final control in regard to which of their data centre facilities a rack of customer equipment is placed. This control allows the operator to position customer equipment across the network such that any unacceptable strain on the cooling system in particular of specific facilities can be avoided. However, this also runs counter to the needs of many customers, who will often ask for a right of first refusal to adjacent rack space in any data centre facility where they have deployed their equipment in order to simplify maintenance and operation. The operator has the opportunity to negotiate with the customer and determine which route to take.
2) Limitations on rack density for customer equipment
    a) An operator may need or want to place limitations on the density of racks which are deployed within their infrastructure edge data centre facilities. These requirements may be driven by the capabilities of the facility cooling

systems or the power feeds to the racks and are in some cases necessary to protect the operation of customer equipment. It may not be necessary, however, to publicly state the limitation in terms of kilowatts per rack when it can be shown through a power delivery system breaker limit. This allows the operator to retain some flexibility in the market and still position any edge data centre facilities with such limitations as effective densification locations.

3) Oversized cooling system deployment for facility
   a) The cooling system for an edge data centre facility should be sized appropriately to support the heat output which is expected if all of the customer equipment racks are filled to their maximum supported density, unless the operator has arranged their customer contracts such that the operator always has the final say over where any customer equipment is deployed. As this is not likely to be popular with some of the customers for these facilities, a combination of cooling systems with enough room to operate at a safe margin such as 85% of system capacity in order to cool all of the equipment that is within the limitations on rack density for the facility is sensible.

Consider the example where multiple infrastructure edge data centre facilities are able to support the customer equipment which, in the previous example, was colocated at a single facility. The total customer equipment budget for each facility in kilowatts is known for each data centre, and the operator has final control over where customer equipment is deployed as long as the operator can show the customer that the chosen facility will meet the key performance requirements of the users of the customer's services to be delivered from that edge data centre. In this case the operator is able to balance the heat output of each facility by organising the deployment of equipment such that no single facility is overloaded. Although this is a simple example, the movement of equipment which has already been deployed to balance the system is certain to cause application workload uptime concerns with customers. As such, this type of load balancing across the operator's network of edge data centre facilities is practical only at the time of equipment deployment, and if customers agree.

To support this type of asymmetric rack density within an infrastructure edge data centre facility, it may also be necessary to consider a different airflow design. Some designs are capable of providing enhanced cooling within a smaller footprint than a traditional hot and cold aisle-based design when deployed within a self-contained unit without the need to directly modify the customer equipment.

By arranging the rack infrastructure of the edge data centre around a central exhaust, the issue of uneven rack loading is eliminated as the central fan is able to draw air evenly through all racks and expel it through the top of the exhaust. This allows even cooling to be applied to all equipment in the facility. Such a system is an example of an advanced airflow design, which can make sense in an infrastructure edge data centre where the central exhaust is built into the middle of the customer equipment area of the facility and all of the rack infrastructure within the facility is arranged around it with sufficient space remaining on all sides for personnel to access the equipment. For facilities in size categories 4 and above, these airflow systems become more feasible due to these facilities most likely being self-contained units. However, in edge data centre facilities of this scale, the established hot and cold aisle-based airflow designs may already provide suitable cooling, removing the need for these more innovative designs which may introduce any additional operational or design complexity.

The future of non-traditional cooling system designs in infrastructure edge data centre facilities will depend on the efficiency of traditional cooling system designs and the need for rack density in each facility. Where traditional systems are capable of providing adequate cooling, there is a limited need for an advanced or more esoteric airflow design, which may introduce additional complexity for both the operator and their customers. As was previously mentioned, the best solution to a problem may not be the solution which is technically superior at its primary purpose, which in this case is cooling customer equipment within the data centre facility. Cost and complexity are other key factors too.

In cases where more extreme rack densities are required, however, it is likely that operators will be able to make the case to their customers that a degree of modification to their equipment is needed in order to utilise technologies like water cooling where heat blocks are applied directly to the heat generating components of that customer equipment. In this way air cooling systems will continue to be used to support low to medium rack densities, with other systems taking over at or above 50 kW.

6.5 Power Distribution

Although an infrastructure edge data centre is physically smaller than a traditional data centre, the same principles of power distribution apply. However, due to the reduced size of the edge facility, the different power offerings may be constrained compared to a larger data centre. These smaller facilities are more likely to support one type of power to the customer's rack and then either have the customer or the operator supply voltage conversion or rectification equipment as needed by specific pieces of customer equipment which have any specialised power delivery requirements.

As in RNDC facilities, the majority of customer equipment is designed to accept standard 120 or 208 V power in the US, with the choice of which voltage and phase being determined primarily by the power usage of the equipment. Smaller infrastructure edge facilities typically will supply 120 V of single phase power to the customer, whereas larger edge data centres can supply 208 V single or three phase power, which the customer can connect to their in rack Power Distribution Unit (PDU).

For infrastructure edge data centres either deployed in facilities which provide −48 V DC power or are designed to support equipment which use this type of power, such as many existing telecoms network structures which may be used for the brownfield deployment of infrastructure edge data centres, it is likely that the power feed will either need to be replaced or will require augmentation by expensive inversion and power conditioning equipment. This introduces efficiency losses during the conversion process and represents an additional point of failure in the system for the operator.

An infrastructure edge data centre of any size category can support a battery backup system, which provides a key period of runtime for the operational systems of that facility as well as the customer equipment. The length of this period depends on the power usage of those operational systems and customer equipment but may typically be anywhere from five minutes to half an hour. The larger the size category of the edge data centre facility, the more likely it is to incorporate such a system and the larger that system must be in order to support customer equipment in a fully filled facility.

Size category 1 infrastructure edge data centres require the simplest power distribution system as they may support only a single piece of equipment which may even be preinstalled by the customer or the infrastructure edge computing network operator. In these cases, the power distribution that is required is very simple and resembles a standard power supply feeding a single piece of customer equipment and, where included, a battery backup system while supporting external power inputs.

Ultimately there is not a significant difference between the power distribution configuration in an infrastructure edge data centre and the equivalent systems in a regional or national scale facility. Where edge data centre facilities differ is in the varying scales at which they operate, which creates unique limitations and characteristics for the design of a power distribution system; although the difference in terms of kilowatts is much larger between a 500 and a 900 kW facility than between a size category 2 data centre and a size category 5 facility, there is a greater difference between the latter two classes of edge data centre facilities in terms of the power distribution design required.

6.6 Redundancy and Resiliency

Due to their limited physical size, an infrastructure edge data centre may not support the same level of physical redundancy that is possible in a larger traditional data centre facility. Although this would appear to conflict strongly with the measures taken in traditional data centre facilities to ensure the uptime of the facility and the customer equipment within it from a physical perspective, there are ways to limit the impact of these design choices on the overall resiliency of the infrastructure edge.

The challenge of physical redundancy at the infrastructure edge data centre is not just due to the available space at each facility; the economics of data centre site design and operation are also a factor. On a per kilowatt of capacity basis infrastructure, edge data centres are more expensive than an equivalently physically redundant facility which is several times larger due to economies of scale in their design and operation. These costs will then be passed on to the customers of these facilities. The following three categories are the primary areas considered for physical redundancy measures:

1) Electrical power delivery and generation
   a) The ability to maintain clean and uninterrupted power at the data centre facility is often the most crucial requirement for maintaining operation, as it is a prerequisite for functioning network connectivity and for cooling system operation. Although a power grid outage may be unavoidable for the infrastructure edge data centre, a range of power redundancy methods can be implemented to lessen their impact.
2) Network connectivity
   a) This is especially crucial for resiliency measures which rely on a distributed service resiliency model where software workloads are migrated to another infrastructure edge data centre facility by using the network in the event of a failure of the onsite electrical or cooling systems. Should the network fail in these circumstances, any workloads or data at an infrastructure edge data centre will be stuck there until the required network connectivity is restored, typically impacting the user experience.
3) Cooling systems
   a) If the required temperature and environmental controls such as internal humidity cannot be maintained within the infrastructure edge data centre facility, it is likely that after a short period of time customer and operator equipment will begin to fail either on a temporary or permanent basis. Equipment may operate in a degraded state to lower its temperature, or it may shut off entirely due to thermal overload protections built into the equipment. Permanent damage is unlikely due to a rise in temperature, but if that temperature increase results in damage to a power delivery system such as a battery backup, then a fire or other avoidable damage may result.

Note that standard system resiliency practice specifies three instances of a critical system element, such as an infrastructure edge data centre facility, so that in the event of one site being taken down for maintenance, there remains a pair of system elements to preserve uptime should one facility fail. This means that infrastructure edge computing networks should deploy three facilities at minimum.

In this section, we will now explore each of these areas of redundancy and resiliency in more detail.

6.6.1 Electrical Power Delivery and Generation

Consider a few of the issues which could occur that would interrupt electrical power delivery to or at an infrastructure edge data centre facility. These situations are listed in increasing scale and severity:

1) In rack power delivery failure
   a) A busbar, PDU, or piece of cabling could fail within a single rack. These failures would cause an interruption of power delivery to the customer equipment within that rack and may also cause a loss of power to any facility operation systems which utilise a shared component of the rack power delivery system. In this failure scenario, only a single rack of customer equipment is down until the fault can be manually repaired.

2) Site power feed failure
   a) The power feed from the local electrical utility company to the edge data centre fails due to an event such as a nearby cable cut by construction equipment in the street, or a substation shutdown. In this scenario, although power to the site has been lost, the failure has not been caused by any equipment which the infrastructure edge computing network operator is responsible for. This means that the issue cannot be corrected by the operator beyond contacting the utility company to report the issue.

3) Wide-area power failure
   a) Electrical power is unavailable across a wide area, such as a city suburb due to the overloading of a local substation. This issue causes two infrastructure edge data centre facilities in the area to lose power. In this case, for the period of time which any power backup systems at these sites are able to remain operational, customers with equipment located in these facilities can take action to move their application workloads and working set data to another nearby data centre facility, only if one is available which is not also experiencing a power failure. Unless a power surge event has caused damage to the infrastructure edge data centre facilities, this is another scenario where the operator must report the issue and wait for it to be remediated.

For each of these scenarios, there are physical redundancy measures which may or may not be used depending on the cost and complexity of doing so, combined with the estimated likelihood of each scenario occurring over the course of a year. This list follows on from the previous list of scenarios:

1) Redundant power delivery within facility
   a) A secondary power path to the rack with redundant components can be used to provide protection against the failure of components on the primary path such as the PDU or cabling within the rack. In a highly redundant scenario, the system can detect a failure of the primary path and then switch to the

secondary path with a minimal amount of downtime for the customer equipment in that rack. However, this type of redundancy does entail additional expense which may be shared by an operator and a customer depending on whether the operator provides the PDU and all other power delivery components within the rack, which is not always the case.

2) Power backup systems at facility

a) A battery backup system, also referred to as an uninterruptible power supply (UPS), is a standard redundancy measure which should be expected in infrastructure edge data centre facilities of size categories 2 through 6 and, even in some cases, in small size category 1 facilities as well. These systems will provide some amount of runtime for customer and facility operations equipment at the edge data centre facility when external power is lost. The amount of time provided by the battery backup system is determined by the size of the batteries and the power draw of the equipment inside the facility. These systems are highly effective at protecting equipment from the risk of improper shutdown due to sudden power failure and can provide a period of time which can be used to migrate application workloads over to another nearby facility. Infrastructure edge data centre facilities of all sizes can also accommodate external power generators, typically burning diesel fuel, to provide a day or more of uptime in the event of a long-term power outage. During this time, however, the operator may remove power from some customer equipment to preserve facility operation.

3) Multiple interconnected facilities

a) In the event of a wide-area power failure, multiple edge data centre facilities may be forced to rely on their battery backup systems and have a limited amount of time to maintain operation, during which time customer equipment will be moving any key application workloads and working set data to other edge data centre facilities that are not suffering from power outages. A key component of this is for the customers of these facilities to have visibility to the operational state of each edge data centre, which will be discussed further in a later chapter. The use of multiple facilities in an area to mitigate the impact of site power failures is a particular strength of the full infrastructure edge computing model as long as network connectivity remains in a performant and available state and customers have distributed their equipment. In an extreme case where all of the infrastructure edge data centres in an area are in a state of power supply failure, application workloads may be moved to a RNDC; or in the most extreme case, the customer equipment must be safely shut down before the power to that equipment from the power backup at the facility expires and those customers must wait until power to the facility is restored.

Due to their severity, power failures at an infrastructure edge data centre facility are concerning to customers and to the infrastructure edge computing network operator themselves. The amount of physical redundancy and power supply protection equipment which is deployed at a specific site is entirely at the discretion of the operator as this equipment incurs significant costs in terms of the design, deployment, and ongoing operation of the facility. However, any infrastructure edge data centre which is highly vulnerable to temporary fluctuations in power supply is likely to cause many issues for both the operator and their customers to warrant both battery and generator systems.

6.6.2 Network Connectivity

Where and to what extent network connectivity to the infrastructure edge data centre facility is physically redundant should be considered during the design phase. The physical redundancy of network connectivity can be put into three categories without significant overlap between them:

1) Network disconnection in rack
   a) Network connectivity to a rack of customer equipment may occur due to the failure of a top of rack (TOR) switch, of its corresponding port on the operator's network infrastructure, or more rarely due to a physical failure of the patch panels or cabling which connect these two endpoints together. The most common type of failure in this category are various human errors due to misconfiguration of the network or poor cable labelling, which result in the affected customer equipment being disconnected until personnel can either replace all of the failed network equipment or correct a misconfiguration.
2) Site network interruption
   a) An external event such as roadworks cutting into a fibre cable buried underground may cause an interruption or degradation of the network service to the edge data centre facility itself. Where multiple physical network paths are available from the facility, a cut of one path should result in a degradation only in terms of the paths, redundancy, and total aggregate speed of network connectivity available from that facility to external locations. However, where only a single path is available or when multiple paths are cut, the facility may be isolated entirely from the network. The location where the external network failure occurs is crucial to understanding its impact on the infrastructure edge computing network, including whether failure occurs between an edge data centre facility and its connected access or last mile networks or between that facility and its neighbouring edge data centre facilities.
3) Wide-area network failure
   a) In some cases, a wide-area network connection used by multiple edge data centre facilities in an area may fail, cutting off connectivity from those sites

to other areas but leaving connectivity between those sites in the same area intact. This results in an isolated segment of the infrastructure edge computing network which is still able to operate between multiple local facilities but which cannot utilise any resources in remote locations, whether for facility operation or customer application workloads.

Unlike power, if network connectivity exists between two or more infrastructure edge data centre facilities, it may be possible to operate the facility in a degraded state by utilising network paths to provide reachability to the facility and to the customer application workloads operating inside it. To address the specific scenarios described in this list, however, there are design choices available:

1) In facility redundancy
    a) To protect the network against network infrastructure device failure, two of each of the key switches and routers in the network can be deployed as a pair in a 1+1 hot standby configuration. Some customers may also choose to deploy their TOR switch in this configuration as well. Although this does considerably increase cost, where a single network infrastructure device is an unacceptable point of failure, this is a valid solution. To protect against physical failure of components such as cabling and patch panels, correct installation to avoid exceeding cable bend radii and other design and deployment practices are the best options as these parts rarely fail under proper use.
2) Street level redundancy
    a) The physical diversity of the way in which fibre cabling enters the edge data centre facility from the street or another nearby location of fibre aggregation is key in how protection against fibre cabling cuts or other physical connectivity interruptions can be achieved. In an ideal scenario, an infrastructure edge data centre facility is fed by multiple physical paths into the site. However, this may be prohibitively expensive or impossible in some areas due to the geography of the existing fibre networks, and so separate conduits and cabling inside of a single point of entry may be used instead.
3) Wide-area redundancy
    a) Within a given area such as a city, multiple infrastructure edge data centre facilities may be the interconnection point for wide-area network connectivity. In many cases, these connections will be provided through the backhaul connectivity from an edge data centre to a RNDC facility. In this case, it is prudent to arrange multiple physically distinct paths to multiple regional or national facilities in areas where this is possible. In others, bringing wide-area network connectivity in to one or more of the infrastructure edge data centres directly provides redundancy in the system by limiting the risk of one network connection isolating that segment of the infrastructure edge computing network. However, where possible, also consider where the specific

wide-area connections being used are aggregated, as a cut further along the line may impact all of the network connections which otherwise appear to be redundant within the city itself. In such a case, that risk should be clearly noted.

The network topology of the infrastructure edge computing network is a key component in providing a reliable and redundant system. As discussed in Chapter 5, there are many ways to design networks for infrastructure edge computing which can support various levels of redundancy depending on the cost and design complexity that the infrastructure edge computing network operator is able to incur. Much like the case of determining the acceptable level of cost as an operator for redundant network connectivity across the infrastructure edge computing network, the answer must be a result of a full understanding of the customer and operational requirements of these facilities over the long term.

6.6.3 Cooling Systems

Although the most obvious cause of cooling system failure is an electrical power supply failure, there are several other issues that can develop with these systems, which then force customer equipment to fail and cause the infrastructure edge computing network operator significant difficulties in facility maintenance and operation. Three of the most prevalent causes of real cooling system failures are:

1) Degradation of cooling capability
   a) The performance of a cooling system can progressively worsen over time due to the absence of maintenance or a design issue with the system. In these scenarios, it is a possibility that all of the components of the cooling system appear to function as per usual, but the temperature of the facility and the customer equipment within it rises over time. A slow coolant leak due to a minute gap in a hose system is an example of a problem which may cause this type of cooling system performance degradation to occur and which can be difficult to detect remotely even as it progressively worsens.
2) Partial airflow obstruction
   a) Specific channels for airflow may become blocked in the facility due to debris or the moving of equipment in or outside of the facility. For example, a customer visiting a facility may accidentally leave a cardboard box over an air intake vent or a workman outside of the facility may unintentionally obscure an air exhaust grille which carries hot air out of the facility with a piece of machinery. Although these examples seem simple compared to some of the more technical issues which can cause the cooling system to fail or degrade, issues like this are common. Even with warning signs and personnel training, such problems are unavoidable across the majority of facilities.

3) Cooling system failure

   a) The cooling system at an edge data centre facility may fail entirely without a power supply failure being the cause. Failures of this type can occur due to the mechanical components of the system such as fan motors, chillers, and compressors, which wear over time. These components can experience mechanical failures which result in the sudden failure of the system, which then requires a manual maintenance process to correct. For example, if the compressor fails in an air conditioning system, the air will not be properly cooled as it passes through the system, resulting in what should be a cold airflow across customer equipment becoming warm, which in turn will increase the operating temperature of this equipment and is likely to cause a thermal failure.

Like power and unlike network connectivity, the availability of a functioning cooling system at a nearby infrastructure edge data centre facility does not help counteract the failure or degradation of such a system in another facility. However, when power and network connectivity are present, an issue with the cooling system of an edge data centre facility can be known and be mitigated in some scenarios:

1) Oversized cooling capability

   a) Although it is not an ideal solution, the cooling capability of the edge data centre facility cooling system can be sized such that should a level of degradation occur which limits the capability of the system, the system is still able to maintain those operational temperatures required by the customer equipment within the facility. This method incurs additional cooling system expense, however, and should be used only to provide the infrastructure edge computing network operator with an extra buffer period before any slow system failure becomes a pressing operational issue.

2) Remote detection of system degradation

   a) The ability of the network operator to rapidly detect and remediate issues such as vent or fan blockage contributes directly to their ability to keep the edge data centre facility operating at a high level of efficiency without the need to constantly dispatch personnel to correct issues. Consider the scenario where a customer has left packing material for some of their equipment in the data centre facility and it is blocking an air intake vent. In this case, if the operator is able to identify the issue by using their airflow sensors across the facility and their security cameras viewing the area, if this identification process can occur quickly enough, the customer can be asked to easily remove the packing material before they leave the site. If this issue is detected days later, or if the precise cause of the issue cannot be determined remotely, personnel must then be dispatched by the operator to correct the issue at the operator's cost.

3) Preventative maintenance and rapid dispatch
   a) Due to their importance to the operation of the edge data centre facility as well as their reliance on a complex system of mechanical parts, cooling systems are prime examples of the benefit of preventative maintenance activities. The infrastructure edge computing network operator should maintain a consistent maintenance and replacement schedule for these systems which notes the wear on specific parts as well as the estimated lifetime of the overall system before a failure will occur. This process cannot predict every failure condition, but it will go a long way towards the operator understanding the real health of their cooling systems across the network. When a real issue is detected, the operator must also have the capability to rapidly dispatch site maintenance personnel to the facility in order to reduce its downtime.

In the case of the smallest size category of infrastructure edge data centre facilities, the cooling that is provided by the facility itself may be augmentative to the customer and operator equipment that is deployed inside. Interruptions may be expected to occur on a regular basis, and due to the use of hardened equipment, acceptable temperatures may be sustained during these interruptions until a normal state of operation can be restored. This is dependent, however, on the operating environment and the customer equipment which is being used in the specific size category 1 infrastructure edge data centre facility. The design of these facilities will be more bespoke and use case driven than their larger cousins, and so the operator and customer must work to fulfil an agreed set of requirements.

Although each physical infrastructure edge data centre facility may not be as tolerant of the failure of crucial support systems such as power and cooling as its larger cousins, the network infrastructure interconnecting multiple infrastructure edge data centres in an area such as a city provides a level of service resiliency for software workloads which are comparatively location independent, as long as for a period of time their operation from anywhere on the infrastructure edge computing network in that area is acceptable to the customer and end users in terms of cost, performance, or functionality.

6.6.4 Market Design

When considering how to implement practical redundancy to achieve service resiliency across the distributed data centre and network infrastructure provided by infrastructure edge computing, the market design process is crucial. During this process, a few key questions must be clearly answered:

1) What are the redundancy and resiliency requirements for the application?
   a) In many cases, the answer to this question will be given in terms of an uptime figure that is expected for the underlying infrastructure, such as 99.999%,

which translates to around five minutes of allowable downtime per year. During the market design process, we will need to tease apart this figure to understand its real requirements.

2) Does the application need service resilience or physical redundancy?

    a) This is a key question which determines much of the resulting physical topology for the infrastructure edge computing network in the area and follows on directly from the previous question. An application which requires software service resilience and can be served with lower levels of physical redundancy has very different needs than one which requires high levels of physical redundancy and cannot make full use of a software-based approach to service resiliency due to its own deployment topology.

3) What level of additional cost is a dealbreaker for this application?

    a) As with many things in system design, there is a trade-off in providing high levels of resiliency or redundancy across the infrastructure edge computing network. Many customers and other stakeholders will insist on the highest levels of performance, resiliency, and redundancy until the costs of these measures are put in front of them. The infrastructure edge computing network operator must work with the customer in order to determine an acceptable cost and set of characteristics for the customer.

4) Is it feasible to deploy multi-homed resources for this application?

    a) This question spans both a software service resiliency approach and one that relies on physical redundancy. Is the application workload which the customer intends to use able to make use of the multi-site operation which is possible across multiple of the infrastructure edge data centres in an area, or does its architecture limit it to a single facility? Similarly, does it make sense for cost, performance, and functionality for the customer to utilise multi-site physical redundancy with multiple connections?

5) Are infrastructure edge data centres available to provide multi-site redundancy?

    a) Where it is feasible for the customer to make use of multiple infrastructure edge data centres in the area, which, if any, of these facilities are located in areas which allow a customer to utilise them in this way? For example, are multiple edge data centres in an acceptable latency range to meet the performance needs of the application, or if one of the facilities were to go down, would the application have to cease operating or operate in a reduced performance state? In the case of a customer who needs to connect physical assets such as cellular network towers directly to an infrastructure edge data centre, are multiple such facilities in range of the towers that are needed?

The value of the specific customer to the infrastructure edge network operator will drive the extent to which that operator is willing to tailor a given market design to the needs of that customer. If an anchor tenant, a customer which is not only highly valuable in themselves but ideally will also serve as a means to draw other key customers into the infrastructure edge network over time were the customer in question, the infrastructure edge network operator may see fit to tailor extensive parts of the physical infrastructure in that area to meet that customer's needs. This process is easiest and cheapest to undertake before the physical infrastructure has been deployed, and so the earlier that market design activities can be undertaken with specific anchor tenant customers, the better for the customer themselves and for the infrastructure edge network operator who can then avoid delays.

Service resilience is a different operational and architectural model than physical redundancy. The physical redundancy model relies on extensive duplication of physical infrastructure such as cooling systems in order to provide the means for an individual data centre facility to withstand failures of these systems. The software service resilience model accepts the lack of physical redundancy of the individual edge data centre facilities and uses their distributed and interconnected nature to create resilient software services which can operate from many nearby locations in the event of a failure.

6.6.5 Redundancy Certification

Due to the size of each infrastructure edge data centre facility, the presence of multiple facilities which are interconnected by a redundant network topology in the area, and the ability to utilise a view of the operational state of each facility to make application workload placement decisions as a customer, the traditional tiers of data centre facility redundancy which are based on physical system duplication are not a good fit for infrastructure edge computing as they do not represent the abilities of the system or take account of its limitations. For infrastructure edge computing, a reasonable level of physical redundancy per facility combined with a redundant market design and the capability for a customer to utilise real software service resilience is a more complete way to understand reliability.

No certification process currently exists for this type of service resiliency utilising infrastructure edge computing networks. This means that the process of establishing a design and operational model to make the best use of this resiliency is dependent upon the customer by working with the operator. The concept of this type of distributed software service resiliency is described further in Chapter 11.

As a customer, when analysing what an infrastructure edge computing network operator offers in terms of reliability and resiliency, consider the following factors before traditional redundancy. For an operator, these factors are key to ensuring your network can support practical resilient services:

1) Thought and failure scenarios behind market designs
   a) The infrastructure edge computing network in an area must be designed in such a way that it can support the redundancy and resiliency requirements of

its users and their application workloads. This includes understanding the failure scenarios of the individual components of the network and how they may be isolated or cascade to other areas of the network and the steps which can be taken to prevent any single failure cascading into a larger failure scenario, which impacts many more customers.

2) Ability to assist in solution design for service resiliency
   a) An infrastructure edge computing network operator should be able to assist in the service resiliency design process for its customers by providing them with solution architecture and engineering support. This entails activities such as participating in engineering sessions to understand the requirements of the customer and of their application workloads and providing the customer with design guidelines that allow their services to make optimal use of the infrastructure edge computing network.

3) Infrastructure visibility for application workload placement
   a) Due to the distributed nature of infrastructure edge data centres and the likelihood that they will support lower degrees of physical redundancy than larger RNDC facilities, it is highly beneficial for the customer to have some visibility to the operational status of the infrastructure such as being notified when the failure of a cooling system at a particular edge data centre facility occurs. This provides the customer with the means to then migrate any workloads as required.

Although they are not foolproof, the combination of these three factors does allow a customer to have a level of service resiliency assurance in an infrastructure edge computing network. If any of these three factors are not provided by the infrastructure edge computing network operator, it is challenging for that customer to provide any service resiliency assurance to their own end users.

6.6.6 Software Service Resiliency

Consider a cloud provider as an example customer of an infrastructure edge computing network operator. The cloud provider wishes to provide a software-based service from one or more facilities across the infrastructure edge computing network. Each of these facilities is located in a common area, such as a single city, and in each facility the cloud provider has deployed equipment that can support a specific application workload which requires service resiliency utilising multiple edge data centre facilities. In this example, the application workload is a low latency database for IoT devices.

The ideal infrastructure edge computing network provides this cloud provider with all of the three factors previously described. When an issue with an edge data centre facility where the workload is present is detected, the migration process of the application workload and its working set data can be initiated and, assuming one or more other edge data centre facilities are located within a useful latency envelope from the end users of the application, the application can continue to operate for the duration of the fault, if even in some cases, at a reduced level of performance or functionality.

One challenge with this model of software-based service resiliency is for cases where a data centre facility is terminating one end of a fixed location physical network connection. Consider the example of a cellular network tower which is connected to only one infrastructure edge data centre. In this case, a software service resiliency model relying on multiple facilities cannot prevent the failure of that one tower as the physical layer of the system must be operating before higher layers can work.

This type of software-based service-level resiliency will be explored further in Chapters 10 and 11.

6.6.7 Physical Redundancy

Following on from the previous example, consider a customer of the infrastructure edge computing network operator who is concerned about connectivity for immovable physical assets, such as the tower locations used by cellular network operators. For this customer, the type of software-based resiliency previously described will not prevent a failure which impacts their services. The diagram in Figure 6.6 shows the network topology that this type of customer will use at the infrastructure edge:

As can be seen, the infrastructure edge data centre represents an unavoidable point of failure for the network operator customer. If a failure were to occur at the infrastructure edge data centre, which is on the path between a cellular network tower and its core network, which prevented the transport of data between those two points, the cellular network will experience an outage for at least the duration of that failure. In this case, the physical redundancy of that infrastructure edge data centre becomes a key component for maintaining the uptime of the overall network itself.

These scenarios are a significant challenge for the infrastructure edge computing network operator. As the infrastructure edge data centre is reliant on the presence of multiple access networks in order to achieve its full value as a place of network interconnection, the failure of the edge data centre is likely to cause those access

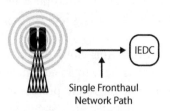

Figure 6.6 Infrastructure edge data centre as single point of failure for network infrastructure.

Single Fronthaul
Network Path

IEDC

networks to suffer localised outages regardless of the software service resiliency that is possible further back in the infrastructure edge computing network for workloads which do not rely on fixed position physical assets like cable network headends or cellular towers.

6.6.8 System Resiliency Example

To put all of the considerations described in this section related to redundancy and resiliency into context, we will explore a step-by-step example of a series of failures occurring to show how the measures to protect against them or mitigate their impact can operate to preserve system uptime. For this example, we will use the diagram in Figure 6.7 as our system configuration. This is a simple setup with two edge data centre facilities operating in an area. In this case the access or last mile network of interest is a cellular network which is dual homed to both edge data centre facilities. This avoids the difficult scenario described in the previous section, at significant expense, but helps to simplify our example for the purposes of this discussion. In its normal operating state, both facilities are up.

During operation, a power failure is detected at one edge data centre facility. Due to the battery backup system present in the facility, there is a short window of time for the cloud provider to be notified of the issue and to then migrate any required workloads and their working set data to the neighbouring infrastructure edge data centre facility. In this case, the cloud provider was notified that there was a power supply issue to the edge data centre facility around 30 seconds after it was detected by the infrastructure edge computing network operator. Such a delay period will often be used in order to avoid overloading customers with information on what may be only very transient faults and which may make the infrastructure appear more unstable than it really is. It is now up to the cloud provider and their own orchestration system to begin the workload and data migration.

In this example, as seen in Figures 6.7–6.9, the simple failure scenario and redundant network topology has ensured that the migration process is easy to understand and no additional faults or issues such as congestion of the infrastructure edge network or localised outages of the access or last mile network have introduced

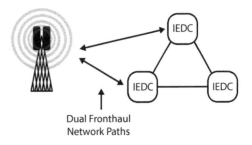

Figure 6.7 System resiliency example: phase one.

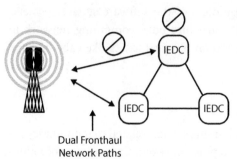

Figure 6.8 System resiliency example: phase two.

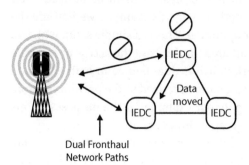

Figure 6.9 System resiliency example: phase three.

additional complexity. The application workload and its working set data have been migrated over to the neighbouring infrastructure edge data centre facility and the end users of the service have most likely suffered no detectable downtime, although this is dependent on the failure and application.

Although these topics and key failure scenarios will be described further in Chapters 10 and 11, it is useful to understand at a high level the difference between software service resiliency which can be enabled through the use of multiple interconnected edge data centre facilities and all of the physical redundancy that can be achieved at any one particular edge data centre facility when the cost and size characteristics of these facilities are considered when compared to a regional or national facility.

6.7 Environmental Control

A traditional data centre is a controlled environment. It is designed to provide the customer and operator equipment that it contains with specific levels of temperature, humidity, and other key factors which allow that equipment to operate within its standard design parameters and to not experience extreme stress during normal operating conditions which would reduce its performance or its efficiency, or result in equipment damage.

Table 6.3 Example infrastructure edge data centre facility environmental controls.

Size category number	Example environment	Mobile operation	Hardened equipment
1	Truck mounted	Possible	Yes
2	Rural tower site	No	Possible
3	Rural aggregation	No	No
4	Cell tower site	No	No
5	Cell tower site	No	No
6	Shopping centre roof	No	No

The level of environmental control provided by the infrastructure edge data centre will vary based on its size category and intended deployment environment. Table 6.3 shows the differences:

For size categories of infrastructure edge data centre where hardened equipment is listed as no, the type of customer equipment to be deployed in these facilities should not require any environmental hardening such as shock proofing, humidity control, or cooling beyond what it would be expected to provide for deployment in a standard RNDC. These facilities provide a level of environmental control which removes all of the need for the customer to harden their equipment.

Environmental control is not limited to maintaining the temperature of all the customer equipment that is deployed in an infrastructure edge data centre facility. The following are also considerations:

1) Vibration and shock
    a) Common and expected levels of vibration and shock must be controlled such that they do not impair the operation of customer equipment within the infrastructure edge data centre. Although an event such as an earthquake may be unavoidable and will introduce very large amounts of vibration and shock, routine events such as the operation of the edge data centre facility cooling plant or a nearby rack being moved in and out of position have the capability to introduce vibration and shock into any customer equipment deployed nearby. The effects of these forces on any customer equipment can be mitigated by the use of rubber dampeners mounted within racks.
2) Humidity
    a) Electronic equipment is sensitive to high levels of humidity, as this may result in the accumulation of water in the vicinity of the equipment, which can make current potentially bridge between electrical contacts on a circuit board and cause a short circuit. This may permanently damage the equipment and render it inoperable. Additionally a high level of humidity within

the edge data centre facility may also result in pooling or standing water over time as water condensates. This can not only be dangerous for its impact on electronic equipment should it make contact, but it can also present a slipping hazard, or in extreme cases even the risk of electric shock, to any visitor or staff present within the edge data centre facility. Humidity can be controlled in the case of the smallest size category of infrastructure edge data centres by the use of humidity and pressure control vents made from materials such as Gore-Tex. In any larger edge data centre facilities, the use of dedicated dehumidification equipment may be necessary if the standard air cooling system does not remove enough of the airborne moisture to fully eliminate the chance of dangerous levels of condensation. Where the external air temperature drops below the dew point for the deployment location, any dehumidification system in the data centre facility must be capable of removing the water vapour from the air that is brought in from the outside to avoid introducing condensation into the facility. Ideally this equipment is part of the main airflow loop in the facility cooling system and does not need to be a separate part.

3) Particulates
   a) The air circulation and cooling systems on customer equipment are designed to be capable of moving cool air across heatsinks, which are affixed to components that are generating significant amounts of heat, in order to cool them and maintain an operationally acceptable temperature. They are, however, not designed to operate with significant levels of particulates in the air, which may lodge themselves in the fans or heatsink fins of the cooling system and reduce its operational efficiency. In extreme cases the amount and type of particulates brought into the system may cause the equipment to overheat and require manual maintenance to remove any physical clogs or obstructions. An infrastructure edge data centre should remove, through filtration steps in its air circulation system, airborne particulates above a certain size in order to reduce the amount which can be ingested by the equipment.

4) Fire suppression
   a) Even in an unmanned data centre facility, fires can still occur, which if not detected and put out as quickly as possible can cause irreparable damage to the customer equipment at the facility, as well as the facility itself. The most common source of fires in an infrastructure edge data centre facility, although very rare itself, is likely to be the battery backup system. The second most likely source is power generation equipment such as a diesel generator due to the use of highly combustible fuel. In this case, the source of the fire may be at the infrastructure edge data centre site but outside of the facility itself as these generators are typically deployed outside.

Just as in a RNDC, the ability of the edge data centre facility to maintain the environmental characteristics of the site within acceptable parameters to ensure the safe and reliable operation of the facility and of the customer equipment it contains is paramount. Without this capability, the infrastructure edge data centre risks being unsuitable for production workloads and therefore not a commercial solution for any practical customer who would require its services.

6.8 Data Centre Network Design

Chapter 5 described the key considerations for the infrastructure edge computing network. As such, this section will focus on the implications for that network on the design and operation of the edge data centre facility itself. Many of these considerations are similar to the general operational and design limitations that the edge data centre model imposes in other areas as previously described.

In many ways, the network infrastructure within an infrastructure edge data centre is a scaled-down version of the networks typically seen within larger data centre facilities. There are, however, several key design and operation considerations that differentiate these networks from their larger cousins:

1) Lack of onsite personnel driving automation
   a) As the infrastructure edge data centre cannot rely on onsite personnel as a RNDC typically can for tasks such as network troubleshooting, the updating of network configurations, or the addition of new customer equipment, an infrastructure edge data centre facility is more likely to incorporate greater levels of network infrastructure automation and remote operation capabilities designed to allow the infrastructure edge computing network operator to avoid expensive and time-consuming personnel visits to distributed edge data centre facilities over time.
2) Smaller and fixed number of customers
   a) Within an edge data centre facility, there is a far smaller variation in the number of customers who may be present in that facility. This simplifies the task of forecasting and scaling the network infrastructure at the facility over time when compared to a larger facility, which may have the capability to open more data halls or otherwise to add more customer equipment space. This simplifies the design of the network in an infrastructure edge data centre facility and allows for more use of standard designs.
3) Differing scale and capabilities across size categories
   a) The network infrastructure that is required within an infrastructure edge data centre of size category 1 is vastly different to that of a facility of size category 6. The scale and functional roles of these two facilities is more

distinct than is apparent in most cases when comparing one regional data centre facility to another. This means that across all size categories, infrastructure edge data centre facilities encompass a wide variation of scale and network capabilities which must be addressed properly so that the performance and functionality required of larger facilities is provided while the cost of the smaller size category facilities can be maintained at an acceptable level.

One key consideration is the physical network infrastructure that is both inside and outside of the edge data centre facility. This has been described earlier in this chapter, and the network should then be designed accordingly based on the limitations of the physical redundancy that is available. For example, where only one fibre connection from outside the site is available, a single site router may be used in comparison to where redundant fibre connectivity from outside the site is available, prompting the use of two redundant site routers, with one connected to each external fibre route.

Much as in larger RNDC, the majority of cabling within an infrastructure edge data centre takes the form of fibre optic cabling for network connectivity. The physical network connectivity available within an infrastructure edge data centre is very similar to that of a RNDC facility; the same type, speed, and topology of all physical network components such as patch panels, cabling, and switching and routing equipment is utilised across the majority of infrastructure edge data centre facilities as it is across regional or national scale data centre facilities.

The network topology and protocol considerations for RNDC facilities that were described in Chapter 4 also apply to the infrastructure edge data centre facility. The same Clos network topologies and mix of protocols are seen in infrastructure edge data centre networks due to these data centres essentially operating as smaller, more physically distributed versions of a RNDC facility. The primary difference in network design between the infrastructure edge data centre facility and the RNDC facility is in terms of the site scale and the number of Data Centre Interconnection (DCI) connections needed between the internal and external data centre networks.

In the case of switching and routing equipment, the scale of the infrastructure edge data centre and of specific customer equipment deployments within these facilities compared to their equivalents in regional or national scale facilities determines the exact switching and routing equipment to be used both for the facility itself and for individual customer racks in TOR switch roles, based on key factors:

1) Customer equipment deployment scale
    a) For the customer, the TOR switch to select depends on many factors including the feature set and physical port capabilities of the equipment, both of which, when at the expected scale of many infrastructure edge data centre

equipment deployments, are likely to be the deciding factors before equipment size and forward capabilities become a key concern. In many cases, the minimum TOR switch which meets the needs of the customer will be used in order to minimise the network infrastructure cost to the customer for what may be a large number of distributed deployments.

2) Edge data centre facility scale

a) The size category of the infrastructure edge data centre facility will in most cases determine the type of switching and routing equipment which is needed in order to support the initial operation of the facility and its expected growth over time. The larger an infrastructure edge data centre is, generally the more network traffic will pass through or be generated by that facility. There are exceptions to this rule of thumb, however, such as a size category 2 infrastructure edge data centre which is being used as a fronthaul network termination point for multiple cellular network towers. The network infrastructure in this facility may be responsible for a larger amount of traffic than its aggregating larger size category edge data centre facility due to routable IP traffic representing a minority of the total radio baseband data.

3) Number of networks present in facility

a) For the infrastructure edge computing network operator, the network infrastructure of the edge data centre facility itself must be capable of providing interconnection and traffic handling capabilities at rates which match the projected growth of the networks present in the facility in terms of both their number and their data rate. Should the infrastructure edge computing network operator fail to do this, networks may be unable to be present and interconnect at their edge data centre facilities or these facilities may become bottlenecks leading to congestion. This will itself then result in external network operators bypassing the infrastructure edge network.

Some network infrastructure equipment utilises a tiered licencing scheme where the same hardware platform can be bought at a reduced cost up front with the expectation that as the traffic load of the network increases, the operator of the network will purchase a software licence for the switch or the router in question, which will unlock additional traffic handling capacity. Although these schemes are unpopular with many buyers, they remain available in the market because of their flexibility in terms of purchasing for their customers and may be used in many edge data centre facilities by operators.

For the sake of comparison, Table 6.4 estimates the average network traffic usage of each size category of infrastructure edge data centre as well as the average network traffic usage for each of the customers who have deployed equipment within that infrastructure edge data centre facility. In this table, the figures used are coarse estimates used to provide comparison, not definitive numbers:

Table 6.4 Example average estimates for network usage per data centre facility size category.

Size category number	Example use case	Facility network usage estimate	Customer network usage estimate
1	Network termination	In 50 Gbps; out 55 Gbps	1 Gbps
2	Network functions	In 250 Gbps; out 25 Gbps	5 Gbps
3	Local aggregation	In 100 Gbps; out 150 Gbps	10 Gbps
4	Low latency workloads	In 250 Gbps; out 300 Gbps	15 Gbps
5	Low latency workloads	In 500 Gbps; out 550 Gbps	20 Gbps
6	Regional edge aggregation	In 700 Gbps; out 750 Gbps	20 Gbps

Ultimately the infrastructure edge computing network does not impose a significant new set of requirements on the edge data centre facilities which it connects to, beyond those which can be already seen at larger scale in RNDC facilities. The wider network design issues and the challenges of providing EX capabilities of varying levels of functionality and scale, as described in Chapters 5 and 7, respectively, are more important to the overall system in terms of its design and operation, but they will work only if the considerations in this section are accounted for.

6.9 Information Technology (IT) Equipment Capacity

Depending on the efficiency of the cooling system in use, an infrastructure edge data centre may be capable of supporting greater rack densification than a traditional data centre. This can lead to some interesting scenarios where the physical space provided for customer equipment is only a handful of racks, but each of those racks is capable of supporting significant amounts of customer equipment. A facility of size category 4 or 5 is typically where these cooling systems become practical, making each of these data centres potentially ideal aggregation points for use cases such as distributed AI, which require densified racks and large amounts of resources located in these infrastructure edge facilities.

6.9.1   Operational Headroom

Like many complex systems, an infrastructure edge data centre, and indeed any data centre, is not designed to operate at 100% capacity for an extended period of time. This tends to put strain on the various components of the system such as power generation, cooling, and environmental control in a way which they were not designed to handle day in, day out. Amongst infrastructure operators, the level of operational capacity which they consider safe for continuous operation varies considerably, but a reasonable estimate is 85% of the total capability of the facility and its supporting equipment.

There are, then, two approaches to capacity estimation. One is to quote your maximum operational capacity for long-term operation, for instance at 85%, and then operate up to that limit; and another is to quote the 100% capacity for the data centre facility but then operate up to only the operational capacity limit. Of these two approaches, the latter has a marketing benefit as it will appear that your facilities are capable of operating at a higher capacity than someone with equal 100% capacity but a stated capacity at 85% of that same figure, and so this is the approach that is most often used today.

In many cases, the customer will not know the current utilisation level of the edge data centre facility and there will be several other customers present within that facility, so any concern about the true capacity of a facility being exposed and creating negative publicity is unfounded. For an organisation which deploys infrastructure edge data centre facilities, these operating capacity limitations will be already known and built into the true capacity of the operational network under normal conditions.

6.10   Data Centre Operation

The highly distributed nature of infrastructure edge data centre deployment requires a different and more automated approach to data centre facility operation than is typically seen at traditional large RNDC facilities. One large RNDC facility which is operating with 10 MW of customer equipment can economically support an onsite team of staff to maintain the facility, conduct daily operations, and respond to customer needs. This same model is not tenable once we apply it to an infrastructure edge computing network, however, which may in that same area incorporate tens or hundreds of infrastructure edge data centre facilities of varying sizes which are distributed geographically. In this case, an operations team in the area cannot be at every edge data centre facility at once and must travel between them based on a maintenance schedule or to respond to customer issues as they become apparent through reports or system monitoring.

Due to the size of a typical infrastructure edge data centre, the type of onsite manned security that is used by many larger data centre facilities is untenable. This necessitates the use of more remote security technologies which allow an infrastructure edge computing network operator to manage security aspects of the operation of an infrastructure edge data centre remotely, using a smaller number of staff who make use of automation in order to operate efficiently as the number of data centre sites for which they are responsible grows over time. Automation can also be used for other key purposes at the infrastructure edge data centre to make unmanned operation more effective.

6.10.1 Site Automation

The inability to economically support onsite personnel at a highly distributed network of a large number of infrastructure edge data centres drives the need for increased data centre facility and supporting site automation, beginning with remote monitoring and progressing to highly advanced uses of robotics to achieve the physical automation of many key tasks which would otherwise need personnel to visit the edge data centre facility in order to perform the task, which could be regularly.

Remote monitoring of the infrastructure edge data centre facility is the first step in achieving new levels of automation at these locations, as it allows vital system statistics to be tracked and graphed over time and for emerging issues to be identified without needing onsite personnel. This can be achieved without the need for automation systems, which use robotics to interact physically with equipment and the data centre facility itself. Additionally, extensive remote monitoring should be considered a prerequisite for deploying such robotic automation systems to ensure that they are operating as expected and can be remotely monitored and controlled themselves by the operator.

There are three primary areas beyond remote monitoring where the automation of infrastructure edge data centres using robotics controlled from a remote operator location is highly promising:

1) Equipment deployment support
   a) Today many data centre facility operators will provide a smart hands service which allows a customer to ship their equipment to the data centre and have it deployed within their rack by an onsite technician. It is feasible with sufficient automation at infrastructure edge data centre facilities to see robotic equipment deployment and integration systems which are capable of taking customer equipment that arrives at the edge data centre facility and then deploying it within that customer's rack space. The variety of equipment and packaging presents a challenge to the practicality of a system like this;

however, the use of standard shipment packaging for equipment as well as purpose designed AI models for this task make it considerably more practical.

2) Data centre facility security

 a) The security of a distributed network of infrastructure edge data centre facilities is an area where the application of automation technologies makes sound economic and technical sense. Along with data centre site technicians, a significant number of the personnel required at a data centre facility are concerned with security both in and outside of the facility in order to prevent issues occurring which may impair the ability of the facility to provide its required services. The use of automation systems to perform functions such as the visual identification of any people at the site using computer vision, establishing a regular patrol of the site perimeter using drones, or using an autonomous wheeled vehicle to simulate a walking security officer are all possible and stand to improve site security without requiring any onsite personnel.

3) Maintenance of site and equipment

 a) In a similar category to equipment deployment support, the ongoing maintenance of many aspects of the site and of the customer equipment that is deployed at that site have the potential to be performed by robotics systems. Consider the failure of the data storage device within a customer's server requiring that physical device to then be replaced. If the device can be shipped to the edge data centre facility, it is feasible that a robotic maintenance system can extract the failed device and replace it with the new one, eliminating the need for personnel to visit the facility. Additionally a task such as refilling the coolant in a cooling system at the data centre facility could be performed by such a robotic maintenance system as well, with the same benefit.

A fully automated infrastructure edge data centre facility would be capable of operating entirely unmanned, even for events which are considered exceptions today, such as the deployment and physical maintenance of customer equipment. Events such as a facility fire or an external attack would require human personnel to visit the site, but such events are very rare compared to the common operational tasks that personnel would otherwise need to travel to the site to perform.

Automation efforts like those described in this section can be greatly accelerated by maintaining a high level of operational consistency across infrastructure edge data centre facilities and, where at all possible, across the equipment that customers are deploying within these facilities. Standards in how edge data centre facilities are laid out and operated make the job of designing and operating a robotics system to maintain them significantly easier. In terms of customer equipment, the use of a standard form factor and design principles such as those from the Open Compute

Project (OCP) or Open 19, each of which are sets of specifications that define various characteristics of the physical server infrastructure to be deployed in data centre facilities, can have a similar automation benefit.

This level of automation, however, does entail a significant development and capital expenditure requirement for the infrastructure edge computing network operator. Many of these capabilities cannot be bought off the shelf today and would in any case need to be tailored to the unique and high performance operating requirements of the infrastructure edge data centre. Infrastructure edge computing network operators are unlikely to either have or wish to build this level of robotics expertise in house, and so partnerships with external specialists in this field are likely to be needed.

The level of site automation which is technically practical and economically feasible will increase over time as the cost of these solutions decreases and as the number of infrastructure edge data centres grows. However, it is worth noting that unlike the level of performance increase and cost decrease which has been seen in computing for the past few decades due to Moore's Law, which was an observation that the number of transistors on an integrated circuit is able to be doubled roughly every two years, this rate of progress does not apply to all areas of technology including robotics. Although advances in computer processing power and especially AI technologies have had significant positive impacts on making robotics more accessible, these technologies do not tend to follow the same curve as CPU or GPU development, for example, and so any plan for the use of these robotic systems for data centre facility automation must be aware of their expected cost over time.

Additionally, the level of site automation which is practical increases along with the size category of the edge data centre facility. At the smallest size categories, beyond the ability to perform remote monitoring, there is far less opportunity to streamline operations when compared to the larger and higher customer equipment capacity edge data centre facilities. Consider a comparison in this regard between a size category 1 edge data centre and another weighing in at size category 6. The former data centre facility is most likely to be used by a single tenant who themselves will not often swap or alter the equipment which is deployed in the facility due to its remote and unorthodox deployment location, such as on a traffic light or attached to a truck. This means that any maintenance or other activities requiring physical intervention will be infrequent for that facility as a whole and may even be several years apart from one another. The larger infrastructure edge data centre facility, however, will typically experience many more events on a regular basis which would require equipment to be deployed, and for that equipment and the site itself to receive physical maintenance. There may be a need for this facility to have personnel onsite multiple times per week, which makes the case for automation significantly stronger and more practical to support from a business model perspective.

Practically speaking the application of this type of robotics system begins to make sense only within infrastructure edge data centres of size categories 4 and above. These facilities have the scale and the operating model required to make high levels of physical automation practical. For smaller edge data centre facilities, there are more limited applications of physical automation which remain valuable:

1) Automated locking of security doors
   a) Consider the example of a size category 2 infrastructure edge data centre which is deployed in a rural location. This facility is being used to connect to a local cellular network tower, and various network functions for that cellular network are being performed within the facility. Although personnel visits to this data centre facility are not as frequent as a larger data centre facility, due to the remote location of the facility, they are typically more expensive and take longer. One common issue that arises after a site visit is verifying the physical security of the facility, which in this case would be the closing and locking of its security doors. These doors could be automated by the use of remote controlled motors in order to open and close the doors on command. Such a system would not only allow keyless access to the facility and therefore reduce the chance of a physical key being lost or stolen, but also the doors could be physically shut should personnel forget to close them fully before leaving.

2) Removal of physical debris from vents
   a) Using the same example, an infrastructure edge data centre deployed in a rural area may have its airflow vents obstructed by plant debris over time, especially during the autumn and winter where leaves and other detritus may accumulate from any nearby trees or foliage. A device similar to that of a car's windscreen wiper could be used to automatically push this material away from the vents of the infrastructure edge data centre facility before airflow in and out of the facility becomes obstructed to the point where it causes an operational issue. This is a task which may need to be repeated in rural areas across a large number of distributed size category 2 edge data centre facilities, and so this physical automation measure can help to reduce the need for personnel to travel to these out of the way sites and limit expenditure.

3) Physical security measures
   a) Beyond the example of the automated locking of security doors, there are examples of physical automation which can either directly improve the security level of a site or contribute to the infrastructure edge network operator having a realistic and real time view of the security level of the location. In rural areas especially, issues may be caused by animals as well as humans, which are often more than capable of finding access to wiring or vents in

order to locate food or places to rest. An automated and remotely monitored drone system deployed at each infrastructure edge data centre facility could provide the light and physical presence to scare away many causes of infrastructure damage or obstruction by performing a regular patrol, with the video data collected being sent back to the infrastructure edge network operator by using the fibre network connectivity of the infrastructure edge data centre facility itself.

Highly extensive robotic automation of infrastructure edge data centre facilities is not inevitable and depends on the economic and technical feasibility of these automation solutions. However, at large scale, its operational benefits can become clear. The following example compares two infrastructure edge computing networks, each incorporating 50 size category 6 edge data centre facilities. These facilities are spread out across multiple areas, so the diagram represents an abstract view of their deployment topology. We can estimate the benefit of site automation by understanding the cost of a personnel visit to the site, the cost of the robotic automation system, and the number of such site visits which may be required over one year, across all of these edge data centre facilities:

1) Calculate the average cost of a site visit by operator personnel
   a) Although there are many potential factors in coming to this figure, for this simple example, we can use the annual salary of a single site technician and assume that other costs are included such as transportation and that only a single technician needs to be at the site for two hours on average to complete any required tasks.
      i) Example: annual salary of $100 000
      ii) Work hours per week: 40
      iii) Salary per hour: $48
      iv) Staff cost per site visit: $96
2) Estimate the number of site visits required per month per facility
   a) To determine this figure, it is helpful to separate those site visits which would have been required had the site been equipped with a high level of automation from the visits which could have been prevented by it. This is difficult to estimate before the efficacy of a site automation system is fully known, but it can be estimated initially and adjusted as the capabilities of a site automation system become clearer later.
      i) Example: site visits per month: 20
      ii) Number of visits for automatable tasks: 15
      iii) Number of visits for non-automatable tasks: 5
3) Multiply the average site visit cost by the number of site visits
   a) Although it is a coarse calculation which does not capture all of the nuance in the scenario, this step provides an indication of the average site visit cost

which is being incurred by a single edge data centre facility. Note that although for a single facility this figure may seem low, a single site technician may be responsible for several of the edge data centre facilities in the area, which could be factored in when creating a more comprehensive version of this cost comparison for a real practical operator.

4) Subtract the cost of site visits required to maintain automation systems
   a) The use of extensive site automation, especially for tasks which will require the automation system to manipulate physical objects, will itself require site visits to maintain mechanical components and ensure the proper operation of the system.
      i) Example: site visits to maintain automation per month: 5
5) Compare the estimated site visit cost to the cost of any automation systems
   a) The upfront cost of edge data centre facility automation systems will be higher than hiring traditional site personnel. Therefore, for the sake of this comparison, the cost of an automation system will be estimated over time with that upfront cost spread out over five years. In terms of the total number of site visits required for each edge data centre facility, we started with 20 per month and ended up with 10 for a fully automated site by accounting for the visits automation can eliminate alongside the visits which it cannot, and the visits which site automation actually requires itself.
      i) Example: total monthly site visit cost: $96 \times 10 = \$960$
      ii) Total upfront cost of automation system: $250\,000
      iii) Averaged monthly cost of automation system: $4167
      iv) Total monthly cost of system and maintenance: $4167 + (\$96 \times 5) = \$4647$

These figures are very rough estimates, and the cost of an automation system will vary greatly based on its complexity, maturity, and the number and variety of physical tasks which it has been designed to perform. However, this process does give us an idea of the scrutiny which is required in order to verify that an automation system for an edge data centre facility will meet the financial goals of the infrastructure edge computing network operator over time. The figures in this example jumped to a complex automation system, but smaller steps can be made over time, which are far easier to justify.

Although this estimation process will result in two dollar figures which can then be compared, there are a host of assumptions behind them, which the infrastructure edge computing network operator must be aware of such as the maturity of automation technology and its operational efficiency gains. These factors are somewhat less tangible than those used in the previous example. Although it will not be possible to eliminate site technician personnel, it may be possible to reduce the number that are required in each area the infrastructure edge computing network is operating in, reducing costs.

Ultimately the automation of an edge data centre facility is a long-term bet which has the potential to result in an enhanced level of operational efficiency which, over time, can contribute to a lower set of recurring costs for the infrastructure edge computing network operator as well as the ability to rectify many potential issues before they impact the operation of the facility or of its customers.

6.10.2 Single or Multi-tenant

An infrastructure edge data centre may be operated for a single tenant or customer, or for use by multiple tenants depending on the business model of the infrastructure edge network operator.

Where an infrastructure edge data centre facility is deployed and operated by an operator who, as is the case with the typical use of that term in this book, will seek to generate revenue by attracting as many unique and valuable customers to that facility and charge them for equipment colocation and the use of network and edge exchange services, the multi-tenant operating model will be utilised.

However, in some cases the organisation which is deploying and operating infrastructure edge data centre facilities may not be an edge data centre facility operator of this type. Consider the example of a cloud provider who seeks to have greater levels of control and integration over their physical infrastructure than they can achieve by using another organisation's edge data centre facilities and sees their ability to deploy and operate these facilities as a competitive advantage in the market. In this example, the cloud provider will operate their edge data centre facilities as the single tenant in the customer equipment which is deployed there while still bringing in network connectivity from many sources. In this scenario, the edge data centre facility operates as a single tenant facility but still uses EX capabilities in order to efficiently route data between their services at the infrastructure edge and any access or last mile networks which are present in any edge data centre facilities to lower latency.

Alternatively, the cloud provider in this example may not operate any EX functionality in their edge data centre locations. However, this approach would make sense topologically only if the cloud provider is also offering their own access or last mile network connectivity from these facilities as otherwise the performance of a service operating from these edge data centre facilities would be hamstrung by the need to inefficiently route data back through an internet exchange (IX) location and on to the facility.

Other organisations who may deploy infrastructure edge computing networks include the largest network operators, such as Verizon in the US or BT in the UK. These organisations already have access to nationwide network infrastructure and either existing structures or pieces of land which could become deployment locations for infrastructure edge data centres. However, the challenges that these organisations face are often more in regard to business focus than their technical and operational capabilities. Where the network operator chooses to operate some infrastructure edge data centre facilities but does not make this part of their business as a business unit with its own goals and strategic imperatives, it is likely to function only as a means to sell more of the existing lines of business which the company operates such as network connectivity. This is a valid strategy, but one which is likely to result in the infrastructure edge business unit being unable to meet its potential.

Many of these factors are not unique to infrastructure edge data centres. Today, there are many organisations who operate regional or national scale data centre facilities as their primary business as multi-tenant facilities. Companies like Digital Realty and Equinix operate this model successfully, and a large part of the value of their infrastructure is that it is home to many different customers, which other customers can potentially interconnect with in these facilities. On the other hand, in some cases entities such as Amazon Web Services (AWS) and Facebook who operate at massive scale will operate their own data centre facilities which utilise the single tenant model. However, these organisations will often also utilise multi-tenant facilities to provide their services where it makes economic sense to do so.

The multi-tenant model of data centre operation allows the operator of those facilities to share their infrastructure across multiple customers. This is an example of the shared infrastructure model, and the economics of this model as have been described previously in this book are appealing to both an operator and their customers due to its ability to spread the significant costs of infrastructure over a number of organisations over time. This is much more difficult to achieve with a single tenant model.

Where an organisation is large enough, however, different business entities within the organisation are often considered to be separate customers, and so for entities operating at massive scale, this variant of multi-tenancy makes sense economically for locations where a very large deployment is required such as at a national or global data centre facility. However, due to this question of single location scale, this model is less applicable to a distributed infrastructure edge computing network.

Over time the landscape of infrastructure edge computing is likely to be fragmented between those organisations who will deploy and operate single tenant facilities, those who will utilise their existing infrastructure but who are not primarily infrastructure edge computing network operators, and the organisations who were established for and dedicated to designing, deploying, and operating this new tier of infrastructure. Due to their focus and expertise in the area combined with their ability to use the multi-tenant shared infrastructure model without appearing to present a conflict of interest to any customer who may wish to deploy equipment in these edge data centre facilities, this latter category of infrastructure edge computing network operators are likely to be the most successful.

6.10.3 Neutral Host

In telecommunications networks, a neutral host facility is one which will accept connectivity to and from any network which is physically present in that facility. As long as a network meets the needs of that facility in terms of physical cabling, logical protocol support, and any fees required to enter that facility, it and any other networks can feed into or out of the facility. If any interconnection services are offered at the facility, this neutral host model becomes especially powerful as the value of those interconnection services increases as the number of networks which are present at the facility grows over time, and the neutral host model removes barriers to entry which otherwise exist for networks.

This is in contrast to a facility which is highly opinionated about which networks will be allowed to be present in that facility. In this case, the operator of the facility will restrict the types and quantities of networks which are allowed to enter the facility. This will typically be the case where a facility owner is a large network operator and sees the presence of other networks as a competitive disadvantage. The extent to which this is an issue for customers who may deploy equipment in an infrastructure edge data centre which uses this model depends on the specific characteristics of the location itself:

1) Service availability
   a) If other network operators are restricted from being able to bring their own services into the facility, those networks which are present in the facility must support the network services required by the customers who may deploy equipment there, as otherwise the facility as a whole will not be valuable as an edge data centre facility.
2) Importance of other networks
   a) Where the organisation operating the facility is not the leading network operator in the area, or where they do not offer network connectivity which meets the feature, speed, or cost needs of customers who may deploy equipment in that facility, access to any other networks logically becomes much more important to these customers.
3) Interconnection services
   a) In cases where no interconnection services are offered at the facility, it matters less whether many or few networks are present at the facility as long as any customers who have deployed equipment at the facility are able to reach the nearest point of interconnection, whether IX or EX, in a performant, reliable, and cost-effective way.

In many ways, whether an edge data centre facility operates as a neutral host is tied to whether that facility is also utilising a multi- or single tenant equipment colocation model. Where an infrastructure edge computing network operator does not own existing network infrastructure or function as their own colocation customer, the ability to utilise any network operator in the areas where they intend to deploy edge data centre facilities provides the operator with significant flexibility in terms of the deployment locations they are able to utilise, the features and speed of the network connectivity that they are able to access, and the pricing which they can achieve from those network operators.

However, there is additional nuance as these two models do not entirely overlap. Consider the case where an infrastructure edge network operator is primarily a network operator, as described in the previous section. In this example, the operator may be ambivalent to which customers are deploying equipment within their infrastructure edge data centre facilities, and so at that facility they will support multi-tenant operation, but concurrently the operator may not want to allow other network operators into that facility. In this case, the edge data centre facility is multi-tenant and single host.

An infrastructure edge data centre network which combines multi-tenant operation in terms of the customer equipment which can be deployed at its facilities with a neutral host model for network connectivity in these facilities presents the most valuable combination for the operator as it provides the greatest flexibility in terms of customers, partners, and suppliers. This approach also provides the most valuable infrastructure for customers as it removes several limitations that make it difficult for equipment and networks to be present across the infrastructure edge computing network. By using the network effect of pulling as many unique customers and partners to these facilities, the operator can create the complete ecosystem for EX services, which makes the entire network more valuable.

6.10.4   Network Operations Centre (NOC)

The infrastructure edge computing network operator must have an efficient means by which to monitor and manage their infrastructure edge data centre facilities and their supporting network infrastructure. Monitoring data is collected from all of the operator's distributed infrastructure and delivered to a central location which acts as a network operations centre (NOC), where all of this data can be analysed, allowing the operator to identify any operational issues and to take any corrective action that is required such as performing remote maintenance or dispatching personnel.

Depending on the density and spread of their infrastructure deployments, an infrastructure edge computing network operator may not have a single NOC location. Consider an infrastructure edge computing network which spans from the East Coast to the West Coast of the US. Assuming that each NOC location has equal and timely access to the monitoring information from all of the operator's deployed infrastructure, a dual or multi-site NOC configuration where each NOC location is distant from the other to make use of geographical diversity in the case of any localised network issues that may impact connectivity is preferable to one NOC location, which may be a single point of failure.

Consider the example of such an infrastructure edge computing network, with one scenario being a single centralised NOC and the other being a distributed network of three NOCs. Those distributed NOCs are themselves interconnected together using network infrastructure that the infrastructure edge computing network operator does not use for the customer traffic. This is an example of out of band (OOB) management and is considered good network practice as it is capable of isolating the impact of any operational network failures which may occur without fully disrupting infrastructure management.

Additionally, key regions such as London or New York City which have especially high visibility to the operator's customers, or which are considered to be flagship deployment locations, may have their own local NOC. This is often more of a business decision driven by the needs of the operator for the perception of their commitment to that region rather than any specific technical factor. However, if such a location is home to a large number of operator personnel who are responsible for operation of the infrastructure, such a mini NOC may make sense and allow for some additional coordination.

Due to the geographically distributed nature of infrastructure edge computing networks, the NOC does not and in most cases should not be the location from which site technician personnel must be dispatched to resolve any identified infrastructure issues. There is no need for the NOC to be within the same state or region to be able to dispatch personnel, who are likely to be home based and live within the area of the infrastructure that they are intended to service. This arrangement prevents the infrastructure edge computing network operator from having to establish office facilities across all of the geographically distributed areas where they have deployed any edge data centre facilities.

Where an infrastructure edge computing network operator has deployed infrastructure between multiple countries, it will typically be preferred by the operator's customers for there to be an NOC available in each country which operates in that country's time zone and speaks the local language. It is possible to have one central global NOC which operates continuously on a 24/7/365 basis and is responsible for coordinating all the national and international operations of the operator, however.

The specific structure and operational requirements for an NOC which is supporting an infrastructure edge computing network are determined by the services which the operator is offering to their end customers. Higher levels of service and tighter levels of service assurance will require a more tightly integrated NOC and services or maintenance organisation within the operator in order to support the expectations which customers will have of these services. This tends to lead towards a multi-site NOC configuration so that staff at each NOC can have a closer understanding of local infrastructure.

6.11 Brownfield and Greenfield Sites

Although the large buildings used by traditional data centres are not typically targets for deployment of an infrastructure edge data centre, unless there is adequate roof or car park space in an area such as a shopping centre, there are many other properties which can be repurposed to be used for this purpose and which are located in distributed locations. Some of the most frequent suitable locations for this purpose include existing telecoms shelter buildings which were used for previous operators or generations of network technology and are now either underutilised or no longer actively used at all. These sites can often be retrofitted in order to operate as an infrastructure edge data centre. The infrastructure edge data centre size category most suitable for these facilities is 2 or 3 due to the size of these telecoms shelter structures as well as their access to power and fibre network connectivity.

One aspect of brownfield deployment which may be difficult with the potential number of facilities is maintaining consistency. It is likely that the buildings or structures used will vary in terms of their size, power infrastructure, cooling system, and other factors, which introduces variability when using them as infrastructure edge data centre locations. This not only introduces operational complexity but also adds additional complications when considering the use of extensive site automation over time. However, the cost of these sites may be low enough for the infrastructure edge computing network operator to bear the additional operational costs and adapt their processes accordingly.

This issue can be addressed by creating a template structure for components, structure, and method of operation for an infrastructure edge data centre which is deployed within an existing structure in much the same way as can be done for infrastructure edge data centres which are self-contained. A template of this type for various scales of infrastructure edge data centre, aligned to the categories of size for these facilities, should be created by the infrastructure edge computing network operator for each of the major site types that they expect to encounter so that when an opportunity presents itself to utilise one of these locations, the operator can quickly determine the initial and long-term cost of deploying an infrastructure edge data centre in that location, reducing any future surprises.

The extent of the work required for brownfield deployment depends heavily on the specific building that is being considered. Consider the following issues which must be evaluated for each building in consideration for edge data centre deployment and the potential challenges that they each create:

1) Building structure
   a) The existing building must be inspected for structural soundness and for suitability in hosting tens of kilowatts of customer equipment. Common points of failure include roofs which may allow water ingress to the facility, doors

which may not support the level of security required by the operator or their customers, and layouts which are not conducive to the optimal positioning of dense data centre rack infrastructure.

2) Power infrastructure

   a) Some existing telecoms shelter structures are designed to provide – 48 V DC power. Others are designed to provide several tens of kilowatts of 120 V AC power and many other types and scales of electrical power depending on the original purpose of the building. A key question is whether the building can provide a type of power which does not commit the infrastructure edge computing network operator to the use of inefficient power conversion equipment, and whether enough power can be drawn using the power infrastructure in and around the building to support the needs of the customer equipment which would be deployed inside it, often at tens of kilowatts.

3) Network infrastructure

   a) In the case of an existing structure which was designed for telecoms use cases, it is likely that there is existing fibre network infrastructure present into the building. It may be, however, that this fibre is not suitable for the bandwidth requirements of the infrastructure edge data centre facility, requiring the existing infrastructure to either be augmented with additional fibre strands or replaced altogether by the operator.

4) Cooling system

   a) Many of the existing structures which will be identified for infrastructure edge data centre facility brownfield deployments were not designed to remove the level of heat which an infrastructure edge data centre of size categories 3 and above will require. This means that the existing cooling system at the building may need to be redesigned, which can be a significant expense, but a necessary one for the facility.

5) Site security

   a) Existing site security measures may be inadequate or non-operational. Any security cameras must be connected to the infrastructure edge computing network operator and their site security monitoring systems, and door or gate locks must be remotely monitorable and ideally controllable by the operator to ensure that the operation of the site can be performed in an unmanned way, without frequent personnel visits.

Multiple suitable sites may be present in an area, and the infrastructure edge computing network operator must then choose between them based on the characteristics of each site as well as the requirements from the operator for the resulting edge data centre facility. For example, consider comparing two sites. One existing building may appear to be more attractive than another because one has a modern cooling system already installed and the other does not. However, the latter site provides sufficient network connectivity while the former would require the operator to pay for the deployment of additional fibre cabling. In this case, the choice of site comes down to the cost that is required in order to bring each site to an acceptable state, using analysis performed by the operator.

In the case of a greenfield deployment, an infrastructure edge computing network operator has two primary options. They can either construct a building and deploy the infrastructure edge data centre components within that building, or they can utilise purpose built, self-contained infrastructure edge data centre designs which are capable of operating outdoors without any additional enclosure. The latter option is preferable for a number of reasons, including several key commercial considerations:

1) Time to market
   a) Consider a case where an infrastructure edge computing network operator has a stock of self-contained infrastructure edge data centres. These facilities are ready for deployment as soon as the sites at which they are to be deployed are ready. In this case, the time required to ready a site for their deployment and to transport a facility to the site is likely to be considerably shorter than the construction time that is required to establish a new building and, in some cases, even faster than a retrofit. The downside to this approach is to achieve this speed, the operator must maintain a stock of edge data centre facilities which are ready to be deployed, which does not allow the operator to ease their own capital expenditure by building or buying each of these facilities only when the deployment sites for them are deployment ready.
2) Differentiation
   a) In the case where an infrastructure edge computing network operator has invested in the design and development of custom edge data centre facilities, the number of locations where these facilities are deployed can be an effective differentiator when compared to other operators who are reliant on off the shelf facilities or the use of retrofitting existing buildings due to the self-contained and highly integrated nature of a custom infrastructure edge data centre facility developed by its own operator.
3) Deployment flexibility
   a) Some infrastructure edge data centre designs will be physically modular and support the addition at a later date after their initial deployment of additional redundancy measures, additional cooling system capacity, or even extra customer equipment. Examples include designs which can be stacked and have cabling fed vertically from one layer of the data centre facility to another in order to achieve integration. This type of flexibility is unique to the self-contained edge data centre facility model and allows an operator to, where it makes economic sense, increase the capacity of a specific site potentially without increasing the footprint of that site. In many cases the operator will be better served by deploying additional edge data centre facilities in nearby locations to expand their footprint, however, where sites are available.

Some infrastructure edge computing network operators will be highly opinionated about the type of physical edge data centre facilities that they deploy and will go so far as to design, develop, and even produce the specific infrastructure edge data centre facilities that they will use. This approach can be highly beneficial as it allows the infrastructure edge network operator to have proprietary and useful integration between the hardware, software, and operational characteristics of the entire system. In this case, however, the operator is saddled with the costs and complexities required to achieve such a level of sophistication. On the other end of the spectrum, infrastructure edge computing operators will emerge who see the edge data centre facilities themselves as commodities and are comfortable utilising off the shelf designs in order to minimise their development expenses and focus on areas of the business, such as operational efficiency or integration with partner infrastructure and services, where they are able to add unique value in the market. However, this approach relies on the general commercial availability of edge data centre facilities, which today are often specialised and bespoke.

Even infrastructure edge computing network operators who design, develop, and produce their own edge data centre facilities may utilise off the shelf designs where they are more economical. These resulting infrastructure edge computing networks will resemble a mix of proprietary and generally available edge data centre facilities interoperating using a common network infrastructure and the same monitoring, management, and operational service layers that are utilised by the infrastructure edge computing network operator. This is vital to ensure that the operator does not end up with an unwieldy collection of non-integrated infrastructures which cause many new operational challenges.

Across an area such as a city, brownfield and greenfield sites can be used together for infrastructure edge data centre deployment. There is no requirement that every data centre facility must be of the same build type or of the same size. There are, however, significant operational benefits to the use of consistent facilities, as previously described, in the form of operational consistency, and so where it is possible, the infrastructure edge computing network operator should strive to maintain that level of inter-site consistency in order to simplify both the customer experience and their own operations.

Ultimately the choice between brownfield and greenfield site deployment will primarily be driven by the upfront cost required by any construction or retrofitting activity that is required in order to fully deploy a functioning and customer ready infrastructure edge data centre facility. The secondary and less visible cost component of this choice is the impact of any inconsistencies between data centre facilities over time in terms of the impact of any operational complexity that they introduce for the infrastructure edge computing network operator by requiring a deviation from standard processes.

6.12 Summary

Throughout this chapter we have explored many of the key factors which make infrastructure edge data centres unique compared to their regional or national scale equivalents. There are discrete size categories of infrastructure edge data centre facilities, each with a unique set of considerations and characteristics which make them suitable for specific use cases and deployment scenarios. By using these size categories to understand the role of a specific edge data centre facility, an overall network design can be created by the infrastructure edge computing network operator, which then supports a software service-based approach to resiliency by utilising many dispersed edge data centre facilities.

Data centre operation is a key consideration for a distributed network of many infrastructure edge data centres. This requires a heavier reliance on automation in order to reduce the significant cost and operational difficulties of maintaining onsite personnel at each of these facilities. Automation itself is a highly complex area which covers the automation of both logical and physical tasks and should be sized appropriately to the problems being addressed, the operational requirements of an infrastructure edge computing network operator, and the maturity of the automation technology.

Although some of their capabilities such as the reduced level of physical redundancy compared to a RNDC may make infrastructure edge data centres appear very different to their larger cousins, they are more similar than not in many ways. Understanding the unique aspects of both types and scales of data centre facilities and how they can be used in a complementary way is key to creating any infrastructure edge computing network of significant value over the long term.

7

Interconnection and Edge Exchange

7.1 Overview

As was described in previous chapters, the internet is a network of networks. To make this system of multiple networks interoperating work as we need it to in order to support new generations of use cases and applications which rely on achieving low latency communications and a minimal cost of data transportation, there must be many distributed points of interconnection between networks present at the infrastructure edge, and the mix of networks present in these locations must match those that are required to support the application workloads required by customers and end users.

Interconnection is the process by which one network is connected to another so that both networks are able to share data. This enables customers connected to one last mile or access network to use resources which are present on another network, such as a piece of content or a cloud service. This interconnection must be possible at the infrastructure edge network for the system to be valuable.

In the infrastructure edge computing network, there must be one or more meet me rooms (MMRs) present in the area. These are the physical locations where the exchange of data between networks occurs. Without an MMR in one of more infrastructure edge data centre (IEDC) facilities, interconnection is at best very limited and at worst non-existent at the infrastructure edge network, limiting its value.

7.2 Access or Last Mile Network Interconnection

The ability to perform access and last mile network interconnection is fundamental to the value of the infrastructure edge computing network. If this is not achieved,

Understanding Infrastructure Edge Computing: Concepts, Technologies and Considerations,
First Edition. Alex Marcham.
© 2021 John Wiley & Sons Ltd. Published 2021 by John Wiley & Sons Ltd.

the infrastructure edge network and its constituent edge data centre facilities are of little value to the operator or their customers.

Without access or last mile network interconnection at the infrastructure edge network, meaning that one or more of these networks is present in one or more edge data centre facilities across a given area such as a city, all of the network traffic which is sent between any end user in the area and the resource they are attempting to access in the IEDC, such as any piece of content or application workload, will not be able to take a direct path either physically or topologically to the edge data centre facility. This is crucial as the ability of the infrastructure edge computing network to support low latency applications and a lower cost of data transportation is entirely predicated on having a direct path physically and topologically for network traffic from the access or last mile network to one or more IEDC facilities in the local area.

This is an issue of crucial importance to the infrastructure edge computing network. If all of the right access or last mile networks do not interconnect in these edge data centre facilities, all of the traffic between end users and their resources of choice will take non-optimal paths, resulting in higher cost and higher latency than is achievable even between an end user and a regional or national scale data centre facility. If two end users are connected to two different access or last mile networks, both of those networks must be present in an IEDC and must also have agreed to interconnect with one another in that facility or another facility which is on the infrastructure edge computing network in the area in order to achieve low latency and a low cost of data transportation.

An IEDC facility is likely in all cases to cost a customer more for the basic services of equipment deployment and colocation than a regional or national scale data centre due to the economies of scale for purchasing, utilities, and operations which are achievable with larger facilities. This means that the only way an IEDC facility can contribute a unique and valuable service to the customer is for it to be capable of providing lower latency or a lower cost of data transportation. As described previously, both of these key factors are completely reliant upon access or last mile network interconnection. Without it, the edge data centre facility is of little value, which means the entire infrastructure edge computing network as a whole is as well.

The diagram in Figure 7.1 shows this network traffic path issue visually. A network path like this is often referred to as tromboning, or hair pinning, due to the sharp out and back path which it imposes on the network traffic. It is highly inefficient and imposes an impassable minimum latency and cost on all network traffic to and from the infrastructure edge computing network which can only then be improved by arranging access or last mile interconnection directly inside edge data centre facilities.

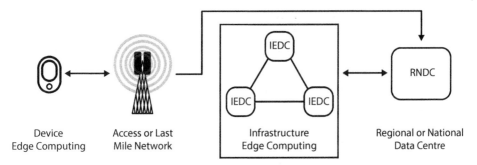

Figure 7.1 Tromboning network traffic path.

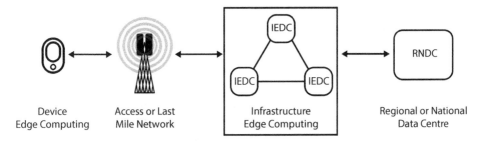

Figure 7.2 Direct network traffic path.

Now, in the case where access or last mile network interconnection has been achieved at an edge data centre facility, the resulting network traffic path is direct between the end user and resources located on the infrastructure edge computing network (see Figure 7.2). The resulting physical and logical topology matches the previous diagrams of network traffic flow from earlier chapters. This is what allows the infrastructure edge computing network to provide lower latency and a lower cost of data transport than a regional or national data centre (RNDC) facility and is the only real way to achieve those capabilities.

It is worth reinforcing the importance of this point for the infrastructure edge computing network operator. In an area where there are RNDC facilities which are providing access and last mile network interconnection and the infrastructure edge computing network is not capable of or has not achieved direct interconnection with these networks in one or more edge data centre facilities, there are no use cases or application workloads for which the edge data centre is a better choice than a RNDC facility in terms of either cost or performance. In such a scenario, an IEDC is relegated to the role of expanding capacity for the RNDCs in the area, which in many cases can be achieved at a lower cost to the end user by adding additional data halls to these larger facilities in centralised locations.

As a customer who may deploy equipment within an IEDC, knowing which access or last mile networks are present and interconnected at the infrastructure edge computing network is key to ensuring that any application workloads which are deployed in that facility can be effectively supported without the need for a tromboning traffic path, which wastes time and money. Consider the following factors when analysing a particular infrastructure edge computing network:

1) Which networks are present in the facility?
   a) An infrastructure edge computing network operator should be able to provide on request a list of the networks who are present in the facility and who have agreed that their presence can be publicly known. This allows the customer to understand the network connectivity options which are available at that edge data centre and to distinguish between individual edge data centre facilities within a specific area.
2) Which of these networks have agreed to interconnect?
   a) Although any particular network operator may be present in any edge data centre facility, they may not have agreed for other customers of that facility to be able to establish an interconnection with their network. For interconnection to occur, both parties, in this example the customer and the access or last mile network operator, must agree to the interconnection. This agreement is typically recorded in the form of a letter of understanding (LOU) between the parties which outlines the intent and terms of the activity. If a network is present in an edge data centre facility but that network will not interconnect with the customer in that facility, the problem described previously of a long, tromboning traffic pattern will persist indefinitely.
3) Which networks are my end users likely to utilise?
   a) Unless the service or application which is being offered is exclusive to a network operator, such as a mobile game launched in partnership with a cellular network, the answer to this question depends on the type of application in question, as well as the user demographics for that application. For example, consider a streaming video service. This application may be oriented towards home viewers who are in one location for the duration of their application session, or it may be oriented to mobile users who are travelling across a city on public transport. The former can most likely be served by a wired network such as Data Over Cable Service Interface Specification (DOCSIS) cable, and the latter will require a cellular network such as fourth generation (4G) Long-Term Evolution (LTE). Once the type of network needed for the application is determined, the question then becomes which networks of that type are available in the area and what is their market share in order to understand the level of user base coverage which will really be achievable for the application itself.

As an infrastructure edge computing network operator, a similar process should be followed in order to determine which access or last mile networks are required to be present and able to interconnect at one or more edge data centre facilities in order for the infrastructure edge computing network to be appealing or at all useful to its intended customers. The importance of this factor cannot be overstressed for the operator as it determines whether or not the substantial investment which must be made in order to deploy the infrastructure edge computing network will have real commercial value.

Upon initial deployment of an infrastructure edge computing network, it may be challenging for the operator to arrange this type of direct access or last mile network interconnection in one or more of their edge data centre facilities. These activities are challenging and require many organisations to agree on the value of the infrastructure edge computing network and the application workloads that it can uniquely support. However, despite this difficulty, an infrastructure edge computing network cannot be considered complete in any way until this access or last mile interconnection is complete.

Where access or last mile network interconnection is achieved with one or more edge data centre facilities, users connected to that network can utilise any application workload which is available to them from a customer on the infrastructure edge computing network in that area. If the network is adequately designed between the edge data centre facilities, an access or last mile network will not need to be present in all edge data centre facilities in the area; however, wherever possible, this is highly preferable as it reduces the latency for the end user and the load on the network as all data can be exchanged between networks at the edge data centre facility it arrives at, without in many cases needing to be sent to another edge data centre facility first. Although this network usage is less likely to limit performance or impose higher costs than a trombone traffic pattern, it remains suboptimal.

However, in cases where the interconnection of access or last mile networks to the infrastructure edge computing network does not occur, the operator is faced with a difficult challenge. In an ideal case, an agreement to interconnect with one or more of these networks has been reached before an infrastructure edge computing network is deployed in an area, but this is itself difficult as well. When over time this interconnection still cannot be achieved, the infrastructure edge computing network in that area must be considered of little value to both the operator and its customers due to its lack of capability to provide the key benefits in terms of cost and performance for the infrastructure edge computing model. There may be some other benefits which can still be retained, such as sovereignty of data compared to a regional or national facility which is located further away, but these are light.

Maintaining backhaul network connectivity to a RNDC facility where the access or last mile networks interconnect does not help significantly as in this case, the larger data centre will be capable of offering lower latencies and a lower cost of data transportation due to the tromboning network traffic path described earlier. Yes, customers who are deploying equipment in an IEDC facility in this scenario can connect to many of the access or last mile networks in the area through the infrastructure edge network which then passes that data to the regional or national facility, but this is not an effective use of all the edge infrastructure at all.

This is an existential issue for the infrastructure edge computing network operator and is beyond perhaps any other factor what determines the value of their infrastructure. If this issue is ignored, the operator implicitly accepts that they will not have a finished infrastructure edge system at all and that their infrastructure will not be attractive to their customers or able to support use cases.

It is worth mentioning here that although infrastructure edge computing requires access or last mile network interconnection, interconnection does not necessarily need edge computing. The impetus to distribute interconnection to the infrastructure edge computing network is to support new use cases and application workloads which require interconnection at the edge to achieve their goals in terms of performance and the cost of data transportation. Although there can be benefits to being able to interconnect at the edge for the current interconnection platform operators who run their services from RNDCs, without solidified use cases which drive customer demand for distributed interconnection, it is difficult to produce a compelling business case for it.

7.3 Backhaul and Midhaul Network Interconnection

Access or last mile networks are not the only important types of network which the infrastructure edge computing network operator must interconnect with in order to provide their customers with performance and cost advantages when compared to a RNDC facility. Just as the access or last mile networks to the left must be interconnected with the infrastructure edge computing network, so must the key backhaul and midhaul networks on the right as shown in Figure 7.3.

In many cases, the infrastructure edge computing network operator will seek to operate their own midhaul network. However, this network may use fibre infrastructure which is deployed by the edge operator themselves, it may use fibre infrastructure belonging to another network operator who is leasing the use of this infrastructure to the infrastructure edge computing network operator, or as is often the case, a combination of both approaches will be used to provide flexibility and cost savings.

A midhaul network in the context of infrastructure edge computing is the network infrastructure that connects IEDC facilities to one another. It is typically the part of the network, when compared to the access or last mile and backhaul

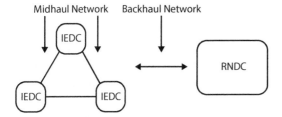

Figure 7.3 Backhaul and midhaul network interconnection.

networks, which the infrastructure edge computing network operator has the most influence over the design of. This is due to the size of the midhaul network and its direct connectivity between IEDC facilities allowing the operator the most opportunity to design and in some cases build the topology that they require between the facilities in an area. Its infrastructure may be owned or leased by the operator.

A backhaul network is composed of all of the network infrastructure which will connect the midhaul network to a regional aggregation point, which is typically a RNDC facility.

Technically speaking there is not a significant difference between interconnecting the infrastructure edge computing network with either of these categories of networks. In the case of any backhaul or midhaul network, the transmission medium is likely to be fibre optic cabling using a data link layer of Ethernet running at 100 Gbps or higher per connection, which is multiplexed through optical network equipment at both ends of the connection to support hundreds of gigabits or several terabits of data per second. Whether the demultiplexing process takes place in or outside of the IEDC, the end result is a network connection present in the facility which can be connected to an MMR. Access or last mile and midhaul or backhaul networks, as well as any customer networks, once present at the MMR, can be interconnected if their operators agree to do so. The operator of the data centre facility in which the MMR is present may choose to be a middleman to this group of agreements between network operators or not, depending on their business model and capabilities.

The phrase customer networks may sound out of place in this context, and it is worth clarifying what it means for this section in particular. Customer network may refer to two different things: customer equipment which is deployed within a data centre whether edge, regional, or national, which is then looking to be interconnected to other networks such as access or last mile networks in order for end users to be able to access resources located on that customer equipment in an efficient manner. Or it may in some cases refer to an external network that the customer has brought to the data centre. In this book, we will use the phrase customer network to refer to the former, for the sake of clarity.

Despite their technical similarities from an interconnection perspective, the business relationships to achieve interconnection with backhaul and midhaul networks are typically different than with access or last mile networks. The former are typically easier to arrange and more amenable to pay for play arrangements whereas with the latter infrastructure edge computing network operator can expect more focus on differentiated services and new use cases in order to motivate the access or last mile network operator to interconnect. This is due to the different business models between the access or last mile network operators and their backhaul and midhaul counterparts, and how they see the cost and new value to them of the whole infrastructure edge computing network evolving over time.

Access or last mile networks are likely to see greater future value in the infrastructure edge network such as the ability to offer new services and use cases, and with this comes more difficulty to prove its value against other competing approaches compared to a midhaul or backhaul network operator who may just see a way to utilise their dark fibre assets to interconnect network endpoints across an area such as a city and whose business is not tuned to providing or developing higher layer services.

This can result in an infrastructure edge network which is adequately connected in terms of backhaul and midhaul networks but is without any access or last mile network interconnection. As described in the previous section, this is a challenging situation for the infrastructure edge computing network operator. The IEDC facilities and their supporting midhaul and backhaul network infrastructure must be deployed first in order to present an otherwise complete system to the access or last mile network operator. In some cases where wired networks are concerned, one entity may be capable of providing both access or last mile networks as well as backhaul and midhaul assets. This is ideal for the infrastructure edge computing network operator as their value to the latter half of the business may help to justify interconnection with the access or last mile business unit as well.

7.4 Internet Exchange

Today the majority of network interconnection which is publicly viewable takes place within a fairly small number of locations across the world which are often within RNDCs. Networks may also interconnect using private venues, but by their nature these are typically hidden.

An internet exchange (IX) is a regional location where many networks are present and have agreed to exchange network traffic. At a broad level, the IX functions as a very large MMR where multiple networks can be present and are able interconnect at the agreement of their operators to exchange data. Although there are many nuances to the operation of an IX and various subcategories of these entities, this is the broad definition which we will use in this book. To be specific, what we refer to as an IX in this book in the majority of cases, especially when discussing a specific physical location, is an internet exchange point (IXP). Although we often use IX for short, where it is important we will still use both terms.

The number of IXs deployed worldwide depends on how an individual facility is classified. Although the exact figures vary, TeleGeography, a company providing telecommunications market research, estimates over 300 IXs utilising over 500 IXPs. Although this data is interesting and provides us with some estimate of the extent of interconnection distribution today, in the context of infrastructure edge computing, we are concerned with specific areas and whether the IX capabilities available in a particular location are sufficient to support the needs of new application workloads and user needs.

Some countries may have only one IX, depending on the scale, population density, and the maturity of network communications technology in the country. This may or may not be an issue for the cost and performance of application workloads operating in that country, or this single IX may be causing significant performance and cost challenges for all the network operators in the area and their users. This can be ascertained only on a location by location basis and should be identified by the operator of the infrastructure edge computing network as part of their analysis of where to deploy facilities.

Between IXs, size can vary drastically. For example, one of the world's largest IXs is IX.br, deployed in IXPs across 31 cities all across Brazil. This IX averages over 7 Tbps of throughput, which is a very large amount of data. In comparison, SAIX, the Salzburg Internet Exchange in Austria, averages around 0.2 Gbps of throughput and is deployed only in the city of Salzburg. This is a single IXP, but even on an individual IXP to IXP comparison basis, SAIX is much smaller than many of the IXPs that are in IX.br.

Although the overall size of an IX is a key consideration, size alone does not necessarily make an IX the ideal choice. If all of the networks that are required by a particular combination of end user and application workload are present in two IXPs, there is a choice to be made in terms of which one to use based on understanding the cost and performance trade-offs of each IXP. An IXP which is closer may actually incur higher costs than one which is further away due to its scale or its business model.

In this example, in theory the IXP which is located closer to the end user of the application workload should be preferable due to the minimum possible latency between the end user and that point of network interconnection; therefore, this IXP has been chosen as the interconnection location to use for this particular application workload. As the diagram in Figure 7.4 shows, these networks are not using

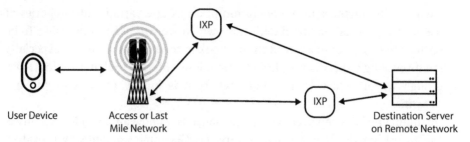

User Device   Access or Last   Destination Server
                     Mile Network   on Remote Network

Figure 7.4 Network interconnection at two IXPs.

just a single IXP and are in fact interconnected at both locations. The choice of which one to use for an application workload's network traffic is controlled by network routing based on operator needs.

Large networks which operate across a wide area such as all of the United States are very unlikely to interconnect in one IXP only. Consider the example of a large cloud provider and a large access or last mile network operator who want to interconnect their networks. Both of these entities operate from coast to coast with networks which each span thousands of miles. For the cloud provider, this footprint may take the form of a data centre presence on the west coast and a matching one on the east coast, whereas for the network operator, their real physical network infrastructure such as fibre cabling may be spanning across the entire country. In this case, it makes sense for these two entities to interconnect on both the west coast and the east coast and at any available locations in between.

This type of multi-point network interconnection helps to limit the network traffic path between the networks from following the trombone pattern which was described previously, which in this case, due to the scale of these networks, could otherwise occur from one coast of the United States all the way back to the other, resulting in a very inefficient network which introduces cost and performance challenges for the cloud provider and the network operator in a way that is entirely avoidable today. The ability to interconnect these networks in multiple locations also sets the stage for using an edge data centre facility to providing supplemental or augmentative interconnection capabilities to the IX.

The example of IX.br shows that the definition of an IX varies depending on the context. On the scale of the global internet, we can treat all of the cities in which IX.br operates as a single entity. However, in the world of infrastructure edge computing, we are also concerned with the specific locations of an IXP down to the level of specific cities so that we can understand the value of interconnection which could be provided by infrastructure edge computing on an area by area basis. So, in this book, when we refer to an IX, we are typically referring to a specific RNDC in which an IXP is located, instead of a number of these facilities spread across a country or region as one entity.

Figure 7.5 A distributed IX utilising several physical IXPs.

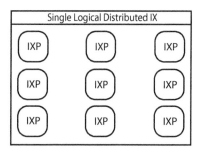

The diagram in Figure 7.5 shows a logical IX which is made up of many physical IXPs across a region. In this example, the IX can be treated as one entity at a macro level, but on a regional level the positions and capabilities of the individual IXPs become important when we consider how to utilise each of them to enable low latency application workloads that may be operating from an edge data centre facility.

An IX is not the only location in which two or more networks may be interconnected. This may also be achieved on a more discrete and limited basis within network operator facilities. An example of this type of arrangement is a content delivery network (CDN) who is deploying content distribution equipment in a number of access or last mile network operator locations. This model allows the CDN to reduce their operating costs by paying for less of the network resources that are required to distribute content to their end users than if the content were located further away from those users in a centralised location, and it allows that network operator to lessen the impact on their network from these same users accessing that content while also being able to provide the customers of that network operator with a better user experience. The CDN equipment must be interconnected with that access or last mile network in the locations where it is deployed, and so this is an example of a private network interconnection.

Comparatively, depending on the IX, it may be possible for network operators other than the parties to an interconnection to see that such an interconnection has occurred and is active. Most network operators will typically want to control who is able to interconnect with their network on a direct basis in order to establish beneficial business relationships and limit their administrative burdens.

In the context of infrastructure edge computing, we care about interconnection in order to achieve a minimum latency for network traffic where traffic must be exchanged between networks in order to meet the performance requirements of key low latency application workloads, or to lower the cost of data transportation by reducing the need to utilise the backhaul and midhaul network. There are physical areas and application workload scenarios where today's IX model may not satisfy all of the required parameters to support these two aims, typically due to the distance between the end user and the nearest relevant IXP. In this case, the edge exchange (EX) can be used to augment the IX system.

7.5 Edge Exchange

Although it offers a similar function to an IX by its capability to interconnect networks so that they can exchange data, an EX differs due to its physical location, its distributed nature, and its access to other networks. Whereas an IX is typically deployed in a larger data centre facility, an EX is deployed in one or more IDECs across the infrastructure edge computing network in an area, as seen in Figure 7.6. Both the EX and IX perform the function of allowing the exchange of network traffic between two or more networks, but their scale and deployment methodology differ.

In the same way as the specific physical instance of an IX is referred to as an IXP, the EX has a similar relationship to the edge exchange point (EXP). An infrastructure edge computing network which is providing EX services can be thought of as a single logical EX composed of one or more physical EXPs where the physical exchange of traffic between networks occurs. The number of physical EXPs which are used depends on the geographical spread of the infrastructure edge computing network as well as that of the access or last mile and backhaul or midhaul networks which are interconnecting to it.

An additional factor to consider in terms of the number of EXPs in an infrastructure edge computing network is the spread of edge data centre facilities by size category across an area, as shown in Table 7.1.

For the infrastructure edge computing network operator, an infrastructure edge computing network cannot be considered complete or ready for production customer application workloads until the sufficient level of access or last mile network interconnection is achieved at one or more edge data centre facilities in the area. The deployment of a functioning EX at one or more edge data centre facilities and interconnection with one or more access networks are the means to achieve this goal.

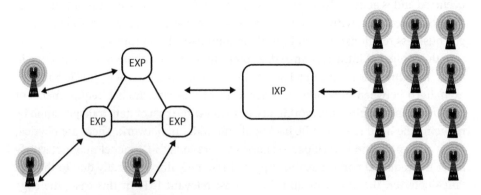

Figure 7.6   EX and IX comparison example.

Table 7.1 Suitability of IEDC facilities for use as an EXP.

Size category number	Example use case	Used as EXP
1	Network termination	No
2	Network functions	No
3	Local aggregation	Maybe
4	Low latency workloads	Yes
5	Low latency workloads	Yes
6	Regional edge aggregation	Yes

This factor makes the EX, composed of one or more EXPs across a given area such as a city, key to realising the value of the infrastructure edge computing network itself. Without the ability of the EXP deployed in one or more edge data centre facilities to exchange data between networks, the infrastructure edge computing network will be of limited value to its users and its operator.

For the sake of completeness, there are cases where a single network is capable of supporting the type of low latency application workloads associated with infrastructure edge computing without the need for localised interconnection. This is the scenario where every component of the service from start to finish is provided by one single network operator. An example of such a scenario is a cellular network operator who is offering a multiplayer video game only for end users of their own network and only utilising their own network, data centre, and cloud resources. These approaches are hamstrung due to the difficulty in one entity providing all of the elements required in order to create a desirable application workload with a large enough potential user case to warrant its use.

As previously described, the same two networks can be and often are interconnected at multiple IXP locations. The diagram below continues this trend while also showing the hierarchical relationship between an EX and an IX. This relationship is similar in many ways to a caching hierarchy; from the perspective of optimising overall system and application performance, where interconnection can be achieved at an EX, then it should be; and in cases where the desired network is not present at the EX, that traffic should be transported to an IX, if all other factors such as the cost of data transportation and network availability are equal between the EX and the IX. In practice, however, these are difficult.

An IX provides access to a significantly higher number of networks directly when compared to an EX. This makes sense due to its much larger physical size and topologically central role within the overall network compared to any individual EX. The IX also has a large head start over the EX as many IXPs have been active for several years, with some for several decades. Another challenge for the EX is the network effect; the more networks which are present at the IX, the more appealing it becomes as a location to interconnect; and the wider this gap is between an established IX and a new EX, the more challenging it will be for the infrastructure edge computing network operator to close the gap.

By definition, an EX is located at the infrastructure edge. This means it is ideally located at the line between one or more last mile access networks and the midhaul network infrastructure, which then connects them to backhaul networks and ultimately to the nearest IX. This physical positioning puts the EX between the access networks and the nearest IX; the distance between an EX and an IX will vary considerably depending on the specific area, but in many cases an EX can be hundreds of miles closer to the access networks, and therefore their end users, than the nearest IX and any of its IXPs.

Where IEDC facilities are connected to one another by their own network infrastructure at the metropolitan area network (MAN) scale, when a network of interest is not present in a specific facility but is available in another across the MAN, that traffic can be transported to the EXP that can serve it and provide access to its destination network. In this way, as long as the network infrastructure between IEDCs is suitably performant, the individual physical EXP facilities available across the infrastructure edge network in a specific area can be treated as one distributed logical EX.

This is similar to how at a macro level, the individual IXPs of even a very large IX such as IX.br can be viewed as a single IX system. From the perspective of an IXP, a nearby EX, itself comprised of multiple EXPs, can be viewed as a single EX system regardless of the number of physical EXP locations within.

The number of IXPs in the area significantly impacts the value of deploying and operating an EX. In a scenario where an IXP is already capable of providing the level of interconnection performance and thus the minimum network latency required for specific application workloads, there is little value in deploying an EX. Because there is little value in deploying an EX in such a location, and the value of an infrastructure edge computing network itself depends on the ability of the EX to perform access or last mile network interconnection at one or more edge data centre facilities, the infrastructure edge computing network itself is of little value in this area as described further in a previous section.

In comparison, in an area where the nearest IX is so far away from the infrastructure edge network that the IX cannot support the latency and data transportation cost requirements of the application workload, an EX can be very useful in that area and then so can the infrastructure edge computing network itself. This combination of technical capabilities, physical infrastructure position, and needs of application workloads is the sweet spot for the infrastructure edge computing model. The more application workloads that require this system in the area, the higher the value of the edge itself.

Whether a point of network interconnection is an IXP or an EXP, many of the core technologies are common between them and differ only in their scale. The next section describes the means by which various network technologies can utilise an IXP or an EXP to interconnect across IXP or EXP facilities.

7.6 Interconnection Network Technology

Although the goal and function of interconnecting with a last mile or access network is the same for an infrastructure edge computing network operator regardless of the specific last mile network that is in question, each type of last mile network must interconnect with the infrastructure edge using a different technical means. The five most common network types will be explored during this section.

The network technologies described in this section are complex and offer various means to achieve the same goal of network interconnection. As such, these descriptions are not exhaustive, but they do show the network elements which must be local to an EXP, for example, for an interconnection in that facility itself to provide all of the desired performance and cost of data transportation benefits.

Conceptually, interconnection at the EX through one or more EXPs deployed in IEDC facilities is appealing for the performance and cost reasons which have been described. However, practically speaking, the locations of the network elements in each type of network that interconnection is desired with, such as access or last mile cellular networks, are typically fixed. This introduces additional levels of complication when understanding the true value of a real world EX.

When a network interconnects with the infrastructure edge computing network, this process will typically take the form of some fibre cabling from that network either entering an IEDC facility from the outside via a cable management conduit or connecting into an external fibre cabinet located at the IEDC site. This connection will then be patched through to an MMR inside the IEDC facility where physical or virtual cross connection between that network and others present in the edge data centre facility can occur, depending on the capabilities of the individual IEDC facility.

From a network perspective the external connection will typically utilise its own public Internet Protocol (IP) address space. Many large network operators will not want to readdress their network segments or to use any of the IP address space of the infrastructure edge computing network operator for their own infrastructure or for the IP addresses assigned to their end users. To that end, the infrastructure edge computing network operator can offer either a layer 2 or a layer 3 interconnection to such a network, with the former option being simpler and the latter offering more configurability.

How each type of network interconnects with the infrastructure edge computing network depends on the network technology in use. To begin, we will use the two most important cellular networks.

7.6.1 5G Networks

Across the fifth generation (5G) protocol stack, there are two major sources of functional separation: distinguishing the radio network from the core network and separating the user plane from the control plane. In the context of network interconnection, the most important element of the 5G system is the User Plane Function (UPF) of the 5G core network. The UPF is the 5G core network entity responsible for the handling of user plane network traffic. It performs functions similar to a standard router in that regard, by forwarding network traffic towards its intended destination within the 5G core network.

Specifically, the type of UPF that matters the most in the context of network interconnection is the packet session anchor (PSA) UPF. This type of UPF is the boundary point between the user plane of the 5G network and any external networks, such as the network of an infrastructure edge computing network operator, another cellular network operator, or a cloud provider. Traffic leaving a PSA UPF destined for an external network can be interpreted by a standard IP routing network, and the PSA UPF functions bidirectionally, acting as the entry point to the 5G network from external networks.

How each cellular network operator chooses to deploy and geographically distribute their UPFs is of critical importance to understanding the value of the infrastructure edge computing network over the next five years as 5G networks are deployed worldwide and become the ideal access or last mile networks to support new generations of low latency applications, due to alterations made from 4G LTE to the 5G radio and core network protocols to support a lower minimum latency for user traffic.

Consider the following example. Although the 5G core network standards and protocols allow an operator to deploy a highly distributed core network utilising a very large number of UPFs across a geographically dispersed footprint, not all 5G network operators will choose to do this and those that do will not do so in all of their deployment areas. There is a trade-off to potential performance and flexibility in the form of an increased cost for the operator in terms of the design, operation, and maintenance of the more distributed core network design which the operator will have to balance.

There are several ways in which a 5G core network could be designed across the same area. In the case where there are a greater number of UPFs, this benefits the EX as there is a chance that more of the UPFs will be in locations where they will be closer to any of the IEDC facilities than a RNDC. Where UPFs are more sparse, it can be challenging for interconnecting the 5G network at the EX to make as much sense; in those cases where the UPF is located closer, physically or topologically, to the local IXP, it may actually increase the minimum end user latency to interconnect the UPF to the EXP instead of using the existing IXP.

5G networks and how they can be enabled by infrastructure edge computing will be described in more detail in Chapter 14 as a key use case for the infrastructure edge computing network itself.

7.6.2   4G Networks

In the case of 4G LTE networks, there are two entities which are key for network interconnection. These are the SGW (Serving Gateway) and the Packet Gateway (PGW). Much as in the 5G case, the cellular network operator controls the number and geographical location of the SGW and PGW that are deployed in their network, and the infrastructure edge computing network operator must work with the cellular network operator to locate where they are to identify the value of interconnection using an EX in a given area. Unlike in the 5G example, these gateway entities are already deployed today ahead of the infrastructure edge computing network and are often fixed function hardware devices which cannot be so easily or cheaply migrated to another location as a software workload.

For infrastructure edge computing, we care only about the data traffic of the 4G LTE network. There is little to no benefit for an infrastructure edge computing network to interconnect with telephony channels carried by the 4G LTE network as these systems have largely already been designed and deployed and are not latency sensitive to the extent that data systems have the potential to be in many new use cases. Between the SGW and PGW, the PGW is responsible for data traffic on the 4G LTE network and its exchange of data with external data networks. This makes the location of PGW entities across the 4G LTE network key for the infrastructure edge computing network operator. As network traffic leaves the PGW for an external network, much like the 5G UPF, the traffic is routable.

The number and location of 4G LTE PGWs is an interesting consideration for the infrastructure edge computing network operator. As 4G LTE cellular network operators today have a footprint of these PGWs spread across their networks to varying degrees, it may then seem easy as the infrastructure edge computing network operator to identify suitable deployment locations for edge data centres using the locations of these PGWs. After all, there are hundreds of millions of end user devices being produced maintain its operational efficiency, but it will be difficult for the cellular network operator to justify large efforts to rearchitect the 4G LTE network. Whether an operator chooses to move from traditional hardware-based 4G LTE network infrastructure to an updated virtualised version which could be deployed in a distributed manner alongside any of their 5G network infrastructure remains to be seen and will be an individual decision for each operator.

Additionally, due to improvements in the 5G radio and core network compared to 4G LTE, a lower minimum latency for end user traffic is possible using 5G than 4G, which makes 5G a more suitable choice for many of the use cases to which infrastructure edge computing itself is targeted. Although the real world efficacy of many of these 5G performance improvements has not been proven at the time of writing, capabilities such as partial frame transmission, more aggressive processing timings, and an asynchronous hybrid automatic repeat query (ARQ) scheme are capable of providing, for a suitably identified application workload, a measurable reduction in the minimum network latency which is achievable. This improvement can be on the order of tens of milliseconds in extreme cases.

All of this is to say, for the infrastructure edge network operator, betting the deployment locations of one or more IEDCs based on the current physical location of PGWs is a gamble which may not pay off as 5G networks are deployed at the same time as infrastructure edge computing networks themselves. Both of these network operators are faced with a bet to make on the maturity of 5G networks in a defined period of time after their deployment, the percentage of end users with a 5G New Radio (NR) compatible device, and the specific application workloads which will help to determine the value of interconnecting the 4G LTE network with the infrastructure edge network.

Although it may leave a gap in time for the infrastructure edge network operator, a strategy which focuses on the specific strengths of the infrastructure edge computing model is likely to be the most successful in the long run. This directs the efforts of the operator towards understanding 5G network deployment locations and timescales, making interconnection with those networks their priority, and then interconnecting with any 4G LTE networks in an opportunistic manner where they are available.

7.6.3 Cable Networks

Although 5G and 4G LTE cellular networks may be the most popular examples of access or last mile networks which come to mind, for the majority of end users, these networks are not how they access most of their services, applications, or content. Due to the amount of time that most end users spend indoors across various locations such as the home and the office as well as their different patterns of network usage in these locations compared to when they are on the move, wired access or last mile networks fill a very important role and are highly useful for the infrastructure edge network operator to interconnect with. Today most end users will use a Wi-Fi router to access these wired networks.

In the United States, the best example of these networks are the DOCSIS networks, many of which span very large tracts of the country from a variety of different network operators such as Comcast. These systems utilise the coaxial cable which was originally laid to millions of homes across the country in order to support cable television services and are often referred to simply as cable networks. Various revisions of the DOCSIS specifications have allowed these cable networks to support hundreds of megabits of data throughput for end users, making them suitable for many home and business locations as their primary network.

Although many of the new low latency use cases which infrastructure edge computing can uniquely support are targeted at mobile devices using cellular network connectivity, there are also use cases which are beneficial to end user devices attached to a cable network connection via a Wi-Fi router. This makes these cable networks attractive for network interconnection at the infrastructure edge.

In terms of the network entities which are crucial for network interconnection, the cable modem termination system (CMTS) is analogous to the 4G LTE PGW or the 5G UPF in that it is the earliest point in the cable network from the perspective of the end user where interconnection can occur. The CMTS is located at a headend location in the DOCSIS cable network. Coaxial cable enters in the front, and either a coaxial or frequently a fibre network cable exits from the back to connect a CMTS to its upstream network elements. This upstream connection from the CMTS is the location where the cable network can be interconnected with the infrastructure edge computing network, as the network traffic on the user plane at this point in the cable network is routable like the 5G PSA UPF.

Despite much of the enthusiasm in the industry, these cable networks are unlikely to be replaced by 5G networks due to the widespread existence of cable network infrastructure and the inefficient use of radio spectrum that the use of 5G as the primary network connection for hundreds of millions of homes and businesses across the United States alone would represent. As can be seen through the continued development of the DOCSIS standards, there is significant throughput available in many cable networks which can be achieved over time as signalling technologies improve and equipment at both the end user location and the CMTS are upgraded to support them. Speeds of 500 Mbps are already achievable using current DOCSIS standards, and many networks support 200 Mbps or more.

For the infrastructure edge computing network operator, the choice of interconnection with a cable network is distinct from that with a cellular network operator. As these cable networks will not be deprecated in favour of 5G, unlike what will eventually happen to 4G LTE networks, they are likely to have lasting value to the infrastructure edge computing network and its customers. However, these cable networks by their nature cannot support the level of mobility of end user devices as a cellular network, even when they are front ended by a Wi-Fi router. This makes the value proposition of an interconnection different than with a cellular network, as a cable network cannot support all of the use cases which make the best use of the characteristics of infrastructure edge computing itself.

To that end, for the infrastructure edge computing network operator, the priority of interconnecting with cable networks must be determined by the value of those applications which can be uniquely supported from the infrastructure edge computing network for a non-cellular end user audience. Many of these use cases such as video conferencing and content delivery are capable of benefitting from infrastructure edge computing but can also be addressed by other means such as a CDN or are of lower value than use cases requiring a cellular network. However, some key use cases such as the use of distributed AI to provide real time computer vision services apply equally well and in some cases better to the cable network due to its considerable throughput capacity and lack of need for spectrum conservation over time. Together, this makes cable networks appealing to the operator.

Much as in the example of a 4G LTE network, the CMTS locations for cable networks have typically already been deployed and were designed due to the spread of the physical coaxial cable plant out to various homes and businesses in the network coverage area. This means that the infrastructure edge computing network operator can work with a cable network operator to determine all CMTS locations across a given deployment area and deploy IEDCs accordingly.

7.6.4 Fibre Networks

Fibre networks may need to be interconnected with for access or last mile network connectivity as well as backhaul or midhaul network connectivity, depending on the topology and physical location of the particular network in question. Fibre networks are unique in the sense that they are the most likely transmission medium for all of the other network types that were previously described in this section when those networks reach an IEDC facility for interconnection. Therefore, almost all network interconnection at the infrastructure edge will be with fibre networks, with the types of networks on the other end of these fibre connections varying between all of the different network types including wireless such as 5G, 4G LTE, and cable, as was described previously.

Unlit or dark fibre links can be terminated in an IEDC facility where the infrastructure edge computing network operator is capable of and willing to light the ends of that fibre circuit using optical network equipment. This is likely to be the case where the infrastructure edge computing network operator is deploying or leasing their own midhaul network infrastructure as well as in some cases for the backhaul network where that connectivity utilises a similar model.

For access or last mile networks, and some midhaul or backhaul networks, it is more likely that one end of the fibre link will have already been lit by the other network operator. In this case, the type of optical networking equipment used at each end of the link must support the same encoding scheme, line rate, laser wavelength, and other parameters in order to achieve operational connectivity. This is not a difficult task as these parameters are standardised and will have to be communicated between both of the network operators involved in order to establish the fibre link. In most cases, this will be achieved using standard off the shelf equipment and so no specialised design at that level is needed.

Although the speed and scale of a fibre network interconnection may vary depending on the scale of the network on the other side of the fibre link, this only increases the amount of physical space and the speed and number of network interfaces on each end of the link that are required. The process and network entities involved in achieving the interconnection remain the same regardless of scale.

7.6.5   Other Networks

There are other types of access or last mile networks which can be useful to interconnect with at the infrastructure edge computing network. Many of these networks are not at the same scale as 5G, 4G LTE, or cable networks but may also be useful to an infrastructure edge computing network operator.

Networks in this category include fixed wireless access (FWA) networks, which utilise a wide range of frequency bands in order to provide wireless network connectivity to endpoints, each of which have fixed physical locations. These networks are often used to provide a residential or business premises with internet connectivity in areas where other network infrastructure is not present or incapable of providing the required performance. Typically FWA networks are deployed in rural or suburban areas which do not have existing or adequate cable network coverage, and so the FWA network provides an equivalent fixed position network connection for those homes or businesses.

Networks of various other types such as DSL can also be interconnected, although at this stage the limitations of the specific access or last mile network technology itself begins to really limit what an infrastructure edge computing network can contribute to the end user. These networks are not capable of supporting the latency or throughput to the end user that would make them attractive for interconnection to support new use cases. However, there may be opportunities to use edge data centre facilities in rural locations as data offload points for these networks opportunistically.

7.6.6   Meet Me Room (MMR)

As described previously, the MMR is a term used to refer to the location inside a data centre facility where a network interconnection can occur. This makes it the focal point of implementing network interconnection. Once the network connections from external networks are brought inside the data centre facility, they are brought to the MMR. Within the MMR, interconnection can be established between networks using cross connections, or cross connects. These connections can be physical or virtual depending on the operating model of the MMR and of the data centre operator themselves.

In a large data centre facility, network operators may deploy their own network equipment inside an MMR. The space inside an MMR is typically much more limited than in the rack space available for a customer to deploy other equipment such as servers, however, and only network equipment will be permitted for deployment. This incentivises any network operators who are present inside the MMR to deploy only what is necessary to support their current and short to medium term projected need. Some data centre operators may also deploy their own network equipment in the MMR and charge any network operators present in the MMR for its usage. This model makes sense where an operator does not see the need to deploy their own equipment and does not need to handle its management.

Due to the size of an edge data centre facility, it is more likely that an infrastructure edge computing network operator will procure, deploy, and operate the network equipment present in the MMR and bring in single or multiple connections from other networks to that network equipment. However, in larger edge data centre facilities there may be space for network operators to be able to deploy their own network equipment in the MMR. This may also be done for certain high value networks that are present in the edge data centre facility, such as cellular network operators. However, due to the size of the edge data centre facility and the corresponding amount of network traffic an individual edge data centre facility can be expected to handle, it is likely that the infrastructure edge computing network operator will push to deploy their own network equipment in the MMR. This also has key advantages for the infrastructure edge computing network operator in terms of the types of cross connects which they are able to offer; as described later, virtual cross connects do not require site visits by edge data centre facility personnel, which is an operational benefit as these are unmanned.

Conceptually, the choice between physical and logical cross connections may seem unimportant as both types of cross connection perform essentially the same function of connecting two networks together inside the MMR so that network traffic can be exchanged between them. Indeed, as long as an MMR is capable of supporting these functions, it has achieved its goal. However, there are a few key differences between these two approaches which are worth understanding for edge computing.

7.6.7 Cross Connection

Whether the entity within the data centre which needs to be interconnected with another entity is an external network such as a 5G network, or equipment such as a server hosting a cloud instance, some form of cross connection must occur between these two entities within the data centre for the interconnection to occur. In the context of interconnection, we will refer to either of these types of entities as networks; either they are a network for the transportation of data such as in the example of the 5G network, or they are a network for the delivery and generation of data such as the server.

In a traditional data centre environment, physical cross connections are the most common type of cross connection. These links take the form of fibre network cabling pulled between both networks, which are seeking to interconnect. Specifically, these fibre links are between the network presence of two networks inside the MMR, between network equipment from each of the network operators.

To establish this cross connection, a letter of intent (LOI) or letter of agreement (LOA) must first be established so that there is proof to the data centre operator that both networks agree on how the cross connection will be performed, as well as any additional terms such as duration, speed, or cost. Depending on the business model of the data centre operator, they may or may not be a party to a business arrangement which is enabled by the interconnection; however, the data centre operator will be paid by one or both of the network operators in exchange for deploying and maintaining the cross connection which enables their networks to be interconnected. The LOI or LOA between the network operators will determine which party pays the data centre operator for this connectivity.

In this way, it can be seen that a cross connection is the physical connectivity between two networks which enables them to be interconnected. It is helpful to think of interconnection as a service layer on top of this physical network connectivity instead of conflating them together as one single entity. This enables us to understand the value of cross connection and interconnection separately whilst knowing that they depend on each other to be realised in the real world between multiple parties.

Once this agreement process has been finalised, the data centre operator must then physically run the fibre cabling between the locations within the data centre where both networks are present. In the data centre, these physical locations do not matter to the networks themselves as long as the data centre operator is able to provide the physical cross connection, regardless of the amount of cabling or the physical cable routing required. Depending on the size of the data centre, its number of MMRs, and other physical factors, the data centre operator may have to route cabling between floors or between rooms in the most complex cases. Ideally, both network operators are present within the same MMR and their racks are reasonably adjacent to simplify the physical connectivity.

As previously mentioned, for data centre operators providing interconnection, the establishment and the maintenance of these physical cross connects is a source of revenue. One or both networks being interconnected will pay the data centre operator for this cross connection for the duration of its existence, typically on a monthly basis. Depending on the value of the cross connection to each network, one network may pay exclusively, or the cost may also be shared across both networks. The data centre operator does not care in the majority of cases which network pays for the cross connection. It is important to note that these cross connections and the interconnection services which they enable are not free; the data centre operator must operate at their expense very large facilities which are required to be fully operational constantly in order to support their customers.

Whether or not a cross connection is permitted by the data centre operator is subject to the various policies and restrictions which they impose on their interconnection customers. It is usual for a data centre operator to maintain a list of interconnection limitations, such as prohibiting customers from bypassing its own services, reselling its services within the data centre operator's facilities, and being able to enforce any network usage restrictions required to protect the network against an attack by one or more of the network operators which connect to it, which may originate from malicious end users of those networks. If a cross connection is requested by a network operator and is determined by the data centre operator to exceed one of these limitations, it will be declined. The data centre is under no obligation to provide their services to people who do not meet their network usage rules.

The model of physical cross connections works in a large data centre where personnel are on hand to perform physical cable routing and configuration as required to establish the cross connections. However, in an unmanned edge data centre facility, this is more challenging. For these facilities, the model of virtual cross connections is an alternative which also enables some other business benefits.

7.6.8   Virtual Cross Connection

Although physical cross connections are currently the main way cross connection is achieved at the data centre, they are not the only solution to the problem of achieving interconnected networks.

In the case of a data centre facility offering physical cross connections, when a customer deploys a rack of equipment, they must have the top of rack (TOR) switch in that rack connected to the network equipment which that customer can use, located in the MMR. Their network equipment can then be connected to that of other customers to achieve cross connection and interconnection. In the case of a virtual cross connection, upon deployment all of the TOR switches deployed by customers in their racks as well as any other networks entering the data centre facility will all be connected to a network fabric which is operated by the data centre operator. At that point, cross connections between networks can be achieved by configuration of that network fabric without the need to alter physical network connections unless more networks or additional ports between networks are required to be added.

The specifics of such a network fabric, along with the way in which the network equipment of each customer who is deployed in the data centre facility, depend on the scale of that data centre facility far more than any other factor. For any small size category edge data centre facility, for example, the network fabric may take the form of a single or redundant pair of Ethernet switches maintained by the data centre operator, to which all customer TOR switches are connected. In a larger facility, it is likely that more complex network fabrics will be required in order to support the facility's customers.

As an edge data centre facility is limited in terms of its smaller physical size and its innate inability to cost effectively support a constant personnel presence, this model of virtual cross connections is a key part of enabling an infrastructure edge computing network operator to offer an EX service with one or many EXPs across a given area. In an infrastructure edge computing network which may have tens of edge data centre facilities over time, each of which is geographically dispersed, the ability to configure and maintain cross connections remotely is a useful operational benefit to the operator.

This approach has a few advantages. Of these, the following three are the most apparent operationally:

1) Remote configuration of cross connects
    a) For the edge data centre facility, the more deployment and maintenance tasks that are possible without requiring personnel to visit the facility, the more operationally efficient the infrastructure edge computing network can be. By physically connecting each customer rack to the network fabric at the time of deployment and configuring each cross connection remotely by configuring the network fabric, the operator can eliminate the need to arrange a personnel visit to a site for each cross connection.
2) Greater network orchestration potential
    a) Due to the removal of a key step in the cross connection process which requires a human to physically add or remove network cabling, even in an otherwise standard and not physically automated data centre environment, the data centre operator can use the establishment or maintenance of a virtual cross connection as a step in the orchestration process of data centre and network resources to support a customer, which allows the operator to then construct more elaborate automation sequences that allow the operator as well as the customer to get more value from the network.
3) Additional opportunity for higher layer services
    a) Building on the previous two advantages, once the remote configuration of virtual cross connections is possible and is then also tied into a wider network orchestration system, the data centre operator can use those capabilities as a foundation for types of higher layer services which rely on automated network orchestration including the interconnection of networks from multiple network operators in a local EXP.

For especially fluid business relationships, the turnaround time that is required to establish or to alter a physical cross connection may be prohibitive. This is likely to be a negligible benefit though, for both the network operator and its customers, beyond the initial configuration of a virtual cross connection. It is difficult to foresee practical business relationships where the cross connection of two or more networks would need to be altered very rapidly on an ongoing basis. If this capability were needed in order to restrict the traffic flows to and from a particular network, it is preferable that this be done using network ingress and egress traffic flow controls rather than bluntly switching on and off a cross connection. The former solution is a technical solution which can be tuned in a far more nuanced fashion than a simple on and off switch. Some data centre operators may seek to be able to provide both of these options, which would provide them with some higher layer capability.

The virtual cross connection model does make point to multipoint cross connection easier between more than two networks. Although such arrangements are not impossible using the physical cross connection model, if more than two networks wish to share the same virtual cross connection, they can be added to one shared virtual local area network (VLAN) or virtual routing and forwarding (VRF) instance, for example, and could then be configured to operate as if they were connected to the same switch or router. As long as all of the networks that are to be interconnected are connected to the data centre network fabric appropriately, this can be a useful function for facilitating cross connections of this type, which are a minority of connections.

However, some of its advantages may be disadvantages to the data centre operator. Without the need for physical network cabling run between two networks within the data centre to point to, it may be challenging to justify the existing cost of cross connection services going forward. As these services represent a method of revenue generation for the data centre operator and still incur an operational cost, it is unlikely that many operators will allow an all-you-can-eat approach without subsequently altering their pricing models and interconnection services. Although over time in the telecommunications and networking industry the value of physical network connectivity alone has fallen and must be augmented with higher layer services in order to remain differentiated, the data centre operator may not be ready or able to provide such services and may be challenged to adapt.

It is important to note that at a basic level, the functionality provided by a cross connection, whether it is physical or virtual, is the same. They are both technical solutions to provide a means for two or more networks to interconnect, regardless of the steps involved in achieving this for the data centre operator. It is not useful to a data centre operator, a customer deploying equipment within a data centre, or a network operator to focus on any one specific method of achieving an interconnection beyond the real capabilities which it provides to solve the problem of interconnecting networks. A virtual cross connection model is useful for smaller unmanned data centre facilities and those which have the intent to offer greater levels of network orchestration. However, a physical model of cross connection may allow a larger data centre facility to scale further. Hybrid approaches are also likely where an existing data centre facility which is primarily using the physical model adds additional new interconnection capacity using a virtual model as they evolve their service offering over time to suit.

As a customer of a data centre facility, it is unlikely that unless the virtual cross onnection model is used by a data centre operator to provide additional flexibility, functionality, or cost advantages over the physical cross connection model, that it will be especially appealing by itself. A technical solution which solves a customer need is always valuable; a technical solution which solves an operator need is valuable to the operator but not necessarily to the customer directly unless it gives them benefits.

7.6.9   Interconnection as a Resource

The question of value when considering an EX is an important one. Consider the scenario where an infrastructure edge computing network is physically and topologically positioned between an access or last mile network and a RNDC, as we have typically shown so far in this book. Returning to our description of the serve transit fail (STF) metric in Chapter 3, we saw that the value of the edge network can be determined by how much of the traffic from the access network is served by some resource which is present on the infrastructure edge access network. A useful question to ask, then, is does network interconnection itself constitute such a resource, and how valuable is it all by itself?

Although a performance improvement in a pure peer-to-peer, device-to-device use case may be an advantage which could be enabled by an EX without any other resource being present at the edge, this is not a widespread use case today as the vast majority of application workloads require some form of server and client structure in order to function, and maintaining peer-to-peer networks that operate only between end user devices is challenging outside of short range, short term use cases such as local file sharing. However, that is not to say it is impossible, and there are unique examples of using all the interconnection capabilities of infrastructure edge computing without relying on the use of any application workload at an edge data centre facility to support a device edge use case.

One potentially useful example of this model is vehicle to vehicle (V2V) or vehicle to everything (V2X) network connectivity. Although much of this communication is envisaged to occur by having direct peer-to-peer network communication between vehicles without the use of local or regional network infrastructure acting as an intermediary, such as a Wi-Fi or cellular network access point, such schemes can be difficult to implement in practice due to the movement of vehicles and the challenges inherent in creating and maintaining an ad hoc network of such devices in a way that supports low latency communications. By using an EXP, the edge data centre can provide a means for these vehicles to exchange data at a local point without the difficulty of ad hoc network creation and operation, even when there is no application workload operating in the edge data centre facility.

Outside of this specific use case, however, it is difficult to see significant value for interconnection at the IEDC network without the support of an application workload which is operating across one or more edge data centre facilities in the network. This does not make having a robust EX constructed from several EXPs in an area any less valuable; it just means that the value of an EX should be considered in the full context of all the other capabilities of the infrastructure edge computing network and not as a means to an end by itself for the vast majority of viable use cases.

7.7 Peering

Beyond the physical interconnection of networks at an IEDC facility, the peering relationship required between networks must also be established. In this context, we are referring to Border Gateway Protocol (BGP) peering as described in Chapter 3. As each of the networks which are going to be interconnected are operated by separate network operators, it is likely that each network is using separate public IP address space and so an EGP must be used to route between them accordingly.

Depending on the scale of each of the networks being interconnected as well as on the operational and business model of those network operators and the data centre operator themselves, there are many variations to how networks may be interconnected from the context of peering. In some cases, networks can be interconnected at only layer 2 or layer 3 of the Open Systems Interconnection (OSI) model, without the need for them to establish and maintain a BGP peering between them directly as external network peers.

The type of peering required between networks is dependent on the network configuration and the business model of the data centre operator who is offering the interconnection service. For example, a data centre operator may provide each of its customers with IP address space and require that any customers with network equipment deployed within the data centre facility be represented to other external networks using this public IP address space. In this case, these customers do not need to be BGP peers with one another or with any other external network; they each utilise public IP address space provided by the data centre operator, and the operator then represents all of these networks to any external networks, to which the data centre operator maintains a BGP peering relationship.

On the other hand, a data centre operator may allow or require customers to use their own public IP address space for their equipment operating within the data centre facility. In this case, BGP peering will exist between customers, or between customers and external networks directly. Because the IP address space being used belongs to those customers and not to the data centre network operator, the operator does not need to be involved in the overall process beyond facilitating the connectivity between networks with the MMR and any higher layer interconnection capabilities which they offer.

In the majority of cases, a large customer such as a cloud provider will prefer that they are able to use their own public IP address space for equipment and services which need to be accessible from external networks. The additional control and transparency which this approach provides allows the network operations teams for organisations of this size to operate effectively. Smaller customers, on the other hand, may not rely on such processes and be amenable to utilising the public IP addresses of a data centre operator. There are numerous hybrid approaches to this problem, and this chapter covers only the two simplest cases; for the data centre operator, it can be valuable for customers to utilise the public IP address space of the operator as it allows the operator to make the deployment experience a bit easier for the customer as well as making it more difficult for them to leave later on.

7.8 Cloud On-ramps

As more key application workloads have moved from operating solely on end user devices or in on-premises data centre facilities to cloud providers whose resources are typically located in a RNDC a significant distance away from their end users, the efficiency and reliability of the network connectivity between those end users and the cloud provider's network has become a point of focus for many large customers of these cloud providers who want to ensure as much as possible that they will be able to achieve their performance and cost requirements using the cloud.

Network connectivity between an end user, such as a bank branch office, and the data centre from which network traffic is able to reach the cloud provider is one part of the equation. The customer and the network operator which they choose to utilise for that connectivity can tune and provision their network infrastructure in accordance with their performance requirements. However, what a customer and a network operator who are external to the data centre facility cannot ensure is that traffic will take an optimal path between their equipment or network and that of a cloud provider once it is inside the data centre facility. This is true whether customer equipment is located in an on-premises data centre, in a rack within the same external data centre facility, or a hybrid of both. To address this issue, a direct connection from the customer to a cloud provider is the ideal solution.

In the context of network interconnection, a cloud on-ramp is a service which provides one or more networks that are present in a data centre facility with a direct connection to the network of a cloud provider in order to provide more consistent performance than alternative solutions. These services can be considered to be very similar to all other versions of network interconnection that have been described in this chapter, although depending on the cloud provider and the data centre operator in question, there may be additional higher layer services offered on top of this interconnection which are integrated with the wider service portfolio of the cloud provider. An example of such a higher layer service is using an awareness of where the application workloads for any specific customer of the cloud provider are located across the infrastructure operated by that cloud provider to create the capability to adjust the on-ramp connectivity to most efficiently deliver network traffic to those locations if they change over time based on resource management by either the user or the cloud.

These on-ramp services are typically provided via similar means to other network interconnections, by connecting the network equipment of a customer to that of a cloud provider in the MMR of a data centre facility. The cost structure for these services, however, may be different for the customer and data centre operator compared to other network interconnections. Many cloud providers are sensitive to the impact which poorly operated cloud on-ramp services would have on their own user experience, and as such, the requirements on the data centre facility itself tend to be more stringent.

Cloud on-ramps have proven to be popular as more large customers rely on cloud providers for their most important application workloads. However, these services are not available across every data centre. To be available in a particular data centre facility, they require the cloud provider to deploy network equipment in that facility and also ideally to deploy server infrastructure in that facility as well in order to offer optimal service between a customer and some resources of the cloud provider where any key application workloads or data storage utilised by that customer could be migrated to. There are other deployment and configuration options available to create a cloud on-ramp, but this is the simplest case for the purposes of this book and does not preclude the use of any of the others.

An IEDC may offer cloud on-ramp services, either directly from one or more facilities or as extensions of cloud on-ramp services being offered from a RNDC which the infrastructure edge computing network is directly interconnected to within the same or an adjacent area. Much like a RNDC, an IEDC which hosts server resources for a particular cloud will be a more appealing location to provide on-ramp services for connectivity to that cloud than one which does not host such servers.

7.9   Beneficial Impact

In the context of infrastructure edge computing, the main point of offering network interconnection services is to be capable of offering benefits for customers in regard to latency and the cost of data transportation. There are additional benefits to the data centre operator in terms of increasing the value of their data centre and network infrastructure and in creating a network effect for customers.

7.9.1   Latency

As has been described previously in this book, where the operation of an application requires data to be exchanged between any two or more interconnected networks, there is a potential improvement in minimum latency for that application where interconnection can occur at a location closer to the end users of that application. However, what is the real benefit of this, and how can it be quantified?

To be specific, light travels at different speeds depending on the medium in which it is travelling. In fibre optical cabling, it is estimated that light travels about 30% slower than it does in free space. For free space, the speed of light is believed to be 186 000 miles per second. This means in fibre optics it will be closer to 130 200 miles per second. Yes, this is still incredibly fast, but it is not the full story.

The speed of light does not tell anywhere near the full story when it comes to network latency. This type of calculation can be easily used to misrepresent whether or not local data centre and network resources are needed in an area by simply drawing a line as the crow flies between a user and a data centre, then estimating only the speed of light in fibre optic cabling between those points on a map.

There are 1000 milliseconds in a second. Some examples of cyber-physical systems are targeting a maximum latency between a user and their application or service operating in the data centre to be 10 ms. Using our 130 200 miles per second figure, this would appear to mean that the user has to be within only 1302 miles of the data centre in order to achieve this latency. However, note that this 10 ms figure is the latency between a user and their application, not between two ends of the fibre optic cabling which forms part of the network connectivity between these two entities. Consider a few of the other important sources of latency across the whole path as described in the following list:

1) Switching and routing time of network devices between user and application
   a) There is a minimum time required by every network device in the path between a user and their application which is required in order for that device to be able to ingest network data, determine its destination, and then send the traffic onward.

2) Number of switching and routing steps between user and application

    a) The longer and more complex the path between a user and the data centre that is hosting the application they need, the larger the number of switching and routing steps there are likely to be, each of which introduces some unavoidable latency.

3) Indirect physical path of fibre optic cabling between user and application

    a) Fibre optic cabling almost never follows a straight path between the user and the data centre due to factors as diverse as physical obstacles, cable pathways, and the design of the network in terms of its hierarchical layers between those endpoints.

4) Data encapsulation and transmission protocols between user and application

    a) Every network system, especially those such as cellular networks which rely on the ability to multiplex their transmission medium such as wireless spectrum amongst multiple users incurs a minimum delay to serve data to and from a particular user due to resource allocation and to ensure the transmission medium is fully usable.

Estimating the real delay of each of these elements is possible, but for figures that would be specific enough to be useful, this estimation would need to be of a real network or network segment. For the purposes of this section, it is enough to say that even with very low latencies for each of these other sources of latency in the network, it is very probable that less than 1 ms is allotted in the overall 10 ms latency budget for the transmission of data across the fibre optic cabling throughout the network. In 1 ms, light will travel roughly 130 miles, and in 500 μs, 65.1 miles. Consider that the real fibre distance between any two points is typically double the straight line distance, and the need for shorter network paths between a user and their application becomes visible for some use cases.

Whether or not this decrease in latency is worthwhile depends on the applications and use cases in question. However, for those use cases, it can be the difference which actually enables the use case. For use cases where this latency difference is not an enabler, it may be of little to no tangible value.

This assumes that all of the resources required by the application, such as compute resources or a particular piece of stored data, are also located in the local location where interconnection can be performed, which is why EX is a key component of a real infrastructure edge network.

7.9.2 Data Transport Cost

One of the goals of a tiered interconnection architecture utilising both EXPs and IXPs across an area is to reduce the cost of data transportation. The theory is that the shorter the physical distance the network traffic has to travel between a user and their application operating in the data centre, the less network infrastructure is required and thus the lower the cost per bit of that network traffic.

The cost of data transportation is variable depending on several factors, including the physical locations of the points between which data must be transported, the speed at which it must be moved, and the level of assurance given on the quality of service (QoS) and reliability aspects of the network used. Commercial considerations are also a factor as for this tiered model to provide a lower cost of data transportation, the infrastructure edge network operator must have access to network infrastructure which provides either an equal cost in terms of bits per mile or a higher cost in bits per mile but a much shorter distance, such that its overall cost is attractive to the operator and to any end users.

In some areas the presence of an EX may have little to no impact on the cost of data transportation. Depending on the commercial factors of the infrastructure edge computing network deployment, it is also possible that the cost may even be higher in some areas to provide data transportation to an EX than for a competing network operator to provide data transportation to the nearest IX, due to the scale of other data centre facilities in the area or the cost of building network infrastructure out to multiple EXP locations in the area. The locality of the data centre to the user is a key contributing factor to the cost of data transportation but is not the sole determinant of all of the resulting costs.

For both the customer and the infrastructure edge computing network operator, it is prudent for a realistic price comparison to be performed in any area where this infrastructure is being considered for use or deployment to ensure that any possible cost advantages are understood and that nobody is surprised by the true operating cost of the system once they have committed to it for a long term.

7.9.3 Platform Benefit

As interconnection is such a key function in terms of network interoperation, a robust collection of interconnection services allows the infrastructure edge computing network operator to present a significantly more valuable infrastructure edge computing network to their customers than if only a lower capability set of services were offered. Much like in the way that adding additional edge data centre facilities and the network infrastructure to support them is one of the most straightforward ways, to the point of satisfying current and near future demand, that an operator can increase the value of the infrastructure edge computing network operator, additional interconnection services, customers, and networks are highly valuable to the operator to increase the value of their platform.

There is a network effect in play with network interconnection which tends to draw more networks and more customer server infrastructure to a data centre facility over time. At any one location, as viewed from the perspective of either an EX system in an area or specific EXPs within that system, the greater the number of potential networks (whether these are discrete customers who have their equipment deployed at a data centre facility hosting an EXP or external networks who are present in that same facility), the greater the impetus for others to join them and interconnect there locally.

7.10 Alternatives to Interconnection

One of the important considerations with any technology is whether there are any alternatives and, if so, what the capabilities of these technologies are to determine whether or not they are useful as a means to solve the same problem when taking into account cost, performance, and functionality.

The primary alternative to interconnection, specifically to the direct network interconnection which has been discussed in this chapter, is public internet connectivity. To be clear, in this case, a series of networks which allow network traffic to get from the customer to their intended destination such as a cloud provider still exist, and each of those networks are using network interconnection to achieve this goal. However, direct interconnection does not occur between the customer's network and the cloud provider. The customer sends traffic on to one network such as their internet service provider (ISP) who then forwards that traffic on to the next best network in the path to reach its destination and so on, using standard hop-by-hop routing and traversing multiple networks until it arrives at the end.

Although basic connectivity between networks is possible in this way, due to the uncertainties that exist when network traffic is transiting multiple disparate networks, each of which has no guarantee of QoS to one another for that traffic, it is challenging to provide the same level of performance as is possible using a direct interconnection between networks. Minimum latency is often not the issue, even though this will not be as low as a direct interconnection; but the average and maximum delays experienced using public internet connectivity can be highly variable, which precludes its use for any latency sensitive application. Differences in latency between average and maximum on the scale of an order of magnitude are not uncommon. Additionally, the cost of data transportation is harder to quantify as many more networks are involved. This type of network connectivity can be provided by a data centre operator hosting an IXP where a direct interconnection has not or cannot be arranged.

This is another example of an area where there are numerous hybrid approaches which cannot all be covered in this chapter. However, this section serves to show that even in a case where some direct interconnection between networks does not exist, they are likely still able to communicate by using the network of networks which is the public internet. However, the connectivity between them will be prone to the vagaries of relying on multiple intermediate networks, which greatly reduce the total consistency of the system and make lowering latency and any data transport costs very challenging.

Not all networks must be directly interconnected in order to function; it is a matter of the use cases they are intending to support and the performance and cost parameters they must achieve in order to do so. Because the applications which infrastructure edge computing is uniquely able to enable are those with stringent performance and data transport cost requirements, we have focused on a direct interconnection model for the exchange of network data between two networks in this book.

7.11   Business Arrangements

As mentioned previously, the business arrangements behind any network interconnection can vary greatly, which then affects the way that the interconnection is paid for, established, and justified on an ongoing basis between those network operators. These factors also influence whether any two networks choose to directly interconnect at all, which is a key consideration for an infrastructure edge computing network operator and their customers who rely on this occurring within an EXP.

   Network interconnection may occur between equal or unequal pairs of networks. There are a few key considerations when determining whether a pair of networks is equal or unequal, which then helps the network operators to establish a real business relationship around the interconnection:

1) Network size and user base
   a) The simplest example of network interconnection is when two networks of roughly equal size, as determined by a combination of geographical reach, user count, and regular traffic volume, are interconnecting together. In these cases, it is often true that there is equal value to each network in the interconnection and so both of the network operators agree to interconnect. This may not always be the case, and if a relationship is particularly uneven, one operator may have to pay the other directly.
2) Type of network and use case
   a) Not every network which may interconnect at an IXP or at an EXP has the same goal. Consider the differences in this regard between an access or last mile network and a backhaul network. If one network is that of a streaming video service or of another content provider, it makes sense that access or last mile networks which provide a direct access for that content to large numbers of consumer end users would be a valuable partner to interconnect with. On the other hand, it may be far less useful for the same content network to connect to a scientific research sharing network.
3) Value of network resources
   a) As well as the size and type of network, the value of each specific network has to be considered as well. Consider the difference in value to a cellular network operator of having a direct interconnection with a popular streaming video service compared to another interconnection with a tiny, niche video service with a very small user base.

The business arrangements in regard to network interconnection have evolved over the past decade primarily as a result of the widespread usage of cloud services and streaming video services. In the case of many network interconnections, it was expected that each network would send and receive roughly equal amounts of traffic to and from the networks that it interconnected with. Consider the example of two networks of equal size and comparable types of end users; a service which users of one network wish to use may be present on one network, and vice versa, creating a reciprocal and roughly even relationship between those networks. Streaming video services in particular, however, change this balance because they are highly desired by users of almost any end user facing network and they are oriented to send traffic almost entirely, rather than to receive it from other networks.

In many cases, smaller network operators will pay the cross connection fees that are required on an initial and ongoing basis to establish and maintain an interconnection to a larger network. These fees may be split when both network operators are of an equal size or see the relationship as more of a partnership where both networks have valuable resources available to offer the other. Ultimately it is up to the network operators in question to determine the nature of their relationship, as well as whether or not any interconnection will actually occur. Data centre operators will not usually insert themselves in the middle of these discussions except in the form of facilitating any interconnection when it has been paid for and agreed to by all the required network operators, recorded in writing.

7.12 Summary

Infrastructure edge computing relies on three main components: edge data centre facilities, their supporting network infrastructure, and interconnection functionality within each of these facilities. Without all three of these capabilities, it is not possible to support the type of low latency workloads for which infrastructure edge computing is ideally suited. The ability to offer EX services from one or more EXPs across the infrastructure edge computing network is key to enabling this and allows the infrastructure edge computing network operator to form a beneficial relationship with a nearby IXP where traffic that can be exchanged at an EXP is, and other traffic is exchanged at an IXP.

In the next chapter, we will explore the key factors related to the deployment of infrastructure edge computing in the physical sense, which will determine where real EXPs may be physically located.

8

Infrastructure Edge Computing Deployment

8.1 Overview

As we have an understanding of the key factors around the design and operation of infrastructure edge computing and the infrastructure edge data centres (IEDCs) within them, we can now explore many of the considerations and challenges inherent in deploying these pieces of infrastructure. This is a topic with many different facets including technical, business, and operational challenges that must be met in order to maximise the value of the resulting infrastructure edge computing network. Considering the implications of deployment and planning accordingly flows directly into the value of the solution.

Additionally, during this chapter we will explore key metrics which allow multiple deployment sites for IEDC facilities to be compared so that data centre facility locations can be determined based on information beyond the availability of the basic underlying physical assets.

8.2 Physical Facilities

The size category of the IEDC facility in question has a significant effect on the deployment considerations for that facility. Where a smaller size category facility may require a 10-ft × 10-ft concrete slab foundation and small scale electrical power and fibre network connectivity, an edge data centre from the largest size categories will require a significantly larger foundation, wider clearance all around the facility, and larger electrical power and fibre network feeds and equipment.

Understanding Infrastructure Edge Computing: Concepts, Technologies and Considerations,
First Edition. Alex Marcham.
© 2021 John Wiley & Sons Ltd. Published 2021 by John Wiley & Sons Ltd.

A site which is ideal for one size category facility may be completely unsuitable for another if it does not support the size of the facility, or it may be overkill and incur unnecessary expenses if the data centre is far smaller than the site itself. Where an available site is not an exact fit for one category of IEDC or where multiple data centre facilities are required, a site may need, where possible, to be expanded or the data centre capacity which was planned for it may need to be split between two or more sites in the area with the resulting facilities then connected to one other.

Size category 1 has its own unique set of deployment considerations which depend on the specific form factor of the IEDC facility. These facilities will be deployed in the most unorthodox locations of all IEDCs, and so it is difficult to provide a comprehensive set of considerations for their deployment. However, due to their specialised use cases, they are also the most likely to be designed and utilised according to a specific deployment where the requirements for that deployment can be understood and designed around beforehand.

Beyond the size of the data centre facility itself, the requirements for any supporting infrastructure must also be considered such as the need for external onsite power generators. Depending on the level of physical redundancy required, the following equipment may take up additional site space:

1) External power equipment
   a) Both electrical power generators and battery backup systems may be located on the outside of the data centre facility in order to maximise internal space and improve the serviceability of the power equipment. Of these, electrical power generators are more likely to be outside than battery backup systems as the latter tend to be more sensitive to environmental variations than any standard diesel-powered generator.
2) External cooling equipment
   a) In many cases, positioning the data centre facility cooling equipment outside of the facility can reduce the size of the facility building, maximise the available space that is available inside the building, and provide maintenance access to the cooling plant, which allows key issues to be repaired without requiring access inside the building.
3) Network termination or equipment points
   a) An infrastructure edge computing site which functions as a connectivity hub for local network infrastructure such as nearby cellular network towers may host an external network connectivity cabinet outside of the edge data centre facility itself. This may be done to provide access to the network infrastructure interconnecting at the site without needing to provide access to the data centre facility or to save space inside.

The physical space required outside of the data centre facility itself, yet still on the site, for these and any other external components is largely determined by the size of that edge data centre facility. For example, consider that the size of a generator is determined in large part by its capacity, and a larger edge data centre facility will require a larger capacity generator; the same principle can be applied to cooling and network equipment which must be deployed at the site. Although the exact dimensions required will vary depending on the equipment needed and any local regulations for clearance space, a rule of thumb of 5 ft of clearance space around facilities or equipment at a site for access and safety should be used and any external equipment should be separated by a few feet for fire safety.

Table 6.1 provides an estimate of the physical size required for each size category of IEDC facility. Ultimately the design and feasibility of a particular site for hosting an edge data centre facility will have to be determined through an analysis of the site and the requirements for the edge data centre facility before any solid determination can be made. Individual equipment choices will also impact the space tolerances of the site due to how they route cables, exhaust heat, or intake air. Although this chapter and others in this book aim to provide an understanding of the key factors affecting an IEDC facility site design, it is an involved process.

8.3 Site Locations

For the infrastructure edge network operator, the choice of where to physically position each of their edge data centres is critical. This sequence of decisions will drive much of the real value of the resulting infrastructure edge computing network and its suitability for key use cases and serve as a set of deployment locations for equipment from customers who want to support those use cases.

Amongst the many factors that go into determining where specific IEDCs should be positioned across the map of a specific area, the infrastructure edge computing network operator must also determine the number of facilities that are required both initially and over time.

Although it may seem preferable to build out a considerable infrastructure edge computing footprint up front in order to showcase the capabilities of the system, this approach runs the risk of having an overbuilt set of infrastructures which must be deployed and maintained for a considerable period of time before there is sufficient customer interest in the area to make full use of them. The expense of doing so makes this approach difficult to justify versus an approach where infrastructure is instead spread across multiple locations to increase the maximum addressable market for the solution, with the ability to support an initial level of customer interest in each location, for example multiple cities, without financial overcommitment.

This scale out rather than scale up approach is also preferable as it indicates to potential customers that they will be able to deploy their equipment, applications and services to more potential users rather than being limited to a deep deployment in a single location.

The locations of other data centre and network infrastructure should also be considered. This is a complex process which by definition varies between each deployment area, but the infrastructure edge computing network operator would be well served to understand that the value of any edge data centre facility if it were to be deployed next door to an existing regional or national data centre (RNDC) would be minimal at best due to the economies of scale advantages achievable at that larger facility.

8.3.1   kW per kM^2

One metric which can be used in the decision of edge data centre facility placement is the minimum kW per kM^2 that is required across the given area to support the types of services and the number of users which are required and expected. This metric seeks to identify the data centre compute power that is required in order to support the needs of each user in the coverage area, and then to multiply that by the number of expected users. This resulting figure provides an indication of the data centre density required to support that population of users within an area such as a city or a nearby suburb.

The kW per kM^2 required for a given area can be estimated through the following sequence of steps:

1) Defining the services the user population is most likely to utilise
   a) The services in this category are those which have a component that is hosted in a data centre. Applications which run entirely locally are not relevant to the resulting figure which will be estimated for this process, so they shouldn't be included here.
2) Identifying the components of those services operating at the data centre
   a) Once a set of services are identified, they can be analysed to determine which parts of their operation require some resource which is located in the data centre. This is a key step as it determines the real requirements on the data centre for these users.
3) Estimating the compute requirements for those service components
   a) Having identified a set of service or application components operating in the data centre, a rough figure of the compute power required to support every 1000 users can be estimated by noting assumptions made in hardware and software designs.
4) Determining the number of likely concurrent users for those services
   a) In the service area, estimate the number of concurrent users on an average and an expected maximum basis for the identified services. Then, multiply

the estimated compute requirement in kilowatts from the previous step to match this number of users.

5) Understanding any unique performance requirements which require locality
    a) Some use cases and applications have specific performance requirements such as a need for low latency which can be satisfied only by certain physical locations. This is vital for understanding the unique value which infrastructure edge computing can provide. If, for example, an application requires a user to application latency of 10 ms, this requirement can be used to create a representation of the physical places which could support such a use case from each proposed edge data centre facility location.

Note that like any estimate of this type, the resulting figure can never be completely accurate as it is subject to constantly changing variations in usage and population. However, comparing the kW per kM^2 estimated for two different areas does provide a useful reference point for the level of density that is required from the data centre infrastructure that is capable of serving that area adequately.

To provide an accurate result, the existing data centre infrastructure in an area must be taken into account when estimating this metric. Consider the example of an area such as a major city which is already home to many large regional or national scale data centres, such as New York City. In this example, step five of the process becomes vital; if the applications to be used by the user population do not require additional data centre locality, any IEDCs deployed in that area will not push the kW per kM^2 metric from unusable to usable, making them less valuable than if they were deployed in any locations where this metric change was achieved. The infrastructure edge computing network operator can use this metric to understand where they can add unique value.

Although helpful in determining the priority of one location over another for the deployment of any IEDC facilities, the kW per kM^2 metric cannot override every reason to or not to deploy edge data centre facilities in a particular area. For example, although it may not be a valuable location technologically due to its proximity to existing regional or national scale facilities, an infrastructure edge computing network operator may seek to deploy an edge data centre in an area with an already saturated kW per kM^2 metric. This location may be chosen as a strategic move in order to establish a physical presence in an area of high visibility or be seen next to competitors.

8.3.2 Customer Facility Selection

As a customer seeking to deploy equipment within an IEDC, an important consideration is which IEDC to deploy it in. Across the infrastructure edge computing network, each edge data centre facility may have different networks present and varied customer equipment. Both of these factors are key in order to determine which data centre facility is the ideal location to deploy equipment, as are factors such as site redundancy and available space.

Customers have two options when selecting a specific IEDC facility which they will deploy their equipment in. Either a customer could attempt to gather all of the information for each edge data centre facility in the area and make an informed decision based on the available data, or they could use the infrastructure edge computing network operator to select a site for them based on a site of criteria they have generated from the requirements of the use cases and services they intend to offer. For many customers, the latter is preferable as it allows the infrastructure edge computing network operator to smooth out the deployment process somewhat for the customer.

8.3.3 Site Characteristics

Once it is determined that IEDC facilities will be deployed in a particular area, the question now becomes which specific locations within that area to deploy them at. While evaluating each area, the infrastructure edge computing network operator will define a polygon, a shape drawn on a map which defines the bounds of the area in question. In the case of a city, this polygon may cover only the city limits or may extend out to cover populous suburbs or transit links in and out of the city. Key transit corridors and infrastructure such as airports should be considered.

Once the polygon is defined, the locations of specific IEDC facilities can be identified. The suitable locations for IEDCs within the polygon depend on several key factors. Although not at all an exhaustive list, amongst these factors are the following:

1) Power availability
   a) The type and quantity of electrical power which is available at a site is a significant contributor to its suitability for the deployment of any size of IEDC facility. Larger size category edge data centre facilities are very likely to require three phase power, and a site which already has access to this type of power and is in a location where the supply of that power is capable of supporting the load will be preferable compared to one where more expense will be required to do so.
2) Network connectivity
   a) In a similar fashion to power availability, sites which have existing access to network connectivity of the quantity and quality required to support the IEDC facility are appealing. Factors to consider include whether there is any fibre conduit passing through or close to the site which is connected to networks in the area, the number of fibre entry points to the site, and any existing cable paths.

3) Location risk profile
   a) A specific location may be prone to events which are likely to impact the operation of an IEDC facility on a regular or irregular but predictable basis. Examples of these events include natural disasters such as hurricanes and earthquakes, extreme weather events such as flooding, and human factors such as dangerous driving hotspots or places where chemicals or explosives may be stored.
4) Land availability
   a) At worst, an otherwise preferable piece of land may not be available at all for the deployment of an IEDC due to size restrictions, local ordinances, or other factors; at best, the land may not be available within a time frame which meets the requirements of the infrastructure edge network operator.
5) Cost of land lease
   a) The cost of land is a significant component of the overall expense required in order to deploy an infrastructure edge computing network. Especially in optimal locations, land with the required combination of assets is often scarce and will become more so as the pace of infrastructure edge deployment accelerates over time. Consider also that the initial cost of land is not the full story. Depending on the length of the lease, price escalators and other measures will come into effect over time which increase the price of the land lease so that the owner can stay ahead of inflation.

To determine which set of physical locations across a given area would be preferable for deployment of a given number of IEDCs, we can also apply the serve transit fail (STF) metric by using a set of key assumptions. These assumptions are the type of use cases to be offered from the facility, the number of users for those services, and the likelihood of achieving interconnection with access networks which these users will use at the edge data centre facility. If a particular use case is of key interest to the customer base of the infrastructure edge computing network operator and it can be shown that one site would provide a better STF metric for that application, that site is preferable.

8.4 Coverage Areas

Although related to the physical locations of each IEDC, the coverage area of each of these facilities is a separate and key consideration. Depending on the design of networks in the area, the coverage area of an edge data centre facility may not even include the specific area in which the edge data centre facility itself is located. This may occur, for example, if the access or last mile cellular networks interconnected at the IEDC facility do not cover the area around the edge data centre facility itself due to terrain or user density issues, which can occur.

The coverage area of a particular IEDC facility varies according to a variety of factors such as the equipment capacity of the site as measured in kilowatts, the key access or last mile networks that are present in that facility, and the type of applications which the facility is intended to serve. Those networks and applications determine the shape of the coverage area; the capacity and network performance, primarily in terms of latency, determine the size of that coverage area. Assuming that all the required access networks are interconnected at the IEDC, we can estimate the coverage area that can be provided by that facility on a use case basis.

There are three primary methods by which the coverage area of an IEDC can be determined. The priority of which method to use depends on a variety of factors including the customer mix. It will also change over the lifetime of the infrastructure edge computing network.

1) Network coverage
   a) As described in the previous chapter, an infrastructure edge computing network must interconnect with access networks in order to provide significant value in the form of performance and cost savings for its customers. In this context, network coverage refers to the ability of the infrastructure edge computing network to be able to interconnect with these access networks in an effective manner by being physically positioned close enough to key network elements in all of those access networks to make such an interconnection efficient and as performant as possible.
2) Population coverage
   a) When combined with access network interconnection, the larger the population that is within a coverage area, the larger the potential user base for services which are operating from the IEDC. However, even if an access or last mile network covers a large number of users, the edge data centre facility must be capable of supporting the compute requirements for the whole population area. If it cannot, the area should be subdivided or otherwise limited to be truly realistic.
3) Points of interest coverage
   a) With all other factors being equal, a coverage area which includes points of interest which function as concentrators of the population for specific use cases, such as a stadium which is providing an interactive experience to visitors using their mobile devices, is preferable to a coverage area which does not. Such locations are likely to introduce bursty usage patterns which may make capacity planning more difficult but which represent significant user populations for a range of specific use cases.

Consider the example of an infrastructure edge computing network which has established decent coverage in its area of operation in regard to network coverage and population coverage. Due to the existing mapping between the network coverage provided by access networks and the areas of high population in an area such as a city, as these networks are deployed in ways to target the greatest number of users, these two coverage criteria are often satisfied in parallel. It may then be useful for the infrastructure edge computing network operator to extend that coverage to a point of interest.

8.5 Points of Interest

The definition of a point of interest is dependent on the specific area in question, but generally it is a location or piece of infrastructure which has significant value in being covered by or attached to the infrastructure edge computing network and which may not be already included in existing coverage.

Depending on the value of a specific point of interest, it may be worth deploying an edge data centre facility which has small population coverage in comparison to another location. Customers may be willing to deploy equipment in such a facility to provide high value services to the user base for that point of interest even if it is active only at certain times of the day or year if the value is significant.

An example of a point of interest for an IEDC is stadium. Although it may not be a population centre for residential purposes, a large stadium can often attract several tens of thousands of people on a regular basis who will benefit from, and may be charged for, use cases that are provided from an infrastructure edge computing network. The stadium operator may provide an interactive application which uses real-time data from the stadium event to augment the experience for the crowd, which requires the use of resources deployed within a nearby edge data centre. In a scenario like this, the choice of use case is paramount as is whether or not any existing RNDC, or some on-premises equipment, can support that same set of needs already.

For smaller size categories of IEDCs, it is likely that they will be deployed close to areas of interest which are the locations of key network infrastructure for networks that are to be interconnected with the infrastructure edge computing network. In some cases, infrastructure of this type may be inside a point of interest such as the video production equipment in a stadium.

Size category 1 is highly unique in that its size allows for IEDCs to be used in mobile deployments. These edge data centre facilities may be deployed in multiple locations at a point of interest such as to support mobile communications stations inside a stadium or a large park.

Typically, outside of the smallest size categories, IEDC facilities will not be deployed inside or at a point of interest. However, if this need arises, many such locations may be capable of supporting a smaller facility in an area such as a big car park to provide local capabilities. The infrastructure edge computing network operator then has a choice in regard to how valuable a particular point of interest is to the operator and to their customers in order to justify all of its costs.

8.6 Codes and Regulations

As they are typically construction projects, the deployment of an IEDC facility requires the infrastructure edge computing network operator, assuming in this case that they are also the entity responsible for the deployment of the required data centre facilities and network infrastructure, must ensure that they are in compliance with all codes and regulations in the area.

Due to the specificity and variation in codes and regulations, this book will not attempt to provide guidance on specific issues related to this topic and instead will focus on the general themes to be aware of when considering this type of distributed infrastructure deployment. When considering an IEDC deployment in an area, always consult local codes and regulations with the services of someone who is familiar with how they operate to avoid any unnecessary issues.

Even infrastructure edge computing deployments which do not require the laying of foundations or for facilities to be craned into position must abide by the appropriate regulations. For example, the smallest size category of IEDCs lends itself well to a variety of deployment scenarios where there is no need for the level of construction required for larger facilities. Even so, consider the local codes and regulations which may apply to an IEDC that is deployed on a lamp post or light pole; individual cities and municipalities maintain regulations that determine who, why, and how such infrastructure may be mounted to and use power delivered from this street furniture. Some of these codes concern power draw and electrical safety while others are focused on the aesthetics of a deployment, sound output, or other factors discussed in this chapter.

The process of establishing compliance with all the required codes and regulations to deploy an infrastructure edge data centre varies heavily on a regional basis, even between cities within the same state in the United States. This introduces complexities into the deployment process for infrastructure edge computing that have to be addressed by specialists who are familiar with each local area which is targeted for an infrastructure edge computing deployment to ensure no unnecessary difficulties.

Some of the key considerations in terms of codes and regulations worldwide, however, include:

1) Noise requirements, especially in residential or residential-adjacent areas
   a) Many areas will limit the frequency and volume of audible noise that is allowed to be generated by infrastructure deployed in those locations. This can be difficult for data centre facilities which are required to remove large amounts of heat from a small space, but measures can be taken such as expelling air upwards or using an enclosing baffle system in order to reduce any noise to an acceptable level outside.
2) Visual obtrusiveness requirements, especially in any non-industrial areas
   a) Townships and municipalities are often keen to maintain the appearance of the areas which they are responsible for. This is understandable; even as the use of modern communications technology has increased, many local opposition groups have been established which protect, for example, historical districts from being visually altered beyond a list of established parameters. Cellular networks have often run afoul of these groups and take extensive measures to get agreements.
3) Localised electrical power and water usage limitations
   a) The utility infrastructure, primarily concerning the electrical grid and the water supply in an area, may have usage limitations in order to preserve the resources provided by these systems to other users within the area. An example is an area with a local power substation which is capacity limited, requiring the data centre facility to draw up to only a specified amount of power to sustain other users.

Although they are not codes or regulations, it is worth understanding the sensitivities around the deployment of distributed technical infrastructure that infrastructure edge network operators are likely to encounter, just as has been the case for cellular network operators and others who must constantly deploy equipment near to people in public and private areas. These key issues include:

1) Health concerns
   a) Concerns over the impact on the human body of new infrastructure are not in any way a recent development. Electrical pylons and cellular network towers have both been subject to many studies and unverified claims of their health impact over the previous decades. As they are typically less visible than either of these entities due to their ability to be deployed at ground height and without the need to maintain a radio signal path to mobile devices, IEDC facilities are at lower risk of being identified as a source of any health concerns, but are not exempt.

2) Intent of infrastructure
   a) Local residents of an area may be concerned that the infrastructure which is being deployed is intended to be used to spy on or otherwise interfere with their lives. In some cases, people can be convinced that the technology is to be used for the aid of law enforcement or government agencies for this purpose. These perceptions can often be handled by communicating the use cases for the infrastructure in a public forum, but in many cases, any intention theories are difficult to completely dissuade.
3) Resistance to technology
   a) In some cases, some residents of an area simply will not want additional technology infrastructure to be deployed. Often this concern is the result of feeling that their way of life will be somehow threatened or changed by this advancement, which may manifest itself as a fear of losing jobs in the area or of the area changing so radically over time that it becomes unrecognisable. These concerns may also manifest using the previous two categories as well, but they typically have a different root cause.

When viewing these concerns from a purely technical standpoint, it may seem easy to ignore them. While there have been no conclusive studies to prove that any danger to the health of humans or other life exists due to the deployment or operation of this type of infrastructure, as people and organisations who are capable of creating and using technology that can make a profound impact on people's lives, we must remember that technology exists to serve the needs of people. Where there is unease around its usage, we should make reasonable efforts to correct the assumptions which are being used and be able to clearly communicate the benefits of the work we are doing to the public.

8.7 Summary

There are many key factors which must be considered to ensure a successful infrastructure edge computing deployment. These range from scoping and locating the initial deployment such that it remains in line with the business model of the infrastructure edge computing network operator to maintaining compliance with local codes and regulations that govern various aspects of deployment and operation for the resulting infrastructure. The goal of this activity is not just to identify the ideal locations for IEDC facilities and their supporting network infrastructure but also to ensure that their deployment can be completed on the required timescale and level of cost.

Key metrics can be used to inform the infrastructure edge network operator on the value of specific locations for data centre facility deployment and should be used in addition to more concrete and physical factors such as network availability and land cost to arrive at a holistic view of the value of each potential IEDC location. This will allow any IEDCs deployed in an area to provide the most unique value to the operator and to its customers.

In the next chapter, we will explore the key factors related to the customer equipment which can be deployed in the IEDC, including what makes a fitting deployment and why.

9

Computing Systems at the Infrastructure Edge

9.1 Overview

Although an ideal infrastructure edge data centre (IEDC) will be capable of supporting any equipment that fits within its internal rack structure, this does not mean that every rack of equipment is an equally good fit for deployment at the infrastructure edge. Some types of equipment make poor uses of the unique considerations of IEDC facilities while others are ideally suited to them, which directly influences the overall success of an infrastructure edge project by a customer.

In this chapter, we will explore the characteristics that make a computing system suitable or not for deployment in an IEDC and describe ways to adapt legacy infrastructure.

9.2 What Is Suitable?

The ideal equipment to be deployed in an IEDC has these characteristics:

1) Physically densified
   a) As the physical size of each IEDC is limited in comparison to a regional or national data centre (RNDC) facility, especially in the case of the smaller size categories of IEDC facilities, equipment that is deployed in these locations should be optimised to fit the most capability into the least amount of physical space. This is to the benefit of both the customer as they can reduce the cost paid for their colocation services in these facilities and to

Understanding Infrastructure Edge Computing: Concepts, Technologies and Considerations,
First Edition. Alex Marcham.
© 2021 John Wiley & Sons Ltd. Published 2021 by John Wiley & Sons Ltd.

the operator as they can enhance the value of all their data centre facilities with more unique customers.

2) Useful for low latency use cases
    a) Many of the primary use cases for infrastructure edge computing are reliant on low latency between a user and the application instance that is operating in the edge data centre facility which is serving them. This means that to the extent possible, equipment deployed in an IEDC should be suited to the operation of these use cases. For example, cold data storage equipment such as a tape drive array is not suited to supporting low latency use cases and should not be deployed at an IEDC, unlike a working set memory array.

3) Minimum manual care and feeding
    a) Although equipment which is not prone to failure and which does not require any physical maintenance beyond that which is normally expected over time is desired when considering deployment in any data centre facility, this is especially true in the context of infrastructure edge computing as edge data centre facilities are designed to operate unmanned, and so any issues may take longer to resolve than if a standby unit of equipment were available and could be immediately deployed by onsite staff.

Equipment which has these characteristics is likely to be suitable for deployment in an IEDC facility, as long as it is also in support of a fitting use case which can make effective use of the capabilities of infrastructure edge computing. Compute hardware is useful only when it is deployed in order to enable a useful application or use case; hardware deployment is not a use case.

9.3 Equipment Hardening

The ideal IEDC will not require any customer equipment operating within it to support any equipment hardening measures beyond those expected of typical equipment which would be deployed at a traditional data centre. This means that environmentally hardened devices which are designed to withstand exceptional physical shock, power spikes, or radiation should not be needed in order to operate effectively in the controlled environment of an edge data centre facility.

However, where an IEDC must be deployed at a particularly small scale or in an especially hostile environment, some hardening of the customer equipment deployed at that IEDC may be required to ensure proper operation. An example of this is a size category 1 facility which cannot supply adequate cooling to maintain operating temperatures within its deployment environment at all times depending on its external power supply or location of use. In this case, additional cooling capability may need to be provided by the deployed equipment.

These scenarios are rare when compared to the bulk of equipment deployments which are expected to occur at IEDC facilities across all size categories. For the majority of the equipment deployments which will occur in these facilities, environmental control by the facility can be assumed, and so additional equipment hardening measures add unnecessary expense. Customers who are concerned about the resiliency of their systems in an infrastructure edge computing context should instead concentrate on designing their deployment and orchestration systems for a software resiliency model, as described in several other chapters throughout this book, to maintain resiliency.

If physically hardened equipment is required, an infrastructure edge computing network operator is responsible for communicating this need to the customer as it is otherwise reasonable to assume a data centre facility regardless of its scale will be capable of providing a controlled environment in as much as the power delivery, temperature, humidity, and other factors will be maintained as needed.

9.4 Rack Densification

To make the optimal use of the limited physical space within an IEDC, the customer equipment deployed in these facilities should be as densified as possible. That is to say in terms of the customer equipment per rack unit (RU), most equipment should be capable of operating in the smallest physical space, as typically measured in kilowatts. This implies that the data centre facility is able to remove the large amount of heat generated from this comparatively small space efficiently under normal operating conditions, but we will assume that this is the case for this section as it is a factor which makes the small size of an IEDC appealing for most of its use cases.

Additionally, over time, the processing capabilities of the device edge will increase due to Moore's Law. If the processing resources available at the infrastructure edge are capable of supporting only similar performance per user when considered across the coverage area of that facility as the device edge, it is much more challenging to justify the value of the infrastructure edge computing network when comparing it to a solution which performs real-time processing at the device edge and other tasks in a regional or national scale data centre facility. If the complexity and processing needs of a function will increase over time to exceed the capabilities of the device edge, then the infrastructure edge computing network must be capable of supporting these processing resources, and the ability to utilise highly densified racks across the infrastructure edge facilities is a key component of this.

As previously described in Chapter 4, according to the 2020 AFCOM State of the Data Centre Report, the average rack density within the data centre increased from 7.2 kW in 2019 to 8.2 kW. This is for a full size, 42 RU 19-in. rack. In comparison, a fully densified rack in that same physical form factor can utilise between 25 and 45 kW with a matching increase in computational power, which allows space to be utilised far more effectively for the operation of application workloads. This is especially key at the IEDC facility, which is necessarily limited in terms of its physical space.

The diagram in Figure 9.1 compares a densified and non-densified rack. Note that in this example the same physical rack space is used, but the achieved density varies considerably. Although the extent of the densification gains which can be achieved and which make sense to achieve depend on the type of application workload which the equipment within the rack will support, in many cases, where the use of specialised accelerators can be employed, this type of rack densification is achievable and useful.

The density of a rack can be measured in many different ways, from the number of application or use case instances which can be concurrently supported to the maximum number of supported users, or many other units of measurement. Although it is possible to calculate each of these and determine the value of densification on a granular basis, an easier measurement is to use kilowatts. This eliminates the need for a deep understanding of a particular application workload and instead will allow a simple comparison between two racks of the same size but of differing equipment densities. It is reasonable to assume a greater kilowatt figure will proportionately benefit all of those other metrics which are limited by compute power.

Although the average rack density is increasing over time and some specialised applications already utilise densified clusters of specialised processors, the typical rack designed for deployment within a traditional large data centre is not designed with significant densification in mind. Historically this has been due to a trade-off between

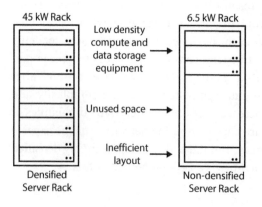

Figure 9.1 Densified and non-densified rack comparison example.

the cost of space within a RNDC and the cost of compute equipment which can be effectively densified to an extent which really matters.

This is an issue for the customer who is deploying their equipment in the IEDC to ensure that they are making the most of what may be more expensive colocation space compared to a traditional data centre facility. However, it is also an issue for the infrastructure edge computing network operator as a whole. The revenue generated from a specific customer and the equipment they choose to deploy in an IEDC is one component of their value to the operator; another is the number and mix of customers present at the IEDC who are capable of interconnecting with one another. The more unique valuable entities that are present and interconnecting in these edge exchange point (EXP) locations, the higher the overall value of the infrastructure edge computing network. This is a classic example of the network effect, where the value of a network itself increases as the number of users of the same system grows over time.

9.4.1 Heterogenous Servers

Within a single server, there are today often a mix of general purpose and specialised compute devices which are used together to process various types of application workloads. This type of server has been considerable deployment in the data centre over the past decade as the types of application workloads being processed within these facilities has diversified to include graphics or parallel computation intensive tasks. Concurrently, the development of these specialised devices which can accelerate particular workloads has continued to accelerate over this period, providing customers with devices that have exceeded the processing power growth curve of general purpose systems over the same period of time and which also appear to be able to do so well into the future.

Alternatively some servers are becoming increasingly specialised towards a particular workload. These servers are often more cost effective for the performance of specific applications at large scale, such as a cloud provider who is offering machine learning (ML) inferencing as a service, but are not as effective when handling a wider range of computational tasks compared to a more general purpose design.

For example, consider the two following example servers. The first is primarily dedicated to the usage of general purpose central processing units (CPUs) for a range of processing tasks and has been augmented by the addition of a graphics processing unit (GPU) accelerator card to aid in tasks which require that form of processing. Servers of this type represent the majority of servers which are deployed today; even in cases where a GPU or other accelerator has not been added, many servers are capable of supporting this expansion by the use of Peripheral Component Interconnect Express (PCIe) slots mounted on the server motherboard.

The second server is designed for a different type of application workload. In this server, the priority of the computational tasks the server has been designed for is the opposite of the first example; the onboard CPUs represent a minority of the capabilities of the server as measured in cost, the space that they require, or their processing power. Instead, the server has been designed GPU first. This means that the vast majority of the server is dedicated to the operation of a dense cluster of GPUs which are interconnected together through the server motherboard. Whereas before the GPU was considered the supplementary component to the CPU, in this case, those roles are reversed, and the CPU is primarily responsible for the operating system and the coordination and execution of tasks which are not suitable for parallelisation. These tasks would ideally not be directed to this server in large volumes just as heavy parallel workloads would see reduced performance on the first server.

This example shows that heterogeneity exists not only within each individual server but also between servers which are designed for different purposes. At a certain level of abstraction, it can be easy to think that one server is equal to another, but as the type of workloads operated from the data centre continue to diversify and specialise, this assumption can lead to a non-optimal use of resources which, if occurring at large scale, can have negative consequences for cost and speed.

This divergence between the two classes of servers can also be seen somewhat in the differences between the RNDC and the IEDC. One is a facility which, due to its scale, is better suited for a wide range of tasks, and the other, due to its physical location, is better suited to a more tightly defined set of use cases. This is not to say that only a data centre facility of a specific size can support either of these types of servers, but in many use cases which fit the infrastructure edge model well, the second class of accelerator-based servers is often preferable as it can be more effectively densified and its resources serve key edge use cases.

9.4.2 Processor Densification

Regardless of which category a particular server belongs to, it will incorporate a significant amount of general purpose CPU resources. Even in the case of a server which is designed primarily to house specialised accelerators, CPUs fulfil a vital role in picking up tasks for which those accelerators were not designed. To that end, as the size of an accelerator-based server increases, so typically does that of its CPUs. This makes processor densification a key consideration for almost every scale of server.

Amongst server grade CPUs, there are a range of options with which densification can be achieved. Where two 1 RU servers currently exist today, it may be possible to replace them and even to greatly improve their processing capabilities by replacing both servers with a single 1 U server that has two or more CPU sockets, supports a greater single CPU core count per socket, or both. As the products available to achieve densification are constantly evolving, this chapter will focus on the concepts a customer can use to achieve rack densification instead of any one specific product or technology.

Modern application workloads are designed to utilise multiple execution threads to make use of a range of multi core and multi CPU architectures. Prior to 2005, multi-threaded applications were a rarity due to the predominance of single core CPUs at that time. As multi-threaded workloads and microservice software architectures have become commonplace, the CPU core count of a server is one of the primary ways its performance can be determined along with measurements such as the instructions per clock (IPC) count and the maximum clock speed of each CPU core. Although CPU performance is a complex topic in itself, this shows that many existing servers can be densified at little additional development expense if their key application workloads are already multi-threaded by moving to a densified design where more cores, whether in multiple processors or not, are used.

The type of processor instruction set in use must also be considered at a certain point. Intel's x86 instruction set powers the majority of CPUs in use today in the data centre for high performance application workloads. The instruction set of a CPU drives much of the resulting performance of a CPU, and as x86 is a complex instruction set computer (CISC), this requires a complex architecture which is able to perform the more elaborate instructions of this instruction set over multiple clock cycles where needed. In comparison, the Advanced RISC Machine (ARM) instruction set is comparatively simple as a reduced instruction set computer (RISC). Generally, the CISC approach places a greater burden on hardware whereas the RISC approach shifts much of that burden to software. There are many grey areas in a comparison like this, however, which muddy the waters and which this book cannot focus on further.

A key challenge with spurring the adoption of ARM CPUs in the data centre has been that there have often been optimisations made to software which runs on x86 CPUs which take advantage of specific capabilities available in those processors due to their instruction set. These optimisations may have been done by hand by the development team or by the compiler. Rewriting an application workload to take advantage of an ARM CPU is often difficult to justify, but for organisations such as large cloud providers and network operators who can see development and operational advantages, including in terms of hardware cost over time, of ARM CPUs, this development work may then be easily justified.

The type of processor architecture to use will depend on the workload and so may vary between two different size categories of IEDC. Due to, in many cases, their more optimised thermal output and power consumption profile, ARM CPUs are considered to be a prime deployment target for the IEDC for use cases such as operating system management and other tasks which do not fit a specialised accelerator. However, x86 CPUs typically offer higher performance per core, albeit with a smaller number of maximum cores, and a familiar development environment within the same power budget as an ARM CPU cluster. For the purposes of this section, consider that CPUs of both types can be effectively densified and that this trend will continue to accelerate as core counts and socket counts per server continue to increase over time.

A clear as possible understanding of the specific resource needs of an application workload is the most important determining factor for rack densification. If a key workload requires a significant amount of parallel processing resources and little general purpose CPU computation, the choice should be that the majority of the compute power and space in the rack is dedicated to a form of specialised accelerator in preference of a large amount of CPUs. If the opposite is true, then a rack should be designed accordingly as well. The difficulty in making this choice is understanding the specific needs of an application workload as well as which application workloads a specific rack should be tasked with. Both of these questions are made easier to answer at medium scale when compared to very small or very large scale; but they are essential for complete rack densification.

Specialised accelerators such as GPUs and their densification will be explored in the next section.

9.4.3   Supporting Equipment

Apart from general purpose and specialised compute devices, there are many other components of a modern server or of the rack itself which can each take up considerable physical space and must be considered when densifying a rack of server equipment. Three of these categories of equipment are:

1) Data storage equipment
   a) The scale and type of data storage that is required on board a particular server or in the same rack is of particular concern to the densification of the overall rack. Where possible, the data storage equipment used should be restricted to memory arrays for the rapid caching of any large working set data that cannot fit into volatile memory.
2) Power delivery equipment
   a) In many cases in a data centre facility, a customer will be required to or may even prefer to provide their own power delivery equipment. By ensuring that this gear is properly designed for the needs of the rack, the physical space required by this type of equipment can be limited, which increases the total space available for servers.

3) Network and management equipment
   a) Each rack of customer equipment deployed within a data centre facility requires a top of rack (TOR) switch or router and a means for the customer to manage that equipment. It is not uncommon for a dedicated management server to be deployed by a customer, which may manage one or multiple racks within a data centre. If this network gear and its management server counterpart can be space reduced – or in the case of the latter, can be replaced by software on a server in the rack – space can be utilised well.

Although this is not an exhaustive list, these three categories of equipment are often overlooked in the discussion of rack densification. Ensuring they are addressed as part of the rack design process alongside the compute equipment to be deployed in the rack is a simple way to create densified rack designs that do not leave any major source of physical space within the rack poorly utilised.

To prevent rack densification having to be a custom development and system integration effort for each deployment, a customer can create a set of densified rack designs which cover the key sets of data centre facilities and rack space size categories ahead of time if they expect to see the regular deployment of their equipment in infrastructure edge or RNDC facilities. This approach does create more upfront effort, but it yields efficiency gains for deployment in time.

9.5 Parallel Accelerators

As the workloads operated from the data centre continue to evolve, so too do the types of compute hardware that is best suited to process them. A significant change in the hardware deployed in the data centre has occurred over the past decade due to the widespread adoption of accelerators that are designed for greater speed at performing specific tasks. The most prevalent of these accelerators are parallel accelerators, which excel at performing tasks which can be divided into many concurrent operations, each of which are similar and can be batched together for processing at the same time.

General purpose scalar CPU architectures are not the optimal solution for highly parallelisable tasks, either on a maximum speed basis or on a work done per watt of energy basis. Compared to parallel accelerators, most modern CPU architectures cannot achieve performance that is within an order of magnitude of a parallel accelerator for the key tasks which the accelerator was designed to perform.

On the other hand, parallel accelerators excel only at parallel accelerable tasks. This makes them less effective than general purpose CPUs at other tasks and makes investing in them more of a gamble in the sense that a dollar spent on a CPU will yield a processor which can perform almost any task, but at a reduced level of performance compared to a specialised accelerator. On the other hand, a dollar spent on a parallel accelerator will yield a processor which can perform a certain subset of tasks at a greatly enhanced level of performance compared to a CPU, but that may be unusable for other uses.

This means that the modern data centre must still incorporate very large quantities of CPUs that are capable of handling any workload at a reasonable level of proficiency as a parallel accelerator cannot be programmed to effectively perform every task at such a high level of performance and efficiency.

Three main categories of parallel accelerators are expected to see deployment at the infrastructure edge in support of key use cases, each with their own unique considerations for usage. These are:

1) Field programmable gate arrays (FPGAs)
    a) As their name suggests, FPGAs allow a developer deep access to the very logic gates which make up the circuitry of the device. With this capability an FPGA can, unlike a typical computing device, be reconfigured to support certain types of computations more effectively depending on the needs of the application workload and after they have been deployed. This programmability in the field makes FPGAs highly flexible and well suited to a variety of tasks including ML inferencing and signal processing.
2) Tensor Processing Units (TPUs)
    a) Emerging from hardware development work at Google [1] to improve the efficiency of the inferencing processing required for ML application workloads, TPUs are capable of greatly enhancing the inferencing capability of a computing system ahead of the performance provided by a general purpose CPU. Although TPUs have been used in ML model training, they are typically utilised in the inferencing role at the moment.
3) GPUs
    a) Although they were originally developed to provide high performance graphics processing for applications such as video games and 3D modelling, GPUs have become much more general purpose parallel accelerators which can then be used for a wide range of tasks. Today they are commonly used to accelerate the functions required for ML inferencing and other workloads, deployed in dense configurations.

As each of these categories of parallel accelerators are very suitable for deployment at IEDC facilities, this section will now explore further detail on each of them as well as for a few additional categories of specialised accelerators which will continue to see use and adoption.

9.5.1 Field Programmable Gate Arrays (FPGAs)

FPGAs have been used for many years in embedded infrastructure devices such as high performance network equipment as their unique combination of hardware, software, and firmware can be tuned to perform specific tasks at speed and, due to their reconfigurability, can be improved after a given product is released by applying a firmware update. This capability has been a significant benefit for many years and will continue to be exploited as these devices find increasing adoption for several types of application workload in the data centre. Additional performance can often be gained for existing workloads, and the FPGA can be updated to optimise its performance for new ones as well.

Some FPGAs are deployed as separate accelerator cards, much like GPUs. Others may be integrated into a CPU, at least to the extent that both the FPGA and CPU are present within the same physical package. A key consideration for an FPGA is its size in terms of the number of programmable logic gates it contains for use by the developer, which has a direct proportional impact on the physical size and power requirements of the FPGA device itself. A size of FPGA can be selected based on its power usage, its number of logic gates, and physical space to serve a specific application workload.

Dedicated servers which primarily house FPGAs also exist, which typically include some amount of general purpose CPU resources so that the FPGAs can be tuned for a specific application workload.

FPGAs will see deployment in the IEDC as a means to accelerate specific application workloads such as signal processing. Although at large scale they may not provide the same amount of raw horsepower for tasks such as ML inferencing as a TPU or especially a cluster of GPUs, FPGAs can also be tuned to operate at lower power requirements due to their configurability, which makes them ideal for lighter workloads or deployment in smaller infrastructure edge facilities.

9.5.2 Tensor Processing Units (TPUs)

TPUs occupy an interesting part of the specialised accelerator space. Out of all the different types of accelerators described in this section, they are one of the newest and are designed for a very specific type of workload acceleration to a greater extent than many of the other categories of accelerators.

The development of an entirely new category of specialised accelerators which are dedicated to the processing of ML functions speaks volumes to the importance of this key use case, and IEDC facilities are in many cases ideal locations to perform the inferencing component of these application workloads as part of a wider distributed AI application such as for computer vision.

Currently, there is contention as to whether TPUs will be able to have the same impact that GPUs have had on the industry due to the prevalence and continuing development of GPUs, which looks set to continue, as well as the performance and commercial model of TPUs as they stand today. A concern for the longevity of TPUs is their applicability to ML model training as well as inferencing when compared to recent GPU developments such as NVIDIA's Ampere architecture, which looks to become increasingly capable of performing both training and inferencing at high performance using the same architecture. The competition between these two categories of accelerator will have to play out over time, but what does appear to be certain is that both TPUs and GPUs will be able to continue to increase their performance for their chosen specialised tasks at a faster rate than CPUs.

TPUs are not commercially available to the extent that FPGAs, GPUs, and other types of specialised accelerators are today. However, this may change in the future as TPUs and their wider ecosystem matures. Regardless, there are some customers who have access to and may choose to deploy a range of TPUs, and due to their capability to perform ML inferencing processing, they are a good fit for deployment at an IEDC facility handling a distributed artificial intelligence (AI) application.

9.5.3 Graphics Processing Units (GPUs)

In 2016, NVIDIA launched the G80 GPU, which introduced the idea of general purpose GPU (GPGPU) computing into the mainstream by incorporating large numbers of parallel processing elements that could be programmed to perform tasks beyond graphics processing [2]. Although the structure of the logic gates cannot be modified by the developer as they can in the case of an FPGA, a modern GPU presents a high performance pipeline for parallelisable computational tasks. Even though technically these modern GPU designs should be referred to as GPGPUs, they are typically referred to as GPUs.

Prior to this generation, the architecture of GPUs was typically formed from high performance but fixed function pipelines to perform specific graphics operations such as texture mapping or shading of 3D objects. Pixel and vertex shaders were implemented in these pieces of fixed function hardware, which allowed them to be performed at speeds which made the applications requiring them possible but rendered the GPU unsuitable for other tasks. As such, any non-graphics computations were still performed by a general purpose CPU in the majority of cases outside of any other accelerator cards.

Over time, GPU architecture has become progressively more separated from this fixed function and inflexible pipeline model. Some GPUs may still use dedicated hardware for small parts of the overall graphics pipeline, such as occlusion, but these components may be removed in the versions of that GPU which are used in the data centre for use cases needing general purpose parallel acceleration.

To that end, even when the underlying GPU architecture is common between a graphics card, which incorporates the GPU for use primarily in 3D graphics applications, and an accelerator card, which is used primarily for other parallel accelerator tasks, there may be hardware differences between the cards such as the amount and type of memory, the type of interconnections to other components including other GPUs within the same or adjacent servers, and the presence of any video outputs.

Today, GPUs are powerful and versatile for a range of application workloads which rely on types of computation which are heavily parallelisable, such as matrix multiplication. Application workloads which make extensive use of parallel operations match well to those which are expected to be key for infrastructure edge computing, such as ML inferencing for distributed computer vision use cases and radio signal processing for fifth generation (5G) networks. Combined with their ability to be deployed at very high densities in both off the shelf and customer rack designs and their relatively mature ecosystem of software tools, GPUs are likely to be the primary type of accelerator and compute resource that is deployed at the infrastructure edge over time, supported by considerable general purpose CPUs.

9.5.4 Smart Network Interface Cards (NICs)

Network interface cards (NICs) incorporating FPGAs or other specialised hardware acceleration are also becoming commonplace on high performance servers. Although it may not be as visible as the processing requirements for tasks such as 3D acceleration, processing network traffic can require a significant amount of processing power. Dedicated network infrastructure devices such as switches and routers have often utilised dedicated fixed function hardware to perform these tasks in order to meet their performance and cost requirements for this reason, and as the volume of traffic that each server in a data centre environment generates or handles over time increases, this becomes an issue for those servers to manage as well and contributes heavily to overall system efficiency and scaling.

By offloading the processing tasks required by the network capabilities of a server from the CPU and onto a smart NIC, significant improvements in CPU utilisation for other tasks can be achieved. This is becoming more important as the number and speed of network interfaces attached to a given server, especially those which house large numbers of parallel accelerators such as GPUs, continues to grow.

As the heterogeneity of the compute resources in the modern server continues to increase, this type of network processing accelerator allows system resources to be more optimally utilised both at the server and at the rack level. For this reason, smart NICs are likely to see widespread deployment at IEDC facilities across racks of any significant scale which generate or sink large amounts of network traffic, which for many of the key use cases which benefit the most from the infrastructure edge computing model, is likely to be a significant proportion of the total racks.

9.5.5 Cryptographic Accelerators

The past decade has seen an exponential rise in the number of applications and services which are implementing cryptographic functions throughout their operations not just to validate the rightful users of these applications but also to verify the safety of their own runtime environment and the legitimacy of any other parts of the application. This capability becomes especially key as workloads become increasingly segmented into smaller microservices which are then each capable of making sure that they are interacting with the software and hardware elements they should be interacting with through means of cryptographic validation, in order to ensure the security of each component of the system and avoid any cases of misplaced trust between components or any unknown entities.

Cryptographic processing functions, such as the generation of encryption keys for symmetrical and asymmetrical encryption systems, become more processor intensive and therefore time consuming as the length of these keys increases. This has led to the use of cryptographic acceleration hardware which can perform encryption and decryption operations at high speed. Some network equipment, for example, uses this type of accelerator to encrypt and decrypt all network traffic at line rate while also offloading these cryptographic functions from the CPU, which increases total system efficiency.

The specific cryptographic algorithm and scheme in use significantly alters the type and volume of cryptographic processing which is required. One of the most commonly used algorithms for public key cryptography, Rivest-Shamir-Adleman (RSA), relies on the difficulty of factoring the product of two large prime numbers which, especially with large key sizes, is difficult. Comparatively, elliptic curve cryptography (ECC) is able to rely on the use of smaller keys in order to provide an equivalent level of security although it does not see the same level of widespread use today. These public key or asymmetric key encryption schemes are complemented by private key or symmetric key schemes which are faster to compute and therefore typically used to encrypt and decrypt data in transit once their shared key has been established using a public key scheme. This does not make them easy to compute at scale, however, and so many cryptographic accelerators focus on a symmetric scheme.

Although modern CPUs have integrated new instructions which aim to speed up commonly used cryptographic operations, in some cases the volume of cryptographic processing required makes it preferable to deploy and operate dedicated cryptographic acceleration hardware and to offload as much of this processing as possible from the available CPUs in the data centre to these accelerators. This trend is likely to continue as overall system security continues to be a concern for customers.

9.5.6 Other Accelerators

There are many other types of dedicated accelerator hardware, but this section has described the main categories which are likely to be encountered in the IEDC. Many types of accelerators are present at the device edge due to the small size and battery life constraints of many of these devices. Use cases such as detecting movement for a fitness tracker or processing pulse oximeter data are useful in these devices but do not apply to their supporting infrastructure.

Digital signal processors (DSPs) are used in many applications where a computer system must be able to interpret and process an incoming signal such as an audio stream or a radio signal. Today, however, much of their niche is now being addressed by FPGA- and GPU-based solutions. In some cases, the term DSP now refers to performing signal processing functions on these accelerators rather than to any specific type of processor hardware itself. Over time this trend will continue as the flexibility and capability of FPGA and GPU accelerators improves for signal processing tasks.

Data processing units (DPUs) are a new and emerging category of specialised accelerator which is targeted at the processing of network data in transit. In some cases, these accelerators will be used in the smart NICs described earlier in this section in order to offload network computation from the CPU, and in the near future, it is likely that they will be integrated directly into servers without the need for an additional expansion card. Although there are varying definitions in the industry today as to what exactly constitutes a DPU, it is generally agreed that it consists of a multi core processor combined with a high performance network interface and a set of programmable acceleration and optimisation engines which can be tuned to outperform a general purpose CPU at its specific tasks.

9.5.7 FPGA, TPU, or GPU?

Each of these general categories of parallel accelerators is moving towards architectures that are capable of acceptable inferencing and training performance for ML workloads. Whereas in the past there was a clearer split between, for example, a GPU architecture which was designed to be suited for inferencing versus model training, this distinction is beginning to disappear due to the efforts of hardware and software architecture teams to provide a single architecture which can be used for both of these application workloads. This benefits the accelerator developer, who now has fewer platforms to support, allowing them to focus their development and production resources in one direction. It also benefits the infrastructure edge network operator, as the more use cases that can be efficiently supported from the infrastructure edge computing network, the higher the potential value of that network. Finally, this trend also benefits the customers buying these accelerators for deployment in an IEDC, as they can develop against and deploy a single type of accelerator in order to support the processing pipeline for both ML inferencing and training.

Of these categories of accelerators today, GPUs present in many ways the optimal type of compute hardware to deploy at an IEDC. They are widely available and supported by many software stacks for a range of parallel accelerator use cases; developers have substantial experience in using them at scale for production services; and they are capable of being deployed in dense and high power usage configurations, which makes good use of the combination of high cooling capability but small physical space that exists within many IEDC facilities.

Additionally, they are well suited to high performance ML tasks such as inferencing for convolutional neural networks, which are designed to perform computer vision tasks. Many computer vision tasks are well suited to being performed in IEDC facilities due to their need for low latency and a low cost for the movement of large volumes of network traffic in many use cases.

9.6 Ideal Infrastructure

There are many different categories of equipment which a customer may consider deploying in an IEDC facility. Although a standard 19-in. rack is capable of supporting any equipment the user wishes to deploy, the unique characteristics of the infrastructure edge model make certain types of equipment more or less desirable depending on its use case and its specifics.

For example, bulk data storage hardware is not an optimal use of the space within an infrastructure edge data centre. The use case that it serves is not latency sensitive on a scale that makes use of the unique capabilities of infrastructure edge computing, and at scale this hardware will take up large volumes of space which can be more economically served from a regional or national scale facility.

Table 9.1 lists several categories of hardware which may be deployed at a data centre facility and describes their general level of suitability for deployment at an infrastructure edge data centre:

Although this list is not exhaustive, it illustrates the types of hardware which are best suited to the unique considerations of the IEDC facility. Equipment that is most highly suitable combines physical densification with optimal support for low latency use cases and as little additional risk for mechanical failure as possible due to the unmanned model of edge data centres.

9.6.1 Network Compute Utilisation

Consider the example of a distributed AI application which is deployed across an infrastructure edge computing network. This category of application workloads requires considerable parallel processing resources deployed across multiple IEDC facilities. In theory, the greater the total amount of suitable compute resource

Table 9.1 Equipment suitability for IEDC facilities.

Hardware category	Category subtype	Use case	Suitability
Data storage	Mechanical disc	Long-term storage	Low
Data storage	Solid state disc	Warm storage	Medium
Data storage	Flash memory array	Working set memory	High
Data storage	Magnetic tape drive	Cold storage	Low
General compute	Sparse x86 CPU	Low intensity workloads	Low
General compute	Dense x86 CPU	High intensity workloads	Medium
Heterogenous compute	Dense CPU, GPU	Dense signal processing	High
Accelerated compute	FPGA	ML inferencing	High
Accelerated compute	TPU	ML inferencing	High
Accelerated compute	GPU	ML inferencing	High
Performance networking	FPGA	High speed overlay	Medium
Performance networking	Dense ARM CPU	High speed overlay	Medium
Performance networking	Dense smart NIC	Network traffic offload	High
Performance networking	Integrated DPU	Network traffic offload	High
Standard networking	Sparse ARM CPU	Network management	Low
Cryptographic accelerator	Public key accelerator	Certificate generation	Medium
Cryptographic accelerator	Private key accelerator	Line rate traffic encryption	High

which is deployed and available across the whole of the infrastructure edge computing network in that area, the greater the value of the infrastructure edge computing network as a whole. One way to estimate this is using network compute utilisation.

We can estimate the network compute utilisation for the infrastructure edge computing network by understanding the total equipment capacity of each edge data centre facility across the network in the area, calculating what amount of that capacity is currently being utilised, and then subtracting that figure from the total equipment capacity of the local infrastructure edge computing network.

The network compute utilisation metric will, in many cases, have a direct impact on the serve transit fail (STF) which is achievable for a specific customer, application, or the entire infrastructure edge computing network. More equipment deployed across the network at each edge data centre facility means more places where traffic from users can be served, providing opportunities to improve the STF metric. If a data centre facility is operating at a quarter of its total equipment capacity as measured in kilowatts, there may be traffic which the infrastructure edge computing network is then forced to transit to a RNDC because the application workload or content the user requires is not present on the infrastructure edge computing network, which may have been avoided if the capacity were used.

For this reason, the infrastructure edge computing network operator should be proactive in helping customers to understand the characteristics of compute density at the edge data centre, and even in working with customers and partners to help design densified racks of equipment which customers are able to deploy in these edge data centre facilities. Fully densified racks utilising equipment which makes optimal use of the power and space budget that is available in IEDC facilities helps the infrastructure edge computing network operator, customers, and end users too.

This utilisation figure is not only valuable for the cloud provider in this example as they are then able to serve the maximum number of application workloads and users from their equipment footprint, but it is also useful for the infrastructure edge computing network operator for several key reasons:

1) Greater facility utilisation
    a) Up to a sensible operating capacity, the infrastructure edge computing network operator is optimally served by there being more equipment, as measured in kilowatts across the edge data centre facilities they operate, than less equipment. The more equipment that is present in each edge data centre facility, the more value that the operator is able to derive from it, both directly and indirectly, through other users.
2) Higher revenue potential
    a) With additional equipment, as measured in kilowatts, deployed in each edge data centre facility comes the opportunity for the infrastructure edge computing network operator to increase the revenue which they are able to generate from each facility. Directly this can be driven by the increased power draw and network resource usage of the equipment, both of which customers of the facility can then be charged for.
3) More network value
    a) As an example of the network effect, the value of the overall infrastructure edge computing network increases the more application workloads and users are able to be served from it. These two factors are driven directly by the density of equipment that is deployed at each IEDC facility. Densification also has the capability to increase the number of discrete customers in each edge data centre facility, which can then enhance the value of any edge exchange (EX) capabilities offered there.

With all other factors being equal, an infrastructure edge computing network with a higher network compute utilisation figure is more valuable to the operator, customers, and end users than one with a lower network compute utilisation figure. The primary way to achieve a higher figure beyond just onboarding customers is to support those customers in densifying their racks to improve densities.

9.7 Adapting Legacy Infrastructure

Many organisations who may deploy equipment at an IEDC have existing racks of equipment they have designed and validated and are familiar with which are used today in on-premises or RNDC facilities. However, these equipment racks may not be well suited for deployment in an IEDC facility as they are likely to utilise only standard rack densities, which creates difficulties in using these existing racks in IEDC facilities where a higher rack density is of significant value to the operator and to the customer, who is then able to make more effective use of their rack space and cooling budget.

Ideally this type of infrastructure adaptation to increase densification can be achieved with no or minimal alterations to the applications and other software operating atop the hardware. Where possible, this is preferable as it reduces the overall cost to the organisation for the deployment and operation of the equipment at the IEDC. For example, where a workload can already utilise a large number of CPU cores, densifying the rack by replacing two servers with a single server that contains a higher core count should have a minimal impact on operating software.

Ultimately the means to achieve densification of existing rack infrastructure is the same as has been described in this chapter for new rack infrastructure. The cost of creating a custom set of racks for higher density deployment must be justified by the number of these racks which the customer can expect to deploy and the value of the use cases they will be supporting both initially and over time.

9.8 Summary

Although an IEDC can technically support almost any type of customer equipment, there are certain characteristics due to the unique nature of IECDs which make specific categories of hardware and densities of deployment desirable. This means that there is another category of hardware and densities of deployment that does not make optimal use of the IEDC and so should be avoided where at all possible.

In the next chapter, we will explore some of the other unique characteristics of the infrastructure edge computing model which influence real system and application workload designs at the edge.

References

1 Google (2020). Cloud TPU [Internet]. [cited 2020 Sep 30]. Available from: https://cloud.google.com/tpu

2 Hruska, J. (2016 Nov 8) 10 years ago, Nvidia launched the G80-powered GeForce 8800 and changed PC gaming, computing forever. ExtremeTech [Internet]. [cited 2020 Sep 30]. Available from: https://www.extremetech.com/gaming/239078-ten-years-ago-today-nvidia-launched-g80-powered-geforce-8800-changed-pc-gaming-computing-forever

10

Multi-tier Device, Data Centre, and Network Resources

10.1   Overview

The deployment of infrastructure edge computing networks adds a new set of data centre and network resources located between the user and the regional or national scale data centre. This creates a gradient of resources where various points along the gradient can then be utilised for application workload operation, with preference between these points being driven by key factors, which include site processing capacity, network connectivity, performance, or physical redundancy.

This chapter will explore several of these key factors including the concept of application workloads which are able to make use of resources at multiple points along the resource gradient concurrently.

10.2   Multi-tier Resources

Infrastructure edge computing introduces new sets of resources spread across potentially multiple physical locations between an end user and a regional or national scale data centre. In the case of an infrastructure edge computing network having direct last mile or access network interconnection, the resources provided by the infrastructure edge computing network are topologically, as well as physically, located between the end user and the regional or national scale data centre. If this type of network interconnection is not achieved, as has been described in previous chapters, the overall value of the infrastructure edge computing network cannot be realised and its resources also cannot be considered to be part of this resource gradient as access network traffic will not flow through any of these

Understanding Infrastructure Edge Computing: Concepts, Technologies and Considerations,
First Edition. Alex Marcham.
© 2021 John Wiley & Sons Ltd. Published 2021 by John Wiley & Sons Ltd.

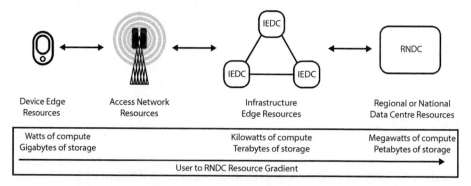

Device Edge Resources   Access Network Resources   Infrastructure Edge Resources   Regional or National Data Centre Resources

Watts of compute
Gigabytes of storage   Kilowatts of compute
Terabytes of storage   Megawatts of compute
Petabytes of storage

User to RNDC Resource Gradient

Figure 10.1   Resource gradient between user and RNDC.

resources at the infrastructure edge computing network directly from any access networks.

The diagram in Figure 10.1 shows the scale of resources available at each stage of the gradient between an end user and the regional or national data centre (RNDC). Although there is considerable variation between different sets of resources which may be present at each point of this gradient, what is important is the scale of difference between gradient steps. This difference of resources between an end user's device and the infrastructure edge data centre, and between the infrastructure edge data centre and the RNDC, is what allows useful multi-tier applications to be created.

Even within the infrastructure edge computing network itself, there are resource gradients when we account for the difference in scale, resources, and intended capabilities between the different size categories of infrastructure edge data centres and their associated network connectivity. Multiple smaller size category infrastructure edge data centres may aggregate back to a smaller number of larger edge data centre facilities; consider the example of five size category 2 facilities which are supporting distributed network functions, which then aggregate back to a size category 5 facility (see Figure 10.2).

Each stage along the gradient is an aggregation point for network traffic. However, through the use of distributed compute and data storage resources along this gradient, the network traffic load on upstream portions of the network can be reduced by processing data at a location that is relatively local to the user. This means that the total aggregate traffic load between two rightmost locations on the resource gradient may not be as large as that on the boundary between the infrastructure edge computing network and the access network, depending on how those networks and the key application workloads they are supporting are designed. This is dependent on many factors, which include the serve transit fail (STF) metric, which has been achieved by the infrastructure edge computing network, as well as the specific design of the application workload and its need for upstream data transmission.

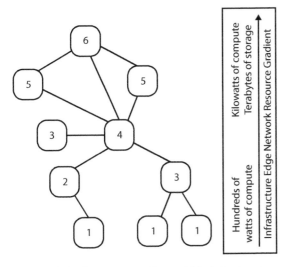

Figure 10.2   Resource gradient within infrastructure edge computing network.

There are typically three main sets of resources along this gradient which can be used by application workloads. Each of these resource sets has a significant amount of nuance, as can be seen in Figure 10.1:

1) Device edge
   a) At the far left of the resource gradient diagram are the processing capabilities that the end user devices possess, such as the onboard central processing unit (CPU) and graphics processing unit (GPU) resources of any modern smart-phone or the image processor within a smart surveillance camera. In real world deployments, there is a wide divergence in capabilities between many of the devices located at the device edge. In terms of network connectivity, some may connect directly to the access or last mile network while others utilise a gateway; in terms of processing, one device may be orders of magnitude more powerful than a different device, such as comparing a desktop computer to an internet of things (IoT) sensor. However, for the purposes of this book, we will treat the device edge as one set of resources.

2) Infrastructure edge
   a) In the middle of the resource gradient is the infrastructure edge computing network, which is located physically and topologically between the end user and the RNDC. The addition of the infrastructure edge computing network creates the gradient, and as has been seen in previous chapters, there may be many different size categories of infrastructure edge data centre facility within this set of resources. For the purposes of this book, we will consider the infrastructure edge computing network as one single set of resources to avoid additional complexity.

3) RNDC

    a) At the far right of the resource gradient is the RNDC. To be clear, this section of the gradient should be considered as two distinct parts; to any regional data centre, there may be as large or more a distance to a nearby national data centre as there is between an infrastructure edge computing network and any regional data centre. However, for the purposes of this chapter, we have combined regional and national data centre facilities into one set of resources on the gradient.

As can be seen from these descriptions of each major set of resources along the gradient, there are a wide range of variations within each of these categories. For example, one infrastructure edge data centre may be twice the scale or density than another, just as a RNDC may be compared to its peers. A device may be exponentially more capable of performing an application workload's processing tasks when compared to another device. Rather than attempt to capture all of the complexity which can exist at each one of these layers, this chapter describes the gradient itself, as well as the primary reasons why an application workload would be processed at a specific location along that gradient. There is then, for a practical deployment, the need to go a layer deeper and look at the specific capabilities of each sublayer of devices within each set of resources on the gradient to ensure that the granular needs of the application workload are then being met in an optimal fashion.

10.3 Multi-tier Applications

Once the physical resources present at each point of the gradient are understood, applications can be architected to make optimal use of them. From an application architecture standpoint, there are functions and components of any application which make sense to operate from particular sets of resources along the gradient from user to RNDC. Some applications may utilise each set of resources along the gradient to some degree, while others may use only a subset or even one set of those resources depending on the needs of their application workloads and the availability of each of these resource sets in the locations where the application workload will run.

The primary concept of multi-tier applications is that once we have a full understanding of all of the resources along the gradient from end user to RNDC, we can understand that each discrete set of resources in that gradient has unique characteristics which make them the optimal location for some elements of an application workload while simultaneously making them undesirable for others. This is crucial as when a set of resources does not offer any benefit to the application workload in terms of performance, cost, functionality, regulatory compliance, or any other key factor, there is no advantage to using it. As with any other decision, technology should be used as a tool to achieve the aims of the overall business and not be used just for its own sake.

For example, the infrastructure edge computing network is the first location along this gradient of resources from end user to RNDC, where collaborative processing can be effective utilised. Data from many device edge entities can be collected and processed together at the infrastructure edge computing network, which is a unique characteristic when compared to the device edge in the majority of cases. The RNDC can also provide this but at the cost of increased latency. Therefore, when an application workload requires the lowest latency while utilising collaborative processing, which is impractical for both the device edge and the RNDC, the infrastructure edge computing network is the best place to operate that component of the application workload. Similar decisions exist for each resource set on the gradient.

The placement of these application workloads will be described in further detail in the next chapter, as will how this placement can be orchestrated at a conceptual level without getting into the specific details of any one particular orchestrator or application operation framework. This is an emerging ecosystem of technologies which will solidify over time, but an understanding of the problems that these technologies are trying to solve is applicable across any resulting solution which solves them.

Regardless of the specific orchestration technologies used to make a workload placement decision along this resource gradient, the benefit of the three sets of resources can be thought of as follows:

1) Device edge
   a) Where the absolute lowest time to complete a processing task is required and the processing capabilities of the device are sufficient, the device edge offers the best location from which to operate an application workload. An example of such a task is in drawing the user interface for an application or rendering a game in real time by using the onboard GPU within a smartphone. As the device edge contains a large number of mobile devices, these devices are often limited by their need to rely on battery power for their standard operations, but where a task can be performed in isolation and the resources at the device are sufficient, it is hard to argue with the low latency achievable with and lack of network resources needed by these devices.
2) Infrastructure edge
   a) The infrastructure edge occupies a middle ground between the device edge and the regional or national scale data centre as the first location along the gradient where a collaborative processing model can work effectively by removing the complications of direct device to device communications while

also introducing the elastic scaling capabilities which users now expect from a public or private cloud service which is operating within a data centre. Additionally, the infrastructure edge can support a lower latency to the end user, although the extent of this latency difference and its value depends on the use case and the physical location of all nearby infrastructure.

3) Regional edge or national data centre
   a) Compared to either of the preceding sets of resources, the RNDC can support unmatched levels of scale for processing power, data storage, and network connectivity, which makes it ideally suited to use cases which are not latency constrained to the extent that they require the capabilities of the device edge or infrastructure edge. Additionally, it is likely that per unit of processing, storage, or network resource, the RNDC is the cheapest option along the resource gradient, which makes it highly valuable for workloads.

As described in the previous section, there is a range of capabilities within each of these resource sets which can also be utilised by a sufficiently sophisticated orchestrator. As a general rule, it is a good idea to incorporate only as much complexity into the orchestration decision as is needed by the application workload, and this will vary depending upon the particular needs of the workload.

There are two primary categories of applications which the introduction of the infrastructure edge computing network into the resource gradient have now enabled: core to edge and edge to core.

10.4 Core to Edge Applications

Some application workloads begin, or are anchored, at a regional or national scale data centre and possess or interact with some components that are best operated from an infrastructure edge data centre. Some examples of core to edge applications include some of the most important use cases:

1) Distributed artificial intelligence (AI)
   a) Before inferencing can be performed in an AI system, the machine learning (ML) model must be trained, and the model must then be distributed out to the locations where inferencing is to be performed. The training process often requires access to large volumes of data which may be expensive or difficult to transport to distributed locations, and so it is best performed in a RNDC which then distributes models which result from the training process to distributed infrastructure edge data centre locations. Due to this process, distributed AI and the many use cases which rely on it can be considered an important example of a core to edge application with key uses.

2) Fifth generation (5G) core networks
   a) Like previous generations of cellular networks, there is a functional separation in the 5G cellular network between the radio access network (RAN) and the core network. The 5G core network is best operated from a location where interconnection with many other networks can occur, such as an internet exchange point (IXP) or a large edge exchange point (EXP), because end user traffic from the 5G network is required to pass through the 5G core network before it can be delivered to another network, such as a cloud provider hosting the video an end user is trying to access. A distributed 5G core network may operate partially from an infrastructure edge data centre and partly from a regional or national scale data centre depending on where specific resources that end users try to access are located for optimal performance.

Core to edge applications are likely to be extensions of existing application workloads which operate today in a regional or national scale data centre facility and that can then benefit from expanding to utilise additional resources located at the infrastructure edge computing network to improve their latency, functionality, or cost profile. For example, current machine vision applications which utilise AI and ML functions operating from a RNDC today can expand out to use the distributed AI model described earlier. This is an example of migrating an existing application workload to become a core to edge application because of the capabilities of the infrastructure edge computing network and the applicability of these capabilities to the specific use case in question.

As they are likely to be extensions of existing application workloads, core to edge applications are more likely to see a clear path to revenue than many examples of edge to core workloads. At the same time, it could be argued that because core to edge workloads are often extensions of current use cases, it is possible that edge to core application workloads may be home to more innovative and unorthodox low latency use cases which hold more potential for creating currently untapped value.

It remains to be seen how many existing use cases will be evolved over time, such as the previous example of distributed AI, to become core to edge applications versus those which will be newly created in order to utilise the resources available at the infrastructure edge. Regardless, the number of application workloads which make use of the resource gradient is a key measure of its value and accessibility, and the choice of whether to rearchitect a current workload or create a new one that utilises these multiple resource sets is mostly immaterial as long as the main end result is the same.

10.5 Edge to Core Applications

In comparison to the previous section, some application workloads begin, or are anchored out, at the infrastructure edge data centre and then have components which are best operated from a RNDC to support them. Some examples of these edge to core applications include:

1) Cyber-physical systems
   a) The core of a cyber-physical system application is in its low latency control of a physical entity, whether that entity is a vehicle, an industrial robot, or something else. As the application cannot exist without this function, and this function is one which is best served from the infrastructure edge, it is considered an edge to core application. Components of the application such as data storage or model training are ideal to operate from a RNDC as an augmentation.
2) 5G RAN networks
   a) Although the 5G core network can be distributed across many physical locations, the 5G RAN is more likely to be distributed in this way due to the physically dispersed nature of RAN infrastructure, which is providing even macro cell coverage for a large area such as an entire country. Small size category infrastructure edge data centre facilities are likely to extend out towards these 5G RAN sites in order to perform the RAN processing tasks required by the virtualised 5G RAN functions, many of which are latency sensitive to the extent that they can utilise this infrastructure effectively.

Edge to core applications may be the most critical category of applications for justifying the value of the infrastructure edge computing network during its initial phases of deployment and operation. A use case in this category is one that cannot be executed effectively or in some cases at all by using a regional or national scale data centre alone, and so where these use cases will also generate revenue, they are likely to be the anchor use cases for an infrastructure edge computing network, supporting enough new and unique value that the business case using this new infrastructure can be approved.

This category of application workloads is likely to generate a lot of excitement as developers seek to create new solutions to a range of problems by using the unique characteristics of the infrastructure edge computing model. However, it is important to retain a focus on the problem at hand as well as on any alternatives, such as using existing technologies, using a RNDC, or simply not developing and deploying the solution if it is not economical or it is difficult to operate.

Not every category of application workload is balancing the RNDC with the use of the infrastructure edge computing network. In some cases, the choice is between the device edge and one or both of the rightmost resource sets in the gradient, which both utilise data centres.

10.6   Infrastructure Edge and Device Edge Interoperation

For the majority of applications today, there is a local component and a remote component. The former operates at the device edge, for example, in the form of a web browser on a user's device while the latter operates from a data centre, whether infrastructure edge, regional, or national in scale and, in this example, may be a streaming video application with data stored in these locations.

There is a class of applications where multiple device edge devices communicate and interoperate directly. Resources at the infrastructure edge may then be used to augment this application or not, depending on the specific use case. Some examples of this category of device edge use cases are:

1) Direct vehicle to vehicle (V2V) communication
   a) There are considerable efforts underway to create ad hoc communication networks between moving vehicles which allow these vehicles to exchange data about road conditions, traffic control, and other key considerations without the need to connect back to a traditional access or last mile network such as a fourth generation (4G) Long-Term Evolution (LTE) cellular network. In these use cases, two or more vehicles, which are device edge entities, communicate directly with each other and also process these communications locally in real time.
2) Vehicle to infrastructure (V2I) communication
   a) In a similar fashion to the previous category, many transportation organisations are creating intelligent infrastructure devices and networking standards which allow a piece of street furniture such as a stop sign to inform nearby connected vehicles of its meaning and position, along with any other useful information which has been generated by its sensors, in order to provide a supplementary source of data which that vehicle can use to support its safe navigation combined with its own abilities.
3) Ad hoc video games
   a) In this use case, multiple user devices such as smartphones create a local ad hoc wireless network in order to host a video game session. Consider the example of an augmented reality (AR) video game where low latency is required in order to provide a smooth gameplay experience and the processing power available in the user group's smartphones is sufficient. One player may host the game session and others may connect to it in an ad hoc fashion to reduce the latency inherent in the network connectivity back to a centralised location which would otherwise be used to support the game session.

The challenge with many of these use cases which require inter-device interoperation is that they require end user devices to operate in a collaborative manner where the battery power and other resources such as processing capacity of a device such as a smartphone must be used to support other users. This is especially challenging for a battery-powered device as the typical users will not want to risk running low on power to enable this class of use cases. Where they do want them to be used will be at the user's discretion, such as when playing a collaborative game, which limits the way that this operational model can be used in any real situation as it cannot be considered "always on."

Additionally, this operating model creates difficulties with enabling collaborative processing. In an application where computation is performed and data is stored in a central location, even if that location is central only for the local area such as an infrastructure edge data centre, every device which uses the application can draw from the knowledge of other devices by getting data from that central point. Processing data from one source in collaboration with others also often reveals key trends which may not be apparent when analysing only a single data source, which creates insights from which every user utilising the service can benefit. This is especially important in the case of an autonomous vehicle, for example, where this processing model can improve safety and efficiency.

For an example of collaborative processing, consider an autonomous vehicle navigation application which is responsible for collecting and processing data on the road conditions that a fleet of cars in a city are generating and then informing them how best to prepare for them to avoid sudden braking or other dangerous driving actions. This use case relies on the ability to collect data from many and possibly hundreds or thousands of vehicles which are operating in an area and then analysing that data to produce actionable insights which can then be distributed back to every vehicle in the area to improve their operating efficiency or safety. There are two ways that this could be architected.

First, this application could be architected using device edge resources only. This means that one or multiple devices, in this case the autonomous vehicles themselves, would need to be the centralised points at which the data from all of the other vehicles in the area is collected and analysed. In regard to the network topology, a heterogenous network must be established directly between the devices without the use of centralised network infrastructure. This can be challenging as these endpoints are moving and will often be using spectrum which cannot easily penetrate any of the nearby buildings.

With this architecture, a few issues become immediately apparent. The key concerns with this are:

1) Use of device processing resources
   a) This is especially crucial for devices which are designed to operate in an autonomous fashion by using their computing capability in order to perceive and navigate their physical environment, often at considerable speeds which could cause injury, death, or damage to property should these systems fail.

As much processing resource as possible should be devoted to these tasks, and the addition of more resources has direct and often large impacts on the cost, size, and power efficiency of the device.

2) Use of device network resources
   a) Each device has a limited amount of network resources, in terms of its processing capability and connectivity to its access network. If necessary, a device could be designed with one or multiple additional transceivers in order to supplement its existing network resources, but this is an additional and often difficult to justify expense which also increases the power draw of the network system of the device.

3) Shortened device battery life
   a) This factor is often the most challenging when considering the practical operation of a device-only collaborative processing application. Users are not typically willing to sacrifice the battery life of their own devices to support the operation of a use case for other users. As the size of mobile devices continues to decrease, there is a real need to optimise the power efficiency of these devices, which makes it difficult to justify the addition of additional battery capacity to support these rare use cases.

Using infrastructure edge computing, however, this application can be architected using both device and infrastructure edge resources in order to optimally serve the needs of the application and limit negative impacts on the devices. The pieces of the application workload which require collaborative processing can be performed in the infrastructure edge data centre facility, as long as the latency for each of the mobile endpoints at the device edge to this infrastructure edge data centre is sufficient.

Where useful, a heterogenous network utilising device to device communication can still be used to augment the system to provide additional resiliency in the event of a localised network issue, but it will be primarily considered to be a backup option and not the primary means of system operation.

With this architecture, the resources of each device, including specifically their battery life and local processing and network resources, are protected against the needs of other users. As long as each of the device edge entities – the mobile endpoints that are autonomous vehicles in this example – have a network connection to the infrastructure edge computing network of sufficiently low latency, this is a more scalable application workload operation model than just relying solely upon the device edge.

However, as standards continue to be developed for these types of device to device applications, it is likely that some use cases such as V2V and V2I will make effective use of this application structure. When this occurs, the other elements of that application workload may not require the combination of low latency to the end user device and elastic resource availability which can be provided by an infrastructure edge computing network, and so the application workload may utilise the device edge and the RNDC. Any combination of resource sets is valid as long as they are the optimal resources for the application workload; one or multiple resource sets may be bypassed by an application workload if it has no use for them or if that use is simply better fulfilled elsewhere.

10.7 Summary

This chapter has described the gradient of resources which the infrastructure edge computing model enables between the end user and the RNDC which allows an application to utilise different sets of resources depending on their unique characteristics and the needs of the application workload. Within each set of resources along the gradient, there is a large potential for variation in capabilities, which introduces additional complexity which should be managed carefully.

In the next chapter, we will explore some of the key factors around creating and orchestrating application workloads which can make effective use of this gradient of resources from the user through to the regional or national facility, by way of the infrastructure edge computing network.

11

Distributed Application Workload Operation

11.1 Overview

The gradient of data centre and network resources between a user and the regional or national data centre (RNDC) which was described in the previous chapter is of little use if application workloads cannot be designed and operated in a way that makes the most effective use of all of these sets of resources.

This chapter will explore the key concepts behind architecting and operating applications in order to make use of the resource gradient introduced by infrastructure edge computing. It will not focus on particular orchestration systems or other software infrastructure implementation details, however, and will instead concentrate on the core issues and choices to be made with any real world solution.

11.2 Microservices

Historically, applications were architected in a monolithic fashion. In the context of this chapter, this means that even though an application may perform many distinct features and functions, when an application is a monolithic entity, all of these functions are part of one single application workload at operation in one specific location. In the case of an application which operates on a user device and utilises a remote component running on a server in a data centre, for example, these are considered to be two separate application workloads, each of which may be architected in a monolithic fashion.

Over time software engineering has evolved to separate individual functions away from the main application. Various approaches have emerged to allow these

Understanding Infrastructure Edge Computing: Concepts, Technologies and Considerations,
First Edition. Alex Marcham.

functions to operate independently such that the application can be architected and operated in a modular fashion where components, which may be separate features, functions, or modules within the code, can be altered separately to create a more robust and manageable way of architecting and operating large applications which is not reliant on maintaining one single monolithic entity where changes to one component may cause adverse effects to another. This approach has led to the concept of microservices, where a workload which was once a single monolith has been separated into a collection of microservices with defined sets of interfaces between those microservices so that the functionality of the original application is maintained while allowing for greater resilience, redundancy, and maintainability for the application.

The segmentation of what would once have been a single monolithic application workload into an array of microservices which are each designed to discretely perform a specific function and a set of interfaces which allow these microservices to communicate effectively with one another is key to an application workload being able to make use of the gradient of resources between the user and the RNDC which was described in the previous chapter. Once an application is separated into such discrete microservices, each microservice can be run at the location along that gradient where it is best suited in terms of performance, cost, and functionality. These decisions are also likely to change over time, which a finely tuned microservice-based application workload can be architected to take advantage of, unlike a traditional monolithic application operating in one place.

The concept of microservices has now become commonplace in software development. However, it is still new territory for many developers to consider the physical location in which their workloads are operating. Ideally the software developer is able to create a framework for their microservices which allows the application to operate from multiple locations across the resource gradient, with the understanding that an orchestration system may migrate individual microservices around to be optimal in terms of performance, cost, and functionality over time as the availability of resources or the cost of utilising those resources changes, such as in the event of network congestion upstream.

11.3 Redundancy and Resiliency

This microservices model is also useful in providing a higher degree of redundancy than is usually maintainable with a traditional monolithic application architecture. In the microservices model, if there is a failure of an application component, it can typically be restarted or replaced without the need to derail the entire application. However, in a monolithic application, this type of issue can often result in application downtime or the need for a longer recovery process if it is remediated.

Once the application has access to a set of redundant resources, in regard to both the underlying gradient of infrastructure and the software capabilities acquired through segmentation, it can be architected and operated to work in a resilient fashion. Again, by utilising the flexibility of multiple microservices which can be deployed at different locations across the resource gradient, it can be possible to deploy an application at multiple physical facilities or devices in order to optimise for resiliency against potential issues with specific network connectivity or sets of resources, such as protecting the operation of the application against the failure of the network connectivity between the infrastructure edge computing network and the regional data centre by operating each of the application services which would normally be at the regional data centre on the infrastructure edge.

It is also possible for one site to operate as a hot standby for another. Consider the example of an infrastructure edge computing network where there are two smaller size category infrastructure edge data centre (IEDC) facilities connected back to a larger facility. Each of these smaller facilities is an ideal location for a particular service, and this service does not require the resources of more than one facility at a time. If an issue is detected at one site, a failover to the instance of the service in another edge data centre facility can be activated in order to preserve overall application uptime.

To be clear, many ways of providing redundant and resilient application operation exist whether a microservices or monolithic application architecture is in use. There are, however, elements of the microservices approach which make this and the use of dispersed physical infrastructure easier to utilise. Microservices are not a panacea, but the disaggregated application workload components with defined communication interfaces they enable map very well to the problem of applying an application workload to the right location across the resource gradient from user to data centre.

11.4 Multi-site Operation

As described in the previous chapter, there are two main ways in which an application workload can be architected to make use of multi-site operation, where sites which are located at different places along the gradient of resources from the end user to the regional or national scale data centre are being used. The first is to utilise different resource sets across the gradient in order to make use of their unique characteristics, for example, by performing tasks at the device edge or infrastructure edge in order to achieve an application performance goal which is far harder to match elsewhere.

Another aspect of multi-site operation is an application workload which operates across multiple sites that are located at the same place along this resource gradient, such as a workload which uses resources positioned across two or more IEDC facilities. This type of multi-site operation may be used to provide scale out capacity or resiliency for an application. Even at one resource set along the gradient, there are many advantages to being able to utilise multiple facilities.

In many ways, these two types of multi-site operation are very similar; they both require information on the capabilities and status of each set of resources which is under consideration, and they both may be used together. For example, an application workload may require a considerable amount of performance or resiliency for its components which are best operated at the infrastructure edge, and so multiple IEDC facilities can be utilised. This means that the decision to deploy those application workload components to the infrastructure edge has preceded, but is also best informed by, the choice of the number of sites across which to deploy within that resource set.

Depending on the needs and the architecture of a particular application, it may not be necessary to duplicate all of the components of that application when operating across multiple sites. The model of microservices is again of benefit here if, for example, an application can benefit from having many instances of a data collection component reporting data back to a single data analysis component to limit the amount of duplication and wasted resources that would occur if the data analysis piece of the application had to be duplicated for every instance of the distributed data analysis component.

To date, in this chapter we have referred to the resources available at each location on the resource gradient as one or more devices or facilities. In reality, especially for the infrastructure edge and the RNDC facilities, the resources which can be utilised by an application are the tenants of these facilities, such as a cloud provider who has deployed accessible servers there.

11.5   Workload Orchestration

To control where individual application workloads are performed, a workload orchestration system that is aware of the unique characteristics of each location where these locations can be performed is required. Depending on the level of sophistication in the reporting of the operational data from each location as well as in the workload placement decisions made by the orchestrator, it is possible to create very complex automated decision trees which will take hundreds of factors into account.

There are several key factors which will drive the orchestration decision for a specific application workload. At any given point in time, these factors may fluctuate based on factors which are outside of the control of the workload orchestration system, the application workload, or the user, and so they must be reacted to as well as possible in order to maintain the performance and cost profile of the application workload. The five key factors which are likely to have the greatest impact on this are:

1) Processing requirements
   a) Application workloads can be divided into two categories in terms of the processing requirements that they have: real time and non-real time. The former category is a class of processing tasks which are required to be performed within a specific time; otherwise the system will fail in some way, potentially completely. This imposes a set of requirements on the system for deterministic operation which does not exist with the latter category, where tasks can be completed within a vaguer period of time and still be valuable. Application workloads often contain both types of tasks.
2) Data storage requirements
   a) The data storage requirements of an application workload can be separated into two categories: short and long term memory. In the former category are structures such as working set memory which are used to support the processing functions of the application, and in the latter category is long term data storage which can be drawn from later should it be required, for example, in a historical data analysis.
3) Network performance requirements
   a) In many cases, this category is the most apparent for use cases which are a good fit for deployment at the infrastructure edge computing network. Many of these use cases are reliant on a certain network latency between a user and their application workload at the nearest IEDC. Should the required level of network performance become unavailable, a workload migration may then occur to a point on the resource gradient which is still capable of providing that performance.
4) Application workload cost profile
   a) Every application workload has an implicit cost profile, even today. Although it may not always be apparent, there is a cost figure which, if an application workload were to exceed, would make that workload uneconomical enough to be no longer viable. Understanding the cost profile for a given application workload therefore enables an application operator to maintain the economic viability of their services over time.
5) Physical redundancy requirements
   a) An application workload may have specific requirements for redundancy which the operators of that workload have determined can be satisfactorily met only using a specific level of physical redundancy at the data centre facilities the workload will be operating at. Although more explicit and less frequently identified than other needs of the application workload in this section, this is nonetheless an important element.

We will now consider the complexity of each of these five key factors to the orchestrator in detail, as well as the concept of resource marketplaces and how a workload may declare its resource needs.

11.5.1 Processing Requirements

The processing requirements of an application workload can be difficult to define. Many developers are not used to identifying the physical resources which will be required to support a function or a feature of the application, as they may be developing at a much higher level of abstraction which is not providing them with that level of visibility to the underlying infrastructure. In many cases, tasks will take the time that they take using the amount of processing hardware which is allocated to the task, whether on a device or a cloud instance. This model, however, does not work for real time use cases where tasks must be performed within an exact time window for the system to function well.

There is an additional level of complexity to the processing requirements of an application workload which is the use of dedicated accelerator hardware such as graphics processing units (GPUs), Tensor Processing Units (TPUs), and field programmable gate arrays (FPGAs). Where the need for these accelerators exist, the availability of a suitable accelerator can drastically alter the cost and performance profile of the application. It may even be the difference between enabling the use case or not for tasks such as 3D rendering or machine learning (ML) inferencing. Thus an orchestrator should ideally be able to make use of the locations and current utilisation of these accelerator resources as an additional but highly valuable layer of complexity when determining the best location for any given workload.

The application workload cost profile may be acceptable only with the use of such an accelerator, due to the capability of these devices to perform specialised computations such as highly parallel operations orders of magnitude faster than is otherwise possible when using standard scalar central processing units (CPUs). This is an example of how any one requirement of the application workload can influence another.

11.5.2 Data Storage Requirements

An application workload's data storage requirements extend beyond the amount of data that must be stored on an hourly, daily, or weekly basis. They also include the speed at which any stored data must be able to be accessed, which adds a performance component to the requirements for data storage for an application workload. This is especially crucial for low latency workloads which may require the processing of large amounts of data which exceed the capacity of typical server Random Access Memory (RAM).

Consider the difference between storing data long term in a cold storage facility compared to the need to store short term data in non-volatile memory as a working set store while an application workload is operating. Other tiers of memory, such as the volatile memory used for server RAM, could also be considered in the workload orchestration decision as this can often be a significant limiting factor for the real performance of any application workload across the resource gradient.

As such, a sophisticated orchestrator should be aware of not only the scale of the data storage that is available at each resource set but also of the performance characteristics of that equipment such that an application workload with specific needs can then be correctly positioned along the gradient.

11.5.3 Network Performance Requirements

As network performance encapsulates the latency between an end user and an application workload when that application workload is located anywhere except the user's local device, even when it is operating from another device edge entity, the requirements in this category are a key determinant of where a particular application workload component should be operated from. If the latency and throughput required by an application cannot be delivered to a specific resource set, that resource set is not a suitable location for the operation of that workload. These factors can also change over time depending on the usage of the network and any upstream rerouting or congestion that occurs.

Should the gradient of resources between the user and the RNDC for any period of time be unable to meet the network performance requirements of an application workload, that workload has two choices: to postpone serving its users until the required level of performance can be reacquired or to continue operating in a degraded best effort state with the ability to then return to normal operating performance once network performance increases to its required level.

The detection and isolation of network congestion is vital in order to fulfil key network performance requirements. Congestion can occur on a macro or a micro scale; the former can occur, for example, between the device edge and infrastructure edge due to last mile or access network congestion or failure, whereas the latter can occur between IEDC facilities due to some localised congestion or the failure of an individual network link between those facilities in question.

11.5.4 Application Workload Cost Profile

The application workload cost profile can change dynamically depending on the level of resources which are currently used at each state of the gradient. As resources become utilised, as an example of supply and demand, the operator of the remaining unutilised resources may choose to increase the price for their usage dynamically.

These types of dynamic pricing schemes are likely to emerge where an ecosystem of use cases exists which are valuable enough to warrant such higher pricing.

There are several key factors which can alter the application workload cost profile with no changes to the scale or operation of the workload itself and which can change over time without any notice:

1) Resource usage
   a) As the number and scale of application workloads increases in a resource set over time, scarcity of resources is likely to become apparent at the smaller end of the scale in times of heavy loading such as during major social or sporting events. A determination must then be made as to who will have access to these resources.
2) Utility costs
   a) The cost of electricity in particular varies over time depending on the contract that an infrastructure operator has with their utility providers and the time of day which intense usage of that infrastructure is occurring at, which may alter the cost basis of the application workload in a case where that workload uses very significant power.
3) Network issues
   a) The operational status of the network is perhaps the most fluid of these variables as depending on the design of the network and the performance which it was created for, it may be subject to frequent unpredictable congestion events which create the need to determine whether the application workload justifies some dedicated quality of service (QoS).

These and other factors help us to understand the application workload cost profile – that is, the level of expense that we as an application operator or an end customer could justify in incurring to keep a given application workload operational as these factors fluctuate over time. Not every use case can be valuable enough to warrant its continued operation if its operational cost were to double due to a network issue which would require the creation and maintenance of a new dedicated class of QoS.

11.5.5   Redundancy and Resiliency Requirements

Each application workload has requirements in terms of the level of redundancy and resiliency that it requires to operate at its desired level of uptime and service continuity. Depending on the way that an application is architected and operated, the level of redundancy and resiliency which is possible may be constrained; however, any form of mission critical or highly valuable application workload is likely to be architected in a way which can make use of many resource sets which meet its needs to support a high level of uptime, even if there are changes to the resources or costs of those sets.

For example, consider an application which is designed to collect real time data from a distributed network of internet of things (IoT) devices. Once this data is collected, it is processed to extract analytical insights and then is stored for later review and additional analysis. The application operator may determine that although the data collection and analysis functions can be performed from data centre facilities that do not support extensive levels of physical redundancy, the data storage function of the application should be operated only from a RNDC facility supporting high redundancy.

With this information in hand, the individual workload components can be operated from resource sets which meet the redundancy and resiliency requirements of that specific component without the need for the application operator to charge their users more to host workload components that do not require the same level of protection in these facilities. This enables an application operator to be capable of supporting the uptime required by their application on a granular and cost effective basis.

11.5.6 Resource Marketplaces

With an established application workload cost profile, it is clear that some means by which to expose the availability and cost of resources across the gradient will be required to make use of this concept and to allow an application operator to utilise the resources which best fit their use case. Where this role can be fulfilled with a cloud provider who has resources within multiple resource sets across the gradient, it is likely that these providers will offer services which expose this information but only for their own resources while ignoring the capabilities or availabilities of resources from other sources.

Resource marketplaces are an emerging concept which aim to expose this information to application operators such that they can purchase access to resource sets based on their application cost profile.

These marketplaces may fulfil a key role in exposing this type of information from multiple cloud or other resource providers at the same time, allowing an application operator to select the cloud that offers the best value for their application while still meeting its performance requirements in a real time fashion. This will provide application operators with the capability to utilise resources from two or more key resource providers, such as cloud providers, enabling them to operate most effectively.

11.5.7 Workload Requirement Declaration

Ideally an application workload is tagged with a set of specific requirements which help the workload orchestration system to identify suitable resources to use for that workload across the gradient from user to RNDC. This workload requirement declaration is the actionable and publicly consumable version of the information within the application workload cost profile; it allows the operator of a resource set, such as a cloud provider, to see the pieces of this information that an application operator has allowed them to see such that orchestration decisions can be made rapidly.

This information could be expressed through parameters carried by the container or other workload isolation and deployment system that is in use. Regardless of the specific means by which it is shown, this information is vital as it allows orchestration to be performed on a workload without a need for manual interaction. The functional split between a private application workload cost profile, which is internal to the application operator, and a public workload requirement declaration allows the level of information about a workload which is shared publicly to be limited, protecting that organisation against any interference to its resources while allowing an orchestration system to work effectively.

To make these decisions, it is key that the orchestrator has visibility of the underlying infrastructure.

11.6 Infrastructure Visibility

A workload orchestration system must have a certain level of visibility to all of the key operating and design characteristics of the resources available on the gradient between a user and the RNDC in order to make optimal workload placement decisions. This need covers both the static factors of these resources such as their general physical locations and the scale of one to another, which may change over time but not regularly, and dynamic factors such as site availability.

Without near real time visibility to the real operation of the infrastructure, workload orchestration cannot make accurate application workload placement decisions. This means that any placement decisions will need to be made in a static fashion, and the orchestration ability of the entire system is limited as it cannot account for changes to the underlying infrastructure in an automated fashion.

One key area of visibility is the ability of a workload orchestration system to understand and react to emerging issues with the operational technology that is present throughout the infrastructure edge computing network. This includes the environmental systems for each data centre facility such as the cooling and humidity control systems, parts of the power delivery infrastructure including any battery backups that are in place, and the state of internal and external facility network connectivity.

However, the majority of network and data centre infrastructure operators today do not expose this level of information to their customers. This is typically an operational choice more so than a limit of the technical capabilities of these operators, as experience has shown many customers assume that notice of faults which occur but which are corrected before they impact that customer means that a network or facility is not as robust as one which does not expose this information. However, this is a flawed mindset which does not fairly represent the worth of the more transparent facility, and in an infrastructure edge computing network where physical redundancy is harder to support at each site than in a RNDC, faults must be detected and worked around in real time.

Consider the following scenario as an example of how visibility to the operating status of these parts of the network and data centre infrastructure can impact the operation of an application workload. An application workload is operating at an IEDC. At this facility, a power outage is detected. There is no generator at this specific facility, and so the application operator has only a few minutes of battery backup system time before their application workload will be offline.

If the workload orchestrator is unaware of these events, the first indication it will have of an issue at the data centre facility is when power at the facility is fully lost and the workloads that were running at that facility are no longer contactable. The orchestrator cannot determine at this point whether a power outage has occurred – and so any users relying on those workloads are cut off from the service that their workloads were providing – or if the network connectivity between the orchestrator and an application workload has failed. The remediation required for these two issues is very different, and without knowing the cause of the failure, the orchestrator is unlikely to make the optimal recovery.

11.7 Summary

Distributed application workload operation and orchestration is a key component of infrastructure edge computing as without it, the underlying infrastructure will not be fully utilised by all of the new and updated applications which can improve their performance, resource utilisation, or costs in using various points along the gradient of resources from the user to the RNDC.

In the next chapter, we will consider the key factors related to infrastructure and application security for the infrastructure edge computing network, including security technologies and security policies.

12

Infrastructure and Application Security

12.1 Overview

As in any area of information technology today, infrastructure and application security is a pressing concern in the context of infrastructure edge computing. Although the majority of security concerns are not unique to an infrastructure edge computing network, they nonetheless apply, and the same care and consideration must be taken from architecture and design through to daily operation to ensure the security of the entire system. In this chapter, we will explore these concerns as well as the countermeasures which can be implemented technically and operationally to address them all.

This chapter will explore the key concerns around system security for infrastructure edge computing.

12.2 Threat Modelling

Any discussion of system security should begin from an agreed understanding of what the threats to that system are and the priority which should be given to their prevention. A realistic threat model for the system, therefore, is an essential step to understanding the security that is achievable given other concerns such as operational efficiency and any budgetary requirements. The outcome of this activity helps to determine the security posture of the system. Attempting to secure the system in a meaningful way before understanding the threats which these security measures are attempting to protect against is inefficient at best and futile at its worst, as it is acting without understanding first.

Understanding Infrastructure Edge Computing: Concepts, Technologies and Considerations,
First Edition. Alex Marcham.
© 2021 John Wiley & Sons Ltd. Published 2021 by John Wiley & Sons Ltd.

In this context, system security refers to the security of the infrastructure edge computing network as well as the equipment which is deployed within the network and the applications that it supports.

It is tempting during the threat modelling process to decree that no level of security risk whatsoever is acceptable and that the system must be entirely free of any security concerns in order to be a real success. This point of view is not without merit, as in an ideal world such a level of security would be practically achievable; however, for any system of even minimal complexity, it is not feasible for this level of security assurance to be achieved. Therefore, we must accept that some security challenges are best identified and accepted rather than attempt to eliminate all possible security issues entirely.

The types of security issues relevant to the infrastructure edge computing network can be separated into three primary categories based on the intent behind any malicious activities which may occur:

1) Confidentiality
   a) An attacker may seek to access confidential information, such as the payment card information held by an application operating at the infrastructure edge or some part of the confidential operational information of the network itself, such as a password.
2) Integrity
   a) Alternatively, an attacker may seek to corrupt the integrity of data or of the entire system itself. An example of this is replacing an application's stored data with some data other than what the original user intended or redirecting any network traffic.
3) Availability
   a) The availability of the system is also a security consideration as if there is an issue which allows an attacker to take the infrastructure edge computing network or one of its customers offline for a period of time, this is a serious breach of system control.

A system cannot be proven to be ultimately secure, as new security issues are uncovered regularly across systems of all levels of complexity. Many attacks target more than one of these issue types in order to achieve a particular aim, such as acquiring confidential information which then allows some attacker to compromise the availability of the system. The importance of each category should then be ranked according to the concerns of each infrastructure or application operator that is involved.

To aid the threat modelling process, we can sort any possible security issues into a few categories that allow us to understand the many unique elements present within each of them. These include:

1) Design security
   a) The initial design of a system can either bolster or hinder the security level which is achievable to a dramatic extent. By applying principles of secure system design, an entire system can be considerably more secure than one which added measures of security as an afterthought to a foundation which was not first designed for them.
2) Operational security
   a) The operational security category includes security issues that may arise due to the ongoing operational activity required to keep the system running, such as how any site maintenance is performed, how security patches are applied, or how strictly the access control mechanisms to a specific restricted part of the system are managed.
3) Technical security
   a) Also referred to as implementation security, this category includes security issues which become apparent due to flaws or design choices in components of the system such as chosen pieces of hardware or software that are used as part of the design.

It is vital to understand each of these categories in order to achieve system security both at the time of initial deployment and on an ongoing basis. Even design security which may appear to be final once it has been defined should be considered set in stone; if a sufficiently serious security issue is found, the ideal design will be modular or alterable enough to accommodate a design solution to the issue which can be addressed by implementing an updated design for that affected part of the system.

Threat modelling is a highly involved activity and this book cannot cover all of the possible activities which it encompasses. However, an understanding of each of the major categories of attack and the categories of security issues which can occur within a system will allow us to better understand the attack surface that the infrastructure edge computing network, its users, and customers really have.

12.3 Physical Security

An infrastructure edge data centre is a facility which, at full utilisation, may be filled with millions of dollars' worth of equipment as well as valuable user data. It is also typically located in a remote area without the benefit of dedicated human onsite physical security measures. These factors make the physical design of the infrastructure edge data centre in the context of being able to maintain multi-tenant security very important to maintain economical and trustworthy operation of each facility.

Some of the challenges related to designing a physically secure infrastructure edge data centre have been described in previous chapters, as well as how a network may be designed in a way that utilises physically diverse paths in order to protect against an accidental or malicious service outage. Some of the operational security procedures which can be used to enhance physical security, such as the use of security cameras and automated security systems, have also been described previously too. Physical security measures such as mantraps can contribute significantly to site security but cannot entirely remove the risk of unwanted access occurring at an infrastructure edge data centre facility. Smaller size category facilities may be equipped only with an alarm and remote notification abilities.

External threats to infrastructure also have to be considered. This is especially true for infrastructure edge data centres which are physical structures deployed above ground in distributed locations that are not economical to staff with full-time onsite security personnel. Although a vandal may not have access to a backhoe or the knowledge of where particular fibre network routes are underground, the infrastructure edge data centre may become a target for someone wanting to disrupt part of a city's network infrastructure or as a general act of vandalism for any other reason. Even when access to a data centre cannot be achieved, damage can occur to the external equipment of the facility such as destroying or spray painting its security cameras and damaging door locks, which would disrupt the standard operations of the facility. Such attacks are much more difficult to prevent but can often be protected against by the use of higher fencing, perimeter security alarms, or the occasional presence of a guard at the facility to introduce an element of doubt for any potential attacker as to whether a facility is manned or not. Again, the cost of protecting against such an attack must be weighed with the impact of the attack were it to succeed in order to verify that any security measures are worth it.

Visually and audibly, any network or data centre infrastructure should be designed in such a way that does not call unneeded attention to itself. While this does not eliminate the risk of external damage, it can help to avoid opportunistic or random attacks perpetrated for unrelated causes or due to factors such as conspiracy theories concerning the effects of technology on the human body as have occurred against cellular network infrastructure during the early stages of fifth generation (5G) deployment.

12.4 Logical Security

The logical security of the infrastructure edge computing network is very similar to that of any other data centre facility and network operator. There are no significant distinctions which infrastructure edge computing imposes on the logical security of the data centre or the network, and so the typical system security measures used for any large scale commercial network system can be applied here.

One of the key logical security concepts which applies to infrastructure edge computing is defence in depth. This is the concept that there is no single point of protection for the system from any external or internal attacks; rather, there are cheques and balances at each point in the network which prevent attacks from developing as best they can. At each point within the infrastructure edge computing network, such as an ingress or egress point for network traffic in and out of an infrastructure edge data centre facility, spoofing detection, protocol filtering, and other firewall functions can be used to reduce the impact of an attacker who is able to gain a foothold within any single piece of the system.

As the majority of access to an infrastructure edge computing network will occur remotely, it is vital that the remote access vectors be properly secured by utilising secure credentials, cryptographically secure protocols, and secure operating procedures that prevent unwanted accesses from occurring.

The core technologies underlying infrastructure edge computing as it relates to remote access and logical security are not unique to the infrastructure edge computing model, and so the usual advice such as updating software on operational systems to remain up to date and reduce the total attack surface of the system, limiting the number of administrative users, and ensuring that credentials are rotated applies to the infrastructure edge computing network operator as it does to other entities.

12.5 Common Security Issues

Many of the security issues described in this section fall into the operational and technical security categories. In some cases, these issues can be avoided or partially mitigated by design security, but they typically require measures which involve elements from all three categories to be addressed.

12.5.1 Staff

Infrastructure edge computing network operator staff are typically in privileged positions and are able to influence the operation of the system in ways which could be used to create or exacerbate security concerns. Whether accidental or malicious, staff are a key contributor to security concerns across the entire infrastructure edge computing network, especially at its edge data centre facilities.

The principle of least privilege applies well to staff in an infrastructure edge computing scenario; it is the idea that a staff member should have access only to the information and resources required for them to do their specific role and that any other access granted on a temporary basis or as part of a previous role should be reviewed and then revoked regularly to prevent any issues from occurring.

Like any role which has access to sensitive information, it a sensible precaution once a staff member leaves to change the access credentials they were using or were aware of to prevent any occurrence of unauthorised access to facilities or their supporting systems. This is a common attack vector that is used by disgruntled ex-staff members across a range of different systems, and an unmanned data centre facility should be considered no different in terms of its risk profile as there is not likely to be anyone else at the site who would be able to identify and prevent the ex-staff member from being able to access the site and potentially disrupt its operation within the timeframe of such an attack.

12.5.2 Visitors

Considering that any multi-tenant data centre is a shared physical space, there should be no surprise that visitors to the facility are a potential source of security issues both for the facility itself as well as for the equipment of any customers within that facility. Visitors from one company may attempt to disrupt the equipment of a competing company which is deployed within the same facility, and if a visitor is left to their own devices, they may either accidentally or maliciously compromise the safety and operations of the site by leaving doors open, sharing access codes, or any other number of easily avoidable issues which can be difficult to troubleshoot and prevent with an unmanned remote site.

Although it is more practical to arrange a site technician from the infrastructure edge computing network operator to be at a particular data centre facility when a customer arranges a site visit compared to 24/7/365 onsite security personnel, it is still not economically favourable when the number of infrastructure edge data centres and customers for these facilities in a single market begins to grow. Some infrastructure edge computing network operators, however, may choose to require this and generally position onsite visitors as unnecessary entirely to dissuade these issues.

If visitors must be allowed onsite, it is sensible to use surveillance cameras and audio recording equipment in and outside of the facility and to remind any visitors that it is in use by noting this throughout a site visitation agreement and via onsite signage to curb any offensive behaviour.

12.5.3 Network Attacks

There are three main categories of network attacks that must be considered by the infrastructure edge network operator. They are listed here in order of increasing severity for the overall system:

1) Undesired access to operator systems
   a) No customer or other non-operator entity must be able to access the control and monitoring systems that the infrastructure edge computing network

operator uses to ensure the operation and security of their infrastructure. If such an attack were successful, individual data centre facilities, network connections, or even the whole system may be taken offline or be made to operate in a reduced or unsafe manner.

2) Undesired access to customer systems

a) The operator must have sufficient protections in place to prevent any customers or other entities from accessing the equipment of other customers deployed in one or many of their data centre facilities. Although the infrastructure edge computing network operator is responsible for the security of the network and of its facilities, the customers of these data centres also must take sensible precautions in order to protect their equipment, as an example of a real defence in depth security strategy.

3) Customer to customer system access

a) Attacks in this category are distinct from the customer to customer communication that is allowed by the network interconnection capabilities offered by the operator. These attacks may not pose any threat to the operations of the customers but may allow them to bypass the infrastructure edge computing network operator and cut them out of the business arrangements required for data to be exchanged between networks. Although referring to this category as attacks may seem odd, an attack is any effort by any party to disrupt the normal operation of the infrastructure edge computing network, and in this example, both of the customers are circumventing the operator, which limits the operator's ability to monetise or benefit from them.

Although these three categories of issues are common concerns for the infrastructure edge operator themselves, the applications running atop their infrastructure will introduce additional complexities.

12.6 Application Security

Two categories of application security exist in the context of infrastructure edge computing network security. First, there are the applications which the operator themselves uses in order to operate the network for purposes such as network management, security system operation, and facility access. As they are part of the operations of the infrastructure edge data centre facilities and their network infrastructure, the security of these applications is the responsibility of the operator even if they are brought in from an external source. Unaddressed vulnerabilities in these applications are especially dangerous as they may be used to control the operational technology of an infrastructure edge data centre facility, resulting in the failure of the facility and potentially deeper penetration in the system.

Second, there are the applications which the customers who have deployed equipment within the infrastructure edge data centre are operating for the benefit of their end customers. These are not the responsibility of the infrastructure edge computing network operator, as long as the operator has met all of the security requirements stated in their service level agreement (SLA), such as maintaining physical separation between customers within a data centre facility, and any specified network security protection such as facility firewalls. As these applications will often be publicly available to many different end users, the task of securing them is complex and dependent on their specific technologies and architecture.

Both of these categories of applications are ultimately reliant on a foundational level of security that the infrastructure edge computing network operator is able to provide, but it is important to draw a distinction between the responsibilities of the application operator and the infrastructure operator.

12.7   Security Policy

Every organisation which is responsible for computer infrastructure, equipment, or data should have a written security policy which defines the security posture of the organisation and its expectations for its partners. These documents can be very complex for an organisation which is involved in key areas such as financial services, but even for other industries they should contain a few key things:

1) Expected threat landscape
   a) As described earlier in this chapter, the expected threat landscape for the assets which the organisation is trying to protect should be determined and documented such that a shared understanding of the accepted and unaccepted threats that the organisation has considered is available for everyone to model any protections on.
2) Designated security officer
   a) The security officer is a single person within the organisation who is responsible for the coordination of the overall system security effort within the organisation and is typically also the point person for any identified breaches or other incidents which are detected. As such, this is a key role with a lot of responsibility and may often be assigned to a Chief Security Officer (CSO), a Chief Information Officer (CIO), or a specific dedicated individual with the right skill set.
3) Issue reporting procedure
   a) A standard method to handle the reporting of security issues is to have a page on the company website which lists an email address suitable for the anonymous and rapid submission of any identified issues. This address will typically forward on to that of the designated security officer to ensure they

are notified of any issues in a timely manner, and they can then begin to coordinate the response to the issue.

4) Breach disclosure policy
   a) An additional level of activity is establishing a bug bounty programme where the organisation incentivises friendly hackers to identify security issues with their systems and then submit them directly and responsibly to the organisation for a reward, which is typically monetary compensation and a mention of their name in any update or patch notes. Even if a bug bounty programme is not utilised, a breach disclosure policy is needed such that customers can be aware of any vital issues.

5) Incident response policy
   a) The incident response policy defines, once a real security incident is identified and categorised, how the organisation will respond. Although this may seem simple to those who have not been through the response process for a live security incident, these are often high stress situations with many unknown factors that bring in many key figures from across an organisation such as the legal and public relations teams. A coordinated response across all of these teams is vital to protect the image of the organisation and to ensure that detail which could lead to more issues is not missed.

6) Issue correction schedule
   a) Once an issue has been identified, it is important that it can be classified and that an understanding of the time and resources that are needed to resolve it can be arrived at using that classification. This schedule can then be communicated out to all of the affected parties, both internally and, where needed, externally to set expectations.

The use of infrastructure edge computing has some implications for the security policy that is used by an organisation, but it is not significantly different from the security policies which already exist due to the use of any cloud computing services, data centre colocation, or infrastructure operation.

Ideally the security policy should be published externally in a reduced form where needed such that customers and partners can easily see the security posture of the organisation and act accordingly.

12.8 Summary

As with all areas of information technology, security is a concern which must be addressed on an ongoing basis in the context of infrastructure edge computing. The path to addressing it in a clear and consistent manner which minimises risk begins by defining key items such as the organisational security policy, the threat model for the organisation and for specific systems, and in understanding that even with high levels of precaution, security incidents can still occur – but that when they do occur, they can be handled well or handled poorly. The majority of these issues are not at all unique to the infrastructure edge computing model, but a good understanding of them will help improve security.

In the next chapter, we will explore some technologies related to infrastructure edge computing.

13

Related Technologies

13.1 Overview

As the definition of infrastructure edge computing has solidified over time, many of its core concepts have interacted with or are related to other technologies. Many of these technologies concern the concept of a gradient of network and data centre resources positioned topologically between a user and the regional or national data centre (RNDC), but they address this idea differently, are adjacent to it, or are simply often mentioned in the same conversation or used interchangeably with infrastructure edge computing. This has been the source of a lot of confusion in the edge computing space to date.

In this chapter, we will explore some of the most prominent of these technologies as well as how or if they relate to infrastructure edge computing. Each of these technologies is complex in its own way, and this chapter does not intend to provide a deep dive into any single one of them but rather will provide the reader with an understanding of how each technology relates to the infrastructure edge.

13.2 Multi-access Edge Computing (MEC)

The core concept behind Multi-access Edge Computing (MEC) is to allow cellular network operators to break out and serve network traffic at locations closer to their end users, at or near the edge of the last mile or access fourth generation (4G) Long-Term Evolution (LTE) or fifth generation (5G) network. The exact definitions of what this means vary from operator to operator, but it is common to see two main definitions: one which says MEC is a set of application programming interfaces

Understanding Infrastructure Edge Computing: Concepts, Technologies and Considerations,
First Edition. Alex Marcham.
© 2021 John Wiley & Sons Ltd. Published 2021 by John Wiley & Sons Ltd.

(APIs) which have been created to allow an operator to create this form of local network breakout and route network traffic accordingly, and one which says that MEC is the combination of these capabilities and the physical facilities from which they will operate.

An infrastructure edge data centre facility can be used as the place from which these MEC solutions operate, as long as the needed network interconnection is achieved. Once network interconnection is established with various types of last mile or access network, as described in Chapter 7, network traffic routing can occur in order to direct that traffic to an edge location where applicable in order to improve performance. This process is made easier in a 5G network where User Plane Functions (UPFs) can be created virtually to support this aim. As such, an operator does not need to deploy a separate set of MEC services to perform this type of local breakout; but in many cases, network operators are calling a range of services such as workload orchestration and operational controls an MEC solution, which introduces additional confusion. Some even use it just to refer to infrastructure edge computing.

However, the term MEC itself belongs to the European Telecommunications Standards Institute (ETSI), which creates many standards, APIs, and documentation [1] for the use of MEC to support new categories of use cases. For a precise written definition of what ETSI defines as MEC, the reader is recommended to read current ETSI documentation while remaining aware that it may not match what is being referred to as MEC by many network operators and that other entities such as large cloud providers are likely to introduce their own APIs to make use of the new resource gradient.

MEC began as Mobile Edge Computing and was later broadened to Multi-access in order to account for the needs of wired network operators such as those operating cable last mile or access networks.

13.3   Internet of Things (IoT) and Industrial Internet of Things (IIoT)

Internet of things (IoT) generally refers to a system model where various small computing devices, typically sensors which utilise wireless network connectivity and battery power, are deployed in a variety of places that to date have not been connected to network resources. This then allows data to be gathered from these places, such as from various points inside of an engine, that can then be analysed. The value of doing this is to perform preventative maintenance or identify otherwise unknown issues with buildings, vehicles, cities, or even people in the case of medical devices sensing key vital signs.

Since IoT has become a popular term in the industry, it has unfortunately been applied to many use cases and devices to which it does not strictly apply. Much like blockchain, artificial intelligence (AI), and edge computing itself, IoT as a term is often misused, and it can be difficult at times to tell what is and is not a real example of IoT. Due to their existence near the edge of the last mile or access network, it has not been too rare to see IoT and edge computing referred to in the same sentence, causing confusion.

The majority of IoT use cases can be classified as a device edge entity which requires the use of some type of resource within a data centre in order to operate. In many cases, IoT use cases, when using a large number of IoT devices, can generate such a significant amount of data that they are best served using an infrastructure edge computing network to reduce network congestion compared to moving all of the generated data to a RNDC. However, this assumes that the data is being generated by the IoT devices in sufficiently large quantities for the locality of the data centre to significantly change the cost of data transportation. Regardless, IoT and infrastructure edge are complementary concepts which can support each other and do not have a large functional overlap.

The industrial internet of things (IIoT) can be considered a subset of IoT which is dedicated to the application of the principles of IoT to industrial environments and use cases such as monitoring the operating statistics of an electrical grid, automating the operating of valves in a water system, and connecting disparate industrial operations systems together such that they can become a part of a single system. Other than this distinction, there is little functional or conceptual difference between IoT and IIoT, and in practice the dividing line between the two is often blurred or just non-existent.

As it is a subset of IoT, IIoT is also complementary to infrastructure edge computing with little to no overlap between the two concepts. Device edge IoT devices may utilise infrastructure edge services.

13.4 Fog and Mist Computing

Fog and mist computing are two terms which have fallen out of favour in recent years but are still referenced in some discussions around infrastructure edge computing and IoT. Historically it has been difficult to arrive at definitive definitions of what these terms mean, which has limited their adoption within the industry. That said, this section will describe their generally used definitions.

Fog computing refers to the placement of compute resources at what we have referred to as the device edge, specifically in the form of a gateway device, which sits topologically between other devices at the device edge and the last mile or access network which ultimately connects those devices to the rest of the system, and to the infrastructure edge computing network. This gateway can then perform some limited processing on the data from other devices before it is passed on to the last mile or access network, such as deduplicating sensor readings or providing a local insight.

Mist computing also refers to the placement of compute resources at what we have referred to in this book as the device edge. Depending on the source of the information, mist computing may refer simply to device edge resources or the deployment of IoT devices which perform computations on their limited local hardware, which is still an example of computation at the device edge, and which then utilise a gateway device which would itself be under the category of fog computing to operate.

Both of these terms are challenging to attach significant value to, as they represent existing concepts and devices, and then attempt to categorise them into two new categories without adding much in the way of a new conceptual framework which allows these concepts and devices to be used in a new and interesting way. However, there is ongoing development in these areas, and so they may emerge over time as unique and valuable subsets of the device edge which enable valuable new use cases.

13.5 Summary

In this chapter, we have briefly described a few of the technologies which are related in various ways to infrastructure edge computing. These technologies have often been discussed and confused with infrastructure edge computing when in most cases they are complementary or even are actually use cases themselves for infrastructure edge computing, rather than being real competing technologies.

In the next chapter, we will examine 5G as a use case example for infrastructure edge computing.

Reference

1 ETSI (2020). Multi-access Edge Computing (MEC) [Internet]. [cited 2020 Sep 30]. Available from: https://www.etsi.org/technologies/multi-access-edge-computing

14

Use Case Example

5G

14.1 Overview

The suitability of fifth generation (5G) networks for deployment at the infwrastructure edge is especially important as by these networks being present at distributed infrastructure edge data centres (IEDCs), the infrastructure edge computing network will carry significant amounts of the total user data for these 5G networks while providing data centre resources which can be positioned locally enough to enable the lowest latency between a user and their application workload, supporting new key low latency use cases.

In this chapter, we will explore some of the ways in which infrastructure edge computing can support the deployment and operation of the 5G radio access network (RAN) and core network at either a regional or national scale.

14.2 What Is 5G?

5G is the latest generation of cellular network technology that has been standardised and, at the time of writing, is beginning to see deployment internationally. The standards for cellular network connectivity had evolved consistently over the previous decades with a new generation appearing roughly every 10 years. Between these major steps of evolution are small standard releases which incorporate various performance and feature updates that allow the network to operate in a higher performance, lower cost, or more functionally rich way than was permitted by the original standard.

Understanding Infrastructure Edge Computing: Concepts, Technologies and Considerations,
First Edition. Alex Marcham.
© 2021 John Wiley & Sons Ltd. Published 2021 by John Wiley & Sons Ltd.

The key 5G standards in the context of infrastructure edge computing can be separated into two main categories: those that are concerned with the radio network (5G New Radio [5G NR]) and those for the core network (5G core network [5G CN]). IEDC facilities and their supporting network connectivity can support either of these categories and so can bridge together the RAN and core in a way that has not been possible before now.

14.2.1   5G New Radio (NR)

The 5G NR radio network is composed of a few key components which interoperate together.

14.2.1.1   Remote Radio Unit (RRU)

The remote radio unit (RRU) is the system component which is responsible for the physical receipt and transmission of radio signals from and to user devices that are connected to the 5G network. It takes the form of a radio unit which is connected to or integrated with an antenna array, which is to be deployed at a location such as a telecommunications radio tower so that it can communicate with the user devices within its coverage area with the least wasted signal energy and chances for errors.

14.2.1.2   Distributed Unit (DU)

As the first 5G NR RAN system component which performs signal processing on the data to and from the RRU, the distributed unit (DU) requires decent processing power and must be located within a specific distance from the RRU, as limited by the maximum latency which is acceptable between the RRU and its associated DU. The DU performs radio signal processing functions and can be supported by specialised software running on general purpose central processing unit (CPU) or on accelerator hardware, including graphics processing units (GPUs).

14.2.1.3   Centralised Unit (CU)

The centralised unit (CU) is responsible for the coordination of multiple DUs which are connected to it. It can be split into halves, one of which performs user plane tasks and another that then performs control plane tasks, both on data passed up from the DU or down from the core network. Each DU must be supported by a CU, and each CU must have at least one DU connected to it to be operating.

14.2.1.4   Functional Splits

To date, this section has described a 5G NR RAN which is using the 7-2 functional split. There are many other functional splits available in the standards which allow for different sets of functional splits, each of which has its own unique characteristics and requirements on the infrastructure that is being used to support the 5G network. Essentially, these splits are numbered 1 through 8, and the higher the split number, the less functionality is present within the RRU. The less functionality that is within the RRU, the greater the opportunity for the network operator to deploy technologies such as coordinated multi-point, which allows the operator to make more efficient use of their radio spectrum.

The 7-2 functional split and the 7-2x functional split are currently the most popular functional splits. The latter is used by the open radio access network (O-RAN) consortium, which is creating ways for network operators to utilise key RAN components from different vendors as part of an open system. This is in comparison to previous generations of cellular technology where vendor lock-in was difficult to avoid due to the prevalence of these vendors providing monolithic single vendor technology sets.

14.2.2 5G Core Network (CN)

In a similar way to the 5G NR RAN, the 5G CN is composed of a set of discrete components which are able to communicate with one another using interfaces defined by the Third Generation Partnership Project (3GPP) standards organisation.

14.2.2.1 User Plane Function (UPF)

For the purpose of this book, the User Plane Function (UPF) is the most important element of the 5G CN. As the user plane and control plane are separated in the 5G network, it is possible to deploy UPF capabilities at a data centre facility which is being controlled by a control plane entity operating in another location, so long as the performance between both facilities is satisfactory. This makes UPF deployment flexible and even software automatable as the needs of the network dictate over time.

The UPF is the point in the 5G network where user data can be taken off of or put onto the network. This provides a standards compliant local breakout function where the 5G network can interconnect with external networks and offload or ingest data without the use of third party solutions. The exact UPF of interest for this scenario is the packet session anchor (PSA) UPF, which represents an external network for routing purposes to the 5G CN. When traffic destined for such an external network, such as a cloud provider or a source of content, reaches the PSA UPF, it can exit the 5G network and utilise standard Internet Protocol (IP) routing to reach its destination. This is a key component of how the 5G CN can support a lower latency between a 5G network user and any application instance operating in the data centre.

14.2.2.2 Control Plane

There are many functions of the 5G CN control plane which are vital to the operation of the network, handling key tasks such as access control, authentication, and handover. However, this is a subject all by itself which could fill a book, and so this chapter will focus on the user plane as this part of the 5G network can achieve the most obvious benefit from the use of infrastructure edge computing. In the example described in this chapter, the control plane will not be shown and may exist at a regional or national scale data centre but may also exist at an IEDC if that is required.

14.3   5G at the Infrastructure Edge

The infrastructure edge computing network can be used to support both the 5G NR RAN and 5G CN.

14.3.1   Benefits

When using the 7-2 functional split or 7-2x functional split, there is a large amount of radio signal processing that is required when all of the tower locations for even a moderate size of 5G network is considered. If the network operator wishes to perform these functions using general purpose hardware, which will allow them to avoid vendor lock-in and have the greatest control and flexibility over the network in regard to operations, upgrades, and purchasing decisions, there is the need for data centre facilities which are located within a certain distance of each RRU across the network so that these facilities can host the DUs and often the CUs. Although the exact figure varies depending on the source and the vendor involved, the latency required between the RRU and its accompanying DU ranges from 75 to 250 μ, which equals the need to have an IEDC facility or another location capable of supporting the processing required by the DU within roughly 10 to 32.5 miles.

Although there are many optimisations in the 5G NR radio standards which allow a lower latency for data transmissions between a user and the 5G NR RAN, if there is a nearby edge exchange point (EXP) in an IEDC which is interconnected with a network of interest, the 5G network operator may choose to deploy a 5G CN PSA UPF in this location and perform local breakout in that facility in order to achieve a lower latency between user and application, as well as lower upstream network usage. This is beneficial for both the 5G network operator and the infrastructure edge computing network. Note that if a UPF is not in a location, network traffic cannot be broken out to any external network and so it will be transported to the nearest PSA UPF in the network, which may increase its latency.

14.3.2   Architecture

An example of how the infrastructure edge computing network can be used to support a 5G NR RAN is shown using the diagram in Figure 14.1. Note that in this

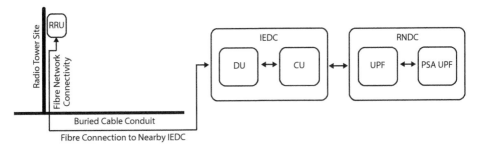

Figure 14.1 Example architecture for 5G RAN deployment using infrastructure edge.

diagram, size category 2 IEDC facilities are used to perform the processing required by the 5G NR RAN at distributed sites.

As can be seen in Figure 14.1, the infrastructure edge computing model with its method of deploying and operating large numbers of physically small, distributed data centre facilities is a good solution to the dispersed processing needs of the 5G NR RAN. In this area it would be challenging to locate any other suitable facilities which meet the security and performance requirements of the network, and so the IEDC facilities are the best option for this 5G network deployment.

14.3.3 Considerations

Although the amount of radio processing which is required by the DUs of the network is quite large in aggregate, individually it may be small enough for even a size category 1 IEDC facility to accommodate depending on the number of RRUs and their specific parameters that include channel bandwidth, transmission layers, and other characteristics. Ideally the infrastructure edge network operator can establish a full understanding of these needs before deploying facilities.

For especially rural locations, the 5G network operator may even choose to deploy their 5G NR RAN utilising a different functional split which eliminates the tight latency bound described earlier, even at the cost of reduced flexibility. This is an economic choice to be made by the 5G network operator at their discretion, which may prove attractive despite the benefits of a higher number functional split.

Additionally, other facilities may exist which provide adequate compute equipment capacity for the needs of the 5G NR RAN. Essentially any facility within the latency bound of the RRUs in question is worth considering for this purpose, although many which are not suitable for use as a data centre will be weeded out quickly from this selection process. Some network operators may also look to deploy their own facilities in order to support these processing requirements, although in that case the economic benefits of the infrastructure edge computing model's use of shared infrastructure will likely be difficult to beat when compared to deploying and operating many single tenant facilities.

Some 5G network operators may utilise their current operational processes and rely on a centralised network architecture, using lower functional splits and aggregating the network at a few key points.

14.4 Summary

In this chapter, we described how an infrastructure edge computing network can support a 5G NR and 5G CN network. Although it is not a magic bullet, infrastructure edge computing can play a key role in supporting both aspects of the 5G network and can have a significant positive impact on both.

In the next chapter, we will explore how infrastructure edge computing can benefit distributed artificial intelligence (AI).

15

Use Case Example

Distributed AI

15.1 Overview

One of the most promising use cases for infrastructure edge computing is distributed artificial intelligence (AI), where the key functional components of an AI system are physically spread out across an example area such as a city in order to provide an optimal level of performance, scale, and cost to the end user. This type of distributed architecture for AI applications relies on infrastructure edge computing and its ability to deploy and operate a number of infrastructure edge data centre (IEDC) facilities across an area that are interconnected both to each other and to regional points of interest such as any larger data centres.

As will be explored in this chapter, there are many use cases for distributed AI which will drive the adoption of both AI and infrastructure edge computing. These use cases include computer vision, where distributed AI resources are used to perform visual analysis of still or moving images such as improving the speed and accuracy of patient diagnoses using medical imaging technologies or using automated video security systems to improve threat detection and tracking. They also include many areas that rely on natural language processing (NLP) such as voice-based AI assistants and analysing data to extract new actionable insights from sources such as large-scale internet of things (IoT) networks in a smart city.

Understanding Infrastructure Edge Computing: Concepts, Technologies and Considerations,
First Edition. Alex Marcham.
© 2021 John Wiley & Sons Ltd. Published 2021 by John Wiley & Sons Ltd.

15.2 What Is AI?

AI is a wide field which has been of interest to scientists and engineers for decades and which has tremendously shaped many areas of science, technology, and pop culture. Although the malevolent likes of HAL 9000 from 2001: A Space Odyssey are not with us quite yet, the technology has advanced beyond what many once considered possible and has accelerated especially rapidly over the past decade due to numerous important innovations across hardware, software, and algorithm design.

Today AI is commonly defined as the simulation of intelligent behaviour in computers. One concept that is integral to this intelligent behaviour is that of an intelligent agent, which can be defined to be any device which is capable of perceiving its environment and then taking actions in order to achieve its goals. Consider the example of a speech recognition system which attempts to analyse the speech from a user to determine which podcast to play or a robotic delivery vehicle which uses cameras to understand its physical environment and navigate around any obstacles which appear along its path.

All of these applications are examples of narrow AI, where an AI system is tuned to provide answers to a specific set of questions, regardless of what they may be. General AI systems in comparison aim to be skilled at a large number of tasks and be able to generalise and apply their knowledge of one problem to another in a similar way to how humans and many animals operate. These systems are difficult to create, and so narrow AI is the focus of operational examples of AI technologies today.

For the purposes of this book, we will use the term AI to refer to the broad category of possible AI, machine learning (ML), and deep learning (DL) techniques which can be applied to solve a wide range of narrow intelligence problems.

15.2.1 Machine Learning (ML)

ML is a subset of AI which is concerned with the ability of a computer system to learn from the events it observes in much the same way as humans do, as opposed to needing to be programmed with a specific output which corresponds to every possible input. This latter approach is familiar to anyone who has written a simple computer programme which utilises an "if this, then that" structure. Although this approach makes sense for the types of logical operations which computers have traditionally performed, it does not fit well for tasks attempting to emulate human reasoning. In such tasks there are often far too many new variables to consider making this approach practical.

How then can a machine learn if not through this type of static programming performed by humans?

Modern ML is centred around the idea of an artificial neural network (ANN). These neural networks are structures which emulate the type of networks present within the human brain which allow us to make decisions. They range from simple enough to draw on a piece of paper and understand to ones which are incredibly complex and may have thousands of potential stages, or layers, and millions of parameters to consider. At even a low level of complexity it is difficult to predict the performance of an ANN from observing its structure; therefore a training process must occur. This trains the network and allows the developer to understand the performance of the resulting ML model as it is trained.

The performance of the ML model can be measured in several ways. The first consideration is the accuracy of the model. For example, in the case of an ML model dedicated to the detection of any car licence plates within an image from a security camera, the accuracy of the model can be found by feeding security camera image data into the model which the model has not seen before. This data should be tagged beforehand by the developer with whether or not a licence plate is in the image and, if so, what the characters of that licence plate are so that these results can be verified.

Another performance measure for an ML model is the resources it required in order to reach a result from some input data. All other factors being equal, an ML model which requires less compute and network resources than another, for example, should be considered superior to one that needs more.

15.2.2 Deep Learning (DL)

DL is itself a subset of ML which has become more practical as the compute power available through parallel accelerators such as graphics processing units (GPUs) has become widely commercially available over the past decade. The same characteristics of ML that have been described in the previous section apply to DL, though DL allows ANNs with more layers to be created, hence its "deep" moniker. These deeper ANNs are often used for computer vision tasks, as deep networks often perform these well.

Not every application benefits from the addition of more ANN layers. For each added layer, there is a cost in terms of computational complexity and maintainability, which must then be balanced against the additional accuracy which that new layer adds to the ML model. Extensive testing, however, has shown that humans and animals employ a multi-layer process in the brain in order to perceive the world around them where simple shapes are identified first and then combined to form any more complex identification which is required. By emulating this process and utilising a large number of layers within the ANN, a DL model can produce accurate results for a wide range of computer vision tasks in a similar way to biological brains as long as sufficient processing power is available to them.

15.3 AI at the Infrastructure Edge

There are two main functions which must occur within an AI system: training and inferencing. The training process must occur before useful inferences can be made, as otherwise the inferencing process will be flying blind, much like a human being asked to perform a task for the first time with no training or context for the activity. Both training and inferencing require significant processing power in order to be performed at scale and to produce accurate results from complex input data; they can also both be sped up by orders of magnitude if processed by a specialised accelerator such as a GPU, Tensor Processing Unit (TPU), or field programmable gate array (FPGA), as described in Chapter 9, in place of a general purpose central processing unit (CPU). The tasks which AI systems are performing see no signs of decreasing in complexity, which is driving the need to have significant parallel processing resources dedicated to them spread across that gradient of resources.

Training can often require large volumes of data to be effective. The amount of data to be used for training varies widely between different use cases, the requirements of different end users, and the architecture of each ANN in use. For example, the users and operator of an augmented reality (AR) game may be fine if the inferencing accuracy of that use case is lower than that of computer vision being used to assist visual diagnosis of oncological issues at a hospital. There is a trade-off between training cost and time, and the impact of an incorrect inference on the application and its end users.

Inferencing, depending on the specific use case, may need to be performed in real time or soft real time in order to be useful. For example, where a system is using a computer vision model in order to control the navigation of a vehicle in the physical world, it must be capable of perceiving the world as well as or better than the average human navigator to ensure that the vehicle can operate safely. This imposes latency constraints on the system which in turn make performing inferencing tasks at locations close to the user, such as at the infrastructure edge or the device edge, highly preferable.

15.3.1 Benefits

By distributing the training and inferencing functions across the resource gradient from the end user to the regional or national data centre based on the needs and cost thresholds of each function of the AI system, a distributed AI model can be created where a single application utilising AI functions can operate each of its components using various resource sets across the resource gradient in order to achieve the vital performance, cost, and functionality goals that are needed for it to be successful.

Distributed AI is applicable to a wide number of potential use cases. For example, many of the most immediately appreciable use cases concern image inferencing where hardware and software that is optimised to identify specific things within a stream of image data and then generate useful insights from that data for the operator of the system are located at the IEDC and capable of operating in a real time or soft real time fashion, providing some human-like intelligence.

Intelligent video analytics (IVA) is the name given to a segment of the market which performs tasks like these using computer vision. Licence plate detection, facial recognition, customer tracking within stores, intent detection for security systems, automated highlight detection for sporting events, and many other use cases are good examples of IVA which can be accelerated by a distributed AI model.

By distributing the inferencing function to the infrastructure edge computing network, the operator of the application can benefit by achieving a lower latency to the resources performing processing of the image data than if they were located in a regional or national data centre facility and lowering the cost of data transmission due to the locality of the IEDC facility. At the same time, training is typically best performed in a regional or national data centre facility which has access to a large number of networks to assemble training data, and the model can then be pushed to each IEDC facility once it has been trained at a fraction of the size of the original training data. This functional split enables the application to be scalable and performant.

15.3.2 Architecture

A key consideration when architecting a distributed AI system which is utilising infrastructure edge computing is the functional split between components of the AI system present in different physical locations. This choice drives many of the architectural decisions across the network, data centre, and application infrastructure required to support the distributed AI system and its use cases. In this case, we will utilise the functional split described earlier, where model training is performed in a regional or national data centre facility while inferencing is performed in real time at the infrastructure edge.

As can be seen in Figure 15.1, the distributed AI system maps well across the infrastructure edge computing network and the regional or national data centre according to this functional split. For our use case, we will use a delivery vehicle which must have accurate image inferencing results from its computer vision application workload component in order to safely navigate the physical world on its way to making deliveries. By operating this component from the infrastructure edge computing network where one or more edge data centre facilities are within a 50-ms round trip of the device, we can provide adequate performance for this use case which would not be possible using the closest regional or national data centre in

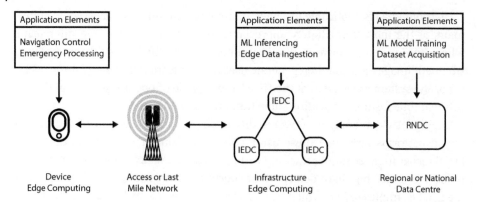

Figure 15.1 Example architecture for distributed AI deployment using infrastructure edge.

this instance. However, due to the scale of the training activity required by this use case, the regional or national data centre is preferable to the infrastructure edge computing network for this component. In many cases, the device itself, which in this case is the delivery robot, will be capable of performing some limited inferencing using its own onboard hardware systems. In this example, we have assumed that this will be limited to ensuring that data which is sent to the infrastructure edge is valid and not obviously corrupted or of irrelevant things.

15.3.3 Considerations

Distributed AI applications are most effective when the major functional roles of the system can be split between distributed data centre facilities at the infrastructure edge and regional or national data centres. Where this cannot be achieved, the benefit of using multiple resource sets is unclear for many use cases and will result in the entire application being deployed at one location instead.

This split between inferencing and model training operations across multiple physically distinct sites poses architectural challenges for some AI applications. In the case where an application cannot use regular training intervals such as performing model training overnight, it may not be worth using a split architecture due to the complexity it introduces for what may be little or no improvement in performance. However, this can be very situational, and so the use of a split architecture should be considered until economic, technical, or operational factors rule it out, due to its potential benefits.

As briefly mentioned earlier, devices are increasingly equipped with their own inferencing capability through the use of dedicated GPUs, FPGAs, or other ML accelerators. If the inferencing requirements of the application can be met effectively with the onboard capabilities of devices alone, then there may be little reason for the use of the infrastructure edge computing network. The counterpoint to this is that there is likely to always be an increased level of computational complexity which can be utilised in order to achieve greater accuracy or more sophisticated insights from the same data and which will outpace the capabilities of devices. However, this assumes that standards around minimal acceptable levels of performance for tasks such as facial recognition will not find widespread usage.

15.4 Summary

In this chapter, we described how an infrastructure edge computing network can effectively support a distributed AI system which is utilising a functional split where inferencing is being performed at the infrastructure edge computing network and any model training is performed at the regional or national data centre to provide a balance of performance, cost, and functionality for the application.

In the next chapter, we will explore how infrastructure edge computing can support cyber-physical systems, which in many cases themselves will utilise this type of distributed AI architecture as well.

16

Use Case Example

Cyber-physical Systems

16.1 Overview

As new generations of vehicles, robots, and other machinery become practical for use in a wide range of environments and use cases, they require support systems that ensure they are able to operate safely and with the efficiency required to make them economically viable. Infrastructure edge computing, by providing an array of physically distributed data centre facilities which can be local to the operating area of a vehicle, robot, or other machinery and provide low latency network connectivity between the machine and its supporting applications when a regional or national data centre (RNDC) cannot, is a key component of making these cyber-physical systems practical for many uses.

This chapter will explore several of the types of cyber-physical systems as well as key use cases for each of those types. The range of potential applications is vast, such as using autonomous drones to inspect potentially dangerous locations such as the scene of an active fire, supporting the practical operation of driverless cars or other automated transit systems, or enabling smart agriculture that makes achieving greater crop yields a reality in many places across the world to support the planet.

16.2 What Are Cyber-physical Systems?

Cyber-physical systems is a catch-all term which refers to devices which are controlled by software but which interact directly with our physical world. They are able to take actions which manipulate tangible things in much the same way that

Understanding Infrastructure Edge Computing: Concepts, Technologies and Considerations,
First Edition. Alex Marcham.
© 2021 John Wiley & Sons Ltd. Published 2021 by John Wiley & Sons Ltd.

humans or animals do, with examples including use cases such as industrial robotics where tasks are completed on an assembly line using precision robotics, using autonomous vehicles to collect visual data for the inspection of transportation infrastructure, and operating autonomous vehicles which can transport people from place to place, such as cars.

There are many examples of cyber-physical systems, but this section will focus on some of the most commonly discussed and most relevant to infrastructure edge computing as a set of key use cases. Notably all of these use cases combine the need for inferencing on some form of data, often using computer vision as was described in the previous chapter, with a latency sensitive control loop that determines how and when a machine moves in the physical world, which is a vital and real time task.

16.2.1 Autonomous Vehicles

One of the most frequently cited categories of use cases for infrastructure edge computing is autonomous vehicles. There are certainly many useful instances where these two technologies overlap and can benefit one another; however, there is significant nuance in determining these.

Although autonomous vehicles and the connected car may appear to be the same thing, these two concepts are not identical. An autonomous vehicle is one which is capable of navigation, propulsion, and collision avoidance without the aid of a human driver. A connected car on the other hand is a vehicle which maintains network connectivity to some resources, such as navigation assistance or entertainment services, which exist in a remote data centre. An autonomous vehicle is very likely to also be a connected car, but a connected car does not need to support any autonomous operation.

It is also worth stating that the fuel source of the vehicle does not matter in regard to whether it is autonomous or connected. Although many of the discussions of autonomous vehicles imagine them to be electrically powered, there is no technical reason why vehicles powered by fossil fuels cannot also be autonomous; in fact, the pioneering work done in this area such as shown in Defence Advanced Research Projects Agency's (DARPA) series of autonomous car races, the Challenge series held multiple times between 2004 and 2018, used a range of diesel and petrol powered vehicles where autonomous control was achieved by computer manipulation of the drive by wire systems within each vehicle, albeit to varying degrees of success.

Using the levels of autonomy as defined by Society of Automotive Engineering (SAE) International, which show the progression from a vehicle where the driver alone is responsible for the control of its propulsion and navigation all the way through to a fully autonomous vehicle, we can see that there are considerable technical and regulatory challenges to achieve the goal of autonomous vehicles operating on public roads with no need for a human driver even in a supervisory role [1]. Table 16.1 shows

Table 16.1 Autonomy levels and the value of infrastructure edge computing.

Autonomy level number	Autonomy level name	Role of infrastructure edge computing	Value of infrastructure edge computing
0	No Automation	None	None
1	Driver Assistance	Driver information services	Low
2	Partial Automation	Driver information services	Low
3	Conditional Automation	Dynamic driving task execution/ driver information services	High
4	High Automation	Dynamic driving task execution/ driver information services	High
5	Full Automation	Driver information services	Low

the name and number of each of these levels of autonomy, matched to the role and value of infrastructure edge computing:

As can be seen in Table 16.1, there is an interesting curve that forms for the usefulness of infrastructure edge computing when plotted across all of these levels of autonomy. The benefit of infrastructure edge computing peaks at Conditional Automation and High Automation, where the benefits of the infrastructure edge computing model are able to assist the execution of driving tasks in real time.

The use of infrastructure edge computing will not be essential for any of these levels of autonomy to be achieved. This would limit the operation of autonomous vehicles to areas which have very low latency connectivity via a wireless network, most likely a variant of fifth generation New Radio (5G NR), back to applications that operate within a nearby infrastructure edge data centre (IEDC). Although this may be suitable for vehicles such as city buses that could, in a city with a widespread infrastructure edge computing network, feasibly remain within the coverage area of an IEDC at every point of their route, it does not sufficiently provide for the needs of a typical family car which may take more rural trips.

However, it is only true that infrastructure edge computing will not be required to achieve a specific level of autonomy over time. As the type and efficiency of compute resources that are deployed in autonomous vehicles continues to improve, there will be a gap of several years where they are not sufficient to provide fully autonomous vehicle operation. During this period, particularly during the gap between Conditional Automation, High Automation, and Full Automation, the role of resources present at the infrastructure edge can be significant as if used appropriately, they can allow a vehicle to progress one or more levels of autonomy without requiring additional onboard hardware, where they are in the coverage area of an IEDC which is supporting the vehicle.

The role of infrastructure edge computing in the operation of autonomous vehicles should be considered to be augmentative. A connected car, for example, with the onboard capability to achieve an autonomy level of Conditional Automation would be able to achieve High Automation with the assistance of resources present at the infrastructure edge computing network when it is in range of these resources, assuming it has achieved acceptable network performance parameters.

In addition to the systems used to support a physical autonomous vehicle operating in real time, it is also important to consider connected infotainment systems which can aid a human driver in the use of the vehicle by supplying real time navigation assistance or other information. If a car is using this type of service, it can be considered a connected car whether or not it is capable of any autonomous operation, and these connected services may be latency sensitive enough to require edge resources.

16.2.2 Drones

Flying drones, also referred to as unmanned aerial vehicles (UAVs) are now a common sight across many parks and other scenic locations today where they are used for aerial photography and other recreational activities. They are available at a wide range of price points and levels of sophistication ranging from entry level hobbyist aircraft through to those designed for professional use. Although many different form factors are available including fixed wing designs for specialised applications, the most common type of drone seen today utilise a quad, hex, or octo drone design, which allows the aircraft to hover in place, rotate, and move at considerable speed all while remaining stable.

Today these aerial vehicles are typically manually controlled by their operators using a handheld remote-control system which is capable of operating with about half a mile, at most, of distance between the user and the vehicle. The controller may be a standalone device, or it may also be a carrier for the user's smartphone, which just provides additional physical input devices such as joysticks and buttons for flight control as well as a long-range antenna system to maintain the wireless network connectivity required between the controller and the drone when it is in flight.

When thought of as a component of an end-to-end computer vision system rather than as a single device, a drone is most valuable as a means through which to collect visual, spatial, and other data such as audio from locations in the physical world which may be challenging to reach regularly or at all. For many use cases, this is the real role of the drone; it is an aerial data capture device, and the fact that it is a drone is of little real interest beyond it fitting a form factor which can carry a suitable camera payload, maintain stability during flight, and offer a reasonable flight time to execute a plan.

Other use cases which utilise drones as a means to deliver packages are in many ways extensions of this same operational model, with some additional mechanical complications in regard to how they may manipulate the item being delivered and ensuring that delivery is achieved without damage. In these systems regardless of the size and equipment handling capabilities of the drone, it remains reliant on the use of a feedback loop where an entity perceives the environment which the drone can see, identifies any risks, and then navigates the aircraft accordingly to avoid those risks and to perform the planned mission. In the manual use case, a human operator performs these tasks; in an automated system, they are performed back in an IEDC by machine learning (ML) algorithms.

Unlike an autonomous car, which has significant power production capability whether it is using an electrical or fossil fuel-powered system and places to physically mount an array of compute, storage, and network equipment onboard, an aerial vehicle the size of a typical drone does not. Every piece of equipment which is attached to the aircraft adds additional weight, which reduces the flight time, and every processing task stands to increase the power draw of the equipment onboard, which also reduces the total achievable flight time for the aircraft, limiting its effectiveness for its key use cases.

These factors make drones a more ideal user of infrastructure edge computing than autonomous cars. The heavy compute requirements of tasks such as allowing the drone to perceive in real time its environment and act accordingly to avoid obstacles are difficult to perform on a small, aerial, and lightweight vehicle which does not have the capability to generate power once it is in the air, such as an autonomous car may be able to do through regenerative braking. The majority of drones operate using batteries as their power source and so are limited to flight times of typically under one hour.

Although flying drones have captured the imaginations of many, they are far from the only example of how drone technology can be used. There are types of drones which operate in many different and challenging environments across land, sea, and air, with some designed for general purposes while others are intended for specialised use cases such as cave or mine exploration, underwater salvage, and other difficult environments. Regardless of their physical form factors, they are all limited by the equipment and power capacity that they can support, which lends them well to utilising the resource available at the infrastructure edge computing network to perform inferencing and other key tasks.

16.2.3 Robotics

Much of the industrial production efficiency gains projected by the work of organisations involved in creating the next generation of factory operations technology, referred to as Industry 4.0, are to be achieved by using low latency communications between a vast array of sensors that are deployed in an industrial location and a data centre to provide real-time control of machinery using insights that are gathered from these sensors to optimise their operational efficiency and minimise the risk of any incidents such as the incorrect manipulation of a piece of steel, which could then cause a safety issue.

Robotics is a wide category under which connected cars and drones could also be grouped. However, robotics in this chapter refers to the use cases for this technology that are not in either group, so as to differentiate them from one another due to the variation in their requirements from the network and data centre resources that they use to operate as well as the different commercial drivers which will push each of these use cases for infrastructure edge computing forward and into real world use.

An example of this type of robotics use case which can be effectively supported by the infrastructure edge computing model are mechanical arms and other tools which are used to manipulate physical materials in a factory during product construction, such as the assembly lines used to produce cars.

16.2.4 Other Use Cases

There are key supporting functions which can be performed using the resources of an infrastructure edge computing network that assist the design, deployment, and operation of cyber-physical systems across all of the categories described previously and which may be difficult if using another resource set.

Digital twins are a concept from the world of manufacturing where a virtual representation of any manufactured product is created at the same time or after the physical product is produced. This virtual entity can then be subjected to testing, which simulates the type of stresses which the real product will be undergoing as it is used in the physical world. The data resulting from this process can then be used to understand how, where, and if components or an entire system may fail or be made to operate in a non-optimal fashion over time, such as the tyres on a car wearing as it moves.

16.3 Cyber-physical Systems at the Infrastructure Edge

16.3.1 Benefits

Many cyber-physical systems such as UAVs are limited in terms of the battery capacity, and thus the amount of local compute resource, that they can provide.

If sufficiently low latency connectivity to a resource set can augment the local compute resource of the device to the extent that new use cases become practical, then the resource set, located at the infrastructure edge computing network, can be the difference which enables that use case and allows the user and application operator to be able to benefit from the value of the use case, such as operating efficiency and safety improvements.

Additionally, even systems which are not constrained by battery capacity may be constrained by the availability of local compute resource and the difficulty of achieving acceptable latency to resources located in a RNDC. It may not be possible or desirable to add local resource, and so in these scenarios, the infrastructure edge computing network provides a middle ground that solves the requirement of that use case for low latency access to sufficient inferencing capabilities.

In some cases, the device manufacturer may not wish to add sufficient compute resource to a device even if the required hardware is available. This may be due to cost targets for the device, due to the usage profile for the features which that additional hardware would enable, or because of a specific choice made by the manufacturer to operate the device as a thin client where almost all processing is offloaded to the nearest low latency resource set along the resource gradient, which can then be the infrastructure edge computing network in an effort to provide very low cost but capable devices.

16.3.2 Architecture

An example of how the infrastructure edge computing network can be used to support a factory robotics system can be seen in Figure 16.1. For this use case, due to the size of and harsh environment within the manufacturing facility, it is desirable to locate the compute resource required for the automated robotics system to

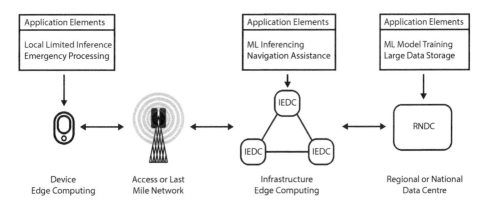

Figure 16.1 Example architecture for cyber-physical systems using infrastructure edge.

operate within the IEDC; in this scenario, the closest RNDC is located more than 50 ms away, rendering it useless.

As can be seen from this diagram, the factory robotics use case is utilising a similar distributed artificial intelligence (AI) framework as was described in the previous chapter. To that end, we have utilised the same split between training in a remote resource set and inferencing in a local resource set to achieve the performance, cost, and functionality required for the factory automation use case to be successful.

16.3.3 Considerations

As was described in Chapter 15, the capabilities of the device edge are increasing at a considerable rate in regard to implementing inferencing resource in devices such as UAVs. As the power usage and processing power of these resources continues to improve, it is possible that most of the real time inferencing can occur on the device itself and will not need to be performed using resource at the infrastructure edge computing network. If this occurs, and the value of additional inferencing which could be performed at these edge data centre facilities is not sufficient for the use case, it is likely that cyber-physical systems will utilise only the device edge and regional or national facilities.

An IEDC, if tasked with performing the inferencing and navigation control for an application such as an industrial robotics system or UAV, must be capable of providing very low latency between the device and its control application operating in the edge data centre facility. The latencies for this task range from 50 to 10 ms depending on the level of autonomy, the speed of operation, and the safety risks of a delayed or missed decision, and so as described in Chapter 7, a direct network interconnection to the wireless network which is being used is absolutely essential.

In some cases, especially for devices or manufacturing facilities which are located in urban areas, it is likely that sufficiently low latency connectivity already exists between that device and the nearest RNDC. Where this is true, there is little real value to using the infrastructure edge computing network instead of the larger facility, which will benefit from its economies of scale.

16.4 Summary

Due to the way in which they merge the need to detect and perceive the physical world in real time with the capability to navigate and manipulate physical objects at high speed, cyber-physical systems are an ideal use case for infrastructure edge computing. However, not every cyber-physical system requires the use of infrastructure edge computing due to the capabilities of the device edge itself.

In the next chapter, we will explore how infrastructure edge computing can be used to support public and private clouds as a key use case. Much like the previous chapter on distributed AI, the deployment of a public or private cloud on the infrastructure edge computing network enables a range of use cases including many of the use cases which were described throughout this chapter.

Reference

1 SAE International (2020). SAE Standards News: J3016 automated-driving graphic update [Internet]. [cited 2020 Sep 30]. Available from: https://www.sae.org/news/2019/01/sae-updates-j3016-automated-driving-graphic

17

Use Case Example

Public or Private Cloud

17.1 Overview

It is fair to say that for many, cloud computing brought the importance of the data centre to the fore over the past decade as it changed how the typical application or service was delivered to its users. Where before applications typically ran on local compute resources, whether an end user's machine or an on-premises data centre or server closet, they are now accessed via the web browser and are operating in a cloud computing instance in a remote data centre which is hundreds or thousands of miles away. The flexibility brought about by this approach in terms of both technology and business has given rise to entire industries which rely on cloud computing, including software as a service (SaaS) and infrastructure as a service (IaaS), which operate applications or platforms remotely, in a cloud.

Cloud computing itself is not a use case per se; rather it is an architecture and supporting ecosystem which can then support a wide range of use cases for a variety of end users. Indeed, these use cases may be others described throughout this book, such as distributed artificial intelligence (AI) or fifth generation (5G) networks; but the needs which come to mind when considering clouds of several different scales make them unique enough to warrant their own chapter as a use case example. Cloud providers will also be some of the most significant customers of infrastructure edge computing network operators, so this focus is sensible.

Understanding Infrastructure Edge Computing: Concepts, Technologies and Considerations,
First Edition. Alex Marcham.
© 2021 John Wiley & Sons Ltd. Published 2021 by John Wiley & Sons Ltd.

17.2 What Is Cloud Computing?

The cloud computing model presents a user with an elastic pool of resources, including processing, data storage, and network capabilities, which the user is then able to use in an on-demand fashion. These resources are typically located and operated remotely from the user, in a large regional or national data centre (RNDC) facility, and their operation is managed by a cloud provider. This entity is then responsible for tasks such as resource allocation amongst users, forecasting the need for any new hardware to meet the projected demand for processing power, data storage, or network capacity and the deployment and operation of these physical resources. The specifics of these resources is typically abstracted away from the user who does not have to care about any models or quantities.

The elasticity of resources is a key component of the cloud computing concept. Unlike when a user has purchased a physical server, for example, to run a particular workload on, if that workload has exceeded the processing capability originally allocated to it, in the cloud model, additional capacity can be allocated to that workload in near real time. In the case where a user has purchased the physical server themselves, they would instead incur a substantial capital outlay in order to either upgrade the server or add one or more to the system in order to provide enough processing power.

Over time, the offerings of cloud providers have become increasingly complex in order to provide their users with fewer reasons to venture outside of their ecosystem. Software orchestration and application development frameworks are now commonly offered by cloud providers, and these are becoming increasingly sophisticated in their own right, allowing cloud providers to differentiate the services they offer from their rivals by focusing on specific tools and features atop their platforms.

There are three main categories of cloud computing which we will explore in this chapter. Each of these categories is distinct from the others by its ownership and operation model, and many of the largest users of cloud computing today have explored all three options and may use them together.

17.2.1 Public Clouds

In public cloud computing, a cloud provider operates server, network, and application resources to allow multiple organisations to access and provide applications and services from these resources. An example of this type of public cloud provider is Amazon Web Services (AWS). These public cloud systems are operating globally today and are some of the largest direct customers of data centre facilities in the world. They support many of the household name applications of the present day, such as Netflix, and are increasingly the primary way in which new applications and services are developed and operated due to their flexibility, lack of requirement for upfront capital expenditure, and global availability.

Public clouds are the classic example of cloud computing. From the user perspective, there is some pool of resources existing at some location, and the user can purchase elastic access to them for an agreed period of time at an agreed rate. Applications which the user creates and operates atop this public cloud infrastructure can be used publicly or privately as the user requires at that point in time.

17.2.2 Private Clouds

An organisation may decide that they want the flexibility of cloud computing but without the need to rely on an external entity to operate the cloud, or they may want an external entity to operate the cloud but for that cloud to be devoted solely to their organisation. In these cases, a private cloud is the ideal solution as it combines the operational elasticity of the cloud with the other requirements of the organisation in terms of ownership or of resource sharing that a public cloud cannot achieve.

Private clouds are typically not of the same scale as public clouds, due to the economies of scale that become present in the public model. However, for a large organisation such as a multinational bank, private clouds can still be of substantial and even global scale. A private cloud may also use the same or similar services as provided by a public cloud to develop and operate some application workloads.

17.2.3 Hybrid Clouds

With the hybrid cloud model, an organisation uses both public and private cloud resources in order to achieve their technical and business goals. Data and applications may be shared between both of these clouds and use this integration to utilise the desired capabilities of both models concurrently.

Some hybrid cloud approaches are the result of a deliberate strategic choice by the user organisation to spread their bets across public and private clouds. Other examples of a hybrid cloud are due to a crossroads in regard to the spending which the organisation is willing to commit to their own data centre infrastructure going forward. A hybrid cloud may combine a public cloud or other resources within a data centre facility with racks of hardware which the customer themselves operates either within their on-premises data centre or at another data centre facility, still separate from the cloud.

A separate topic which is often intermingled with the hybrid cloud is multi cloud. In a multi cloud environment, the user utilises services from multiple cloud providers, typically from one or more public cloud providers. For example, one public cloud may offer preferable machine learning (ML) inferencing abilities whereas another may excel at data analysis. By utilising services from each of these public clouds according to their unique capabilities, the customer can benefit in terms of performance and cost.

17.2.4   Edge Cloud

The term edge cloud has been used in many discussions on the convergence of edge computing and cloud computing and has unfortunately in several instances taken on a life of its own. As this is a key phrase to understand, this section will briefly explain how infrastructure edge computing and cloud computing interoperate, whether one replaces the other, and how the term edge cloud can be used.

To be clear, infrastructure edge computing does not replace cloud computing. Cloud providers are likely to be some of the largest customers for an infrastructure edge computing network operator because they are able to utilise this infrastructure to operate their cloud services from, just as they can utilise RNDC facilities today. Due to the unique characteristics of the infrastructure edge computing network, the cloud provider may be able to support new services.

The presence of the infrastructure edge computing network alone does not make it a cloud. Data centre and network infrastructure by itself does not perform the required functions of any cloud computing system. They are instead a useful foundation for a cloud provider to extend an existing cloud to, or to build a new cloud presence on. If a cloud provider began designing their new cloud system by utilising infrastructure edge computing networks first, it could be referred to as an edge cloud; but this term has become quite loaded with alternate meanings as people have used it to describe a future in which edge computing replaces cloud computing, which, for the reasons that have been stated above, does not make sense as they are actually complementary technologies.

17.3   Cloud Computing at the Infrastructure Edge

17.3.1   Benefits

Cloud computing platforms are likely to support many of the other key use cases which have been described in this book for infrastructure edge computing, including 5G networks and distributed AI. All of these use cases require a set of hardware resources, software infrastructure, and the means to allow developers to make use of them, which the infrastructure edge computing network alone does not provide. By having a cloud provider as their direct customer, the infrastructure edge computing network operator can actually show these use cases operating from their network. Just as network interconnection is required to make the infrastructure edge computing network interesting from a performance and cost standpoint, the presence of a cloud provider is a significant enabler for users to utilise the infrastructure edge computing network at all as cloud systems are now so widely used.

By deploying their hardware and software systems to the infrastructure edge computing network, a cloud provider can utilise the unique characteristics of the infrastructure edge computing network to support new use cases such as those described in this book which require or can benefit from lower latencies between the user and application and a lower potential cost of data transportation. Cloud providers are constantly expanding their list of supported use cases and tools, and the use cases that have been described in this book look set to be key drivers of growth for the usage of cloud services. This necessitates deploying cloud infrastructure in locations along the resource gradient where they can support these vital use cases, which can often be the infrastructure edge computing network.

This can be especially valuable if an infrastructure edge computing network is deployed in a location which is a considerable distance away from a RNDC. The users in that area can be served primarily from the infrastructure edge computing network and the cloud system that is operating there, which not only allows the cloud provider to offer a better user experience, but in addition they may be able to offer new use cases and to offload use from a remote system instance.

17.3.2 Architecture

An example of how infrastructure edge computing can be used to support a cloud system is shown in the diagram in Figure 17.1. For this example, we have chosen the simplistic case of a public cloud which needs to extend its presence to the infrastructure edge computing network in order to support new use cases which rely on a low latency inferencing capability as part of a distributed AI application. As may be expected from this use case, the example is similar to that which was shown in Chapter 15 as the distributed AI functions are operating on top of the cloud infrastructure, hardware, and software.

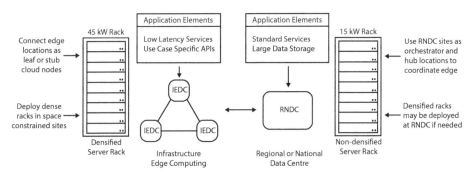

Figure 17.1 Example architecture for cloud computing using infrastructure edge.

As the diagram shows, in many ways, cloud computing itself is not a use case for infrastructure edge computing, as the cloud then requires its own use cases such as distributed AI, for which the customer of the cloud provider will pay. This can be thought of as a relationship with three layers, where the infrastructure edge computing network operator lays the foundation, the cloud infrastructure builds atop that, and the use case which the end user cares about is then deployed on top of both of them.

17.3.3 Considerations

The primary consideration for the deployment of cloud infrastructure at the infrastructure edge computing network is the feasibility of supporting the new use cases described in this section by using existing regional or national data centre infrastructure. If the cloud provider determines that they can utilise this existing infrastructure and still offer the service which they require, there is no compelling reason to utilise the infrastructure edge computing network until the needs of their use cases outstrip the capability of all of the existing infrastructure which they already have access to.

Another consideration is the revenue generation capability of the use cases which are uniquely enabled by the infrastructure edge computing model. The cost of deploying the cloud infrastructure required to support a use case will typically need to be paid back over a period of time in order for the use case to be considered financially successful by the cloud provider, before prompting any further spending on its development and operation. An exception to this is if a use case is considered to be strategically important and will not generate much direct revenue itself, but these are rare.

Lastly, some cloud providers operate at such a significant scale that they already design and operate some of their own data centre facilities. It may be the case that if a cloud provider sees a significant value in the infrastructure edge computing model that they seek to deploy their own network that competes with any other infrastructure edge computing network operators but which is dedicated to the use of that single cloud provider only. This is a key competitive threat to local edge operators.

17.4 Summary

In this chapter, we have explored how infrastructure edge computing can benefit cloud computing as well as some of the key use cases which can utilise this type of distributed cloud infrastructure. Cloud computing is in many ways not a use case for infrastructure edge computing as it is a part of the underlying infrastructure required to support many of the other use cases described in this book.

In the next chapter, we will explore some additional infrastructure edge computing use cases.

18

Other Infrastructure Edge Computing Use Cases

18.1   Overview

Some previous chapters in this book have explored many of the key use cases for infrastructure edge computing and the factors which make it a beneficial solution for those uses. However, these are far from the full list of realistic use cases which can be enabled or supported by infrastructure edge data centres (IEDCs) and their supporting network infrastructure. Other new and existing use cases are discussed in the context of infrastructure edge computing and may or may not be entirely suitable for its use.

Although this chapter does not go into the same level of detail for each of these use cases as earlier chapters did for other use cases, the same principles apply and the same serve transit fail (STF) metric can be used to determine the value of the use case to the infrastructure edge computing network operator as well as the ability of the operator to fully support those use cases, depending on network performance.

18.2   Near Premises Services

Today many organisations who utilise data centre services have two choices: They can deploy their equipment on their own premises, referred to as on-prem, where they are responsible for operating and maintaining that equipment as well as the facility in which it is operating. This may be a smaller scale version of a traditional data centre which the organisation has built or may be a large Information Technology (IT) room within one of their buildings which functions as a local data centre for that organisation's key users.

Understanding Infrastructure Edge Computing: Concepts, Technologies and Considerations,
First Edition. Alex Marcham.
© 2021 John Wiley & Sons Ltd. Published 2021 by John Wiley & Sons Ltd.

The other choice the organisation has is to deploy their equipment within a regional or national scale data centre or to use equivalent services to those which they could deploy themselves on their own hardware on a cloud service which then also operates from a regional or national scale data centre.

Where they are physically close to an IEDC, such as within 15 miles, this type of organisation has a third option: the near premises (or near-prem) deployment model. With this model, the equipment which would otherwise be deployed on-prem or in a regional or national scale data centre can instead be deployed within the IEDC. This approach seeks to combine the best of the on-prem deployment model with those of the data centre, such as:

1) Local-like performance
    a) By being located just a short distance away from the premises of an organisation, an IEDC facility can offer similar or equivalent performance to that of their on-premises data centre, from a network performance perspective.
2) Same data jurisdiction
    a) One challenge that some users of cloud services encounter is ensuring their data remains within a particular jurisdiction and, therefore, a certain physical location. This often applies to sensitive data such as healthcare information, financial data, and digital evidence for law enforcement. As cloud providers begin to segment a region into many smaller regions using more data centre facilities of every scale, ensuring that key data does not leave its original jurisdiction becomes possible.
3) Third party operating facility
    a) Some organisations do not have the onsite IT staff to maintain and operate local compute infrastructure like an on-premises data centre. Despite this, they may still want to own and operate their own equipment. Tasks such as troubleshooting and maintaining network connectivity or power delivery to equipment can be performed by the staff of an infrastructure edge computing network operator instead, which helps decrease the administrative burden on all of the IT staff of the organisation.

For organisations such as healthcare providers or stadium operators, there are logistical challenges with providing access to an on-prem location due to security requirements during events or medical protocols to prevent the spread of infectious disease. This limits the ability of these organisations to bring in external assistance to resolve issues with their technical infrastructure when it is deployed on-prem. These limits are not present when that equipment is instead located at an infrastructure edge data centre, so equipment maintenance can occur even when an on-prem site is locked down.

Examples of near premises services include:

1) Off-site system mirroring
   a) An organisation can use a nearby edge data centre as a new location to mirror their active IT systems to in real time. This real time backup of their operational state can then be used as a quick use backup should any issue occur with the local version. If performance is acceptable, the organisation may be able to operate these systems from the edge data centre while repairing any local equipment which has failed.
2) On-prem data centre expansion
   a) Leasing space within a nearby infrastructure edge data centre facility may be a more economical alternative than expanding the limited space available for an on-prem data centre for many organisations. The space available in such a data centre facility can be used to augment what is already available to the organisation on-prem either indefinitely or for some time, depending on the specific needs of that organisation.
3) Hybrid cloud operation
   a) By expanding their on-prem equipment footprint to an infrastructure edge data centre facility where public and private clouds may have a deployed presence, an organisation can use this data centre facility as an integration point between those systems and may even be able to interconnect directly to them at the edge facility.

The challenge for near premises services is offering a unique service providing which straddles the line between an on-premises data centre and the nearest regional or national data centre (RNDC) facility. One of the challenges in doing this is the densification of the customer equipment that is required in order to make the most effective use of all the limited space of an infrastructure edge data centre facility. Another is ensuring that the combination of performance and cost available with the infrastructure edge computing network is preferable to both alternatives for the specific use case. Although this may seem difficult, there are cases where services of this type are very useful for an organisation.

18.3 Video Surveillance

Whether in private or public spaces, video surveillance systems are in frequent use today across the world by private entities such as store owners and governments on both a national and local scale. The move from analogue to digital systems has made these systems more useful than ever before but has also introduced a challenge in regard to how the video surveillance data is used and stored.

In addition, modern video surveillance systems are a highly valuable data source to be used with a computer vision application which is using a distributed artificial intelligence (AI) architecture. Even a small surveillance system may include 10 or 20 cameras, each of which can be augmented with rapid machine intelligence to indicate to an operator the actors and actions that are being detected in the video steam, providing that surveillance system operator with the ability to act accordingly should any situation arise where the police or a security service need to be called, or another physical action must be taken in order to protect people or property within the range of the surveillance system.

Video surveillance systems then can be used as a data source for a distributed AI system which is performing intelligent video analytics (IVA) on the feeds from many cameras concurrently, and the operator of the surveillance system will not need to deploy significant local machine learning (ML) compute resources at each location where they have deployed cameras in order to support this use case, which allows them to provide more value to their customers than cameras alone are capable of. The benefits of lower latency and a lower cost of data transportation, however, vary depending on the specific use case and customer. Although in many cases an infrastructure edge data centre is well suited to supporting an IVA use case, there are other circumstances where it is not, where latency and data transportation costs are sufficient using a RNDC facility. However, low latency does mesh well with security needs as it can reduce the time required to notify a person or entity who is able to take a corrective action.

18.4 SD-WAN

Over the past decade, there has been substantial interest from enterprises in modernising their wide area network (WAN) connectivity options to ensure that they are getting the performance, cost, and security that they require from these services. As the speed and reliability of internet connectivity has improved, traditional WAN connectivity services have begun to look increasingly expensive in comparison. For an enterprise, a standard internet connection may cost an order of magnitude less than a leased line or Multiprotocol Label Switching (MPLS) circuit and, in many cases, may also actually be capable of higher peak throughput. With this in mind, it is no wonder that these services have come under increasing pressure from their users.

Software-defined WAN (SD-WAN) is a set of technologies which have been developed by many different vendors in order to address this challenge. These solutions take the form of creating an overlay network, an example of network virtualisation and abstraction, which utilises many of the physical networks which are available in order to determine the best set of paths to use between the source and destination of traffic based on various metrics that are important to the user such as the cost, performance, and reliability of the selected paths. This is highly valuable as it allows a customer such as a bank or other large enterprise who must have connectivity between many locations such as branch offices or automated teller machines (ATMs) to avoid being locked in to a single source for this connectivity, such as an MPLS provider, and being unable to utilise other technologies and providers which may offer a significant increase in performance and decrease in cost for equivalent services when combined with the capabilities of the SD-WAN solution to steer traffic around issues.

A user deploys an SD-WAN gateway device at each network location they wish to be a part of their SD-WAN network. These gateway devices are connected to all of the currently active WAN options at each location. They then proceed, by running performance and path reachability measurements between each other over these WAN connections, to establish an overlay network which seeks to make the optimal use of each underlying WAN connection. For example, the internet connection may be substantially cheaper for bulk data uploads to a public cloud, but for critical transaction traffic, the MPLS circuit may be more reliable. These types of traffic can be routed accordingly in order to meet their requirements onto the best WAN link, rerouting around issues as needed.

With infrastructure edge computing, SD-WAN services can be embedded throughout the network between the user and the destination of the user's traffic. Each infrastructure edge data centre facility in the network can be used as an endpoint and routing location for the SD-WAN network.

To be clear, SD-WAN has already seen widespread deployment and does not need infrastructure edge computing in order to function. However, the network and data centre infrastructure which infrastructure edge computing utilises can be used to improve the efficiency of an SD-WAN system and provide the SD-WAN operator with the capability to offer higher layer services such as security or content delivery services delivered from an infrastructure edge data centre through which their SD-WAN system has routed the traffic that is sent to and from the end users of the SD-WAN service.

18.5 Security Services

As the types of network-borne threats become more complex over time, there is a growing market for advanced security services which use compute resources to subject network traffic to a battery of analysis and testing against known threat signatures in order to identify and quarantine problem traffic before it is able to impact its intended target. Where more complex analysis and prediction of potential issues begins to utilise complex ML models which require significant amounts of compute power, a data centre then becomes an ideal environment in which to perform these determinations.

Although these tasks are not new and have been performed for many years in the form of network equipment such as intrusion detection systems (IDS) and intrusion prevention systems (IPS) which have been deployed at the security perimeters of enterprise networks in the form of appliances, an opportunity appears to exist in the market for offering these services without the need for such an appliance. In some cases, this is referred to using a term which originated from Gartner, known as secure access service edge (SASE). Although the adoption of these services remains to be seen, an infrastructure edge data centre facility, due to its proximity to its end users, can be a useful place to operate these services from in order to maintain a lower network latency for those same end users.

In many ways, the use cases in this category are an accessory to an SD-WAN solution. The ideal way to get any enterprise traffic routed through infrastructure edge data centres where these security services are operating is for an SD-WAN solution to do so, with these security services themselves being offered as value-added services to the customers of the SD-WAN solution either by SD-WAN operators directly or indirectly through any partnerships established with security services vendors.

18.6   Video Conferencing

Although it is in some ways similar to content delivery in that video is being distributed to a number of end user devices after it has been collated at a single point, video conferencing has its own unique challenges due to its need to operate in real time, using video and audio streams which cannot be cached ahead of time. In some cases, this use can be improved with infrastructure edge computing.

As the video content generated by a video conferencing application is created in real time and must meet the same performance requirements in regard to latency as a voice call for the system to be able to provide a satisfactory user experience, it cannot be effectively stored ahead of time, unlike the static content that is hosted on a content delivery network (CDN). When these systems experience periods of heavy usage such as during large virtual events or prolonged pandemic situations, the amount of traffic that they generate can be disruptive to other applications that need to use any bandwidth across WAN links.

The value of deploying a video conferencing system at the infrastructure edge depends on where the participants of the video conference are located. When all the participants are physically in an area adjacent to, within, or surrounding the infrastructure edge computing network, this topology can yield significant improvements in video conference performance and resilience to congestion across WAN networks, which does not occur when all conference participants are connected to the metropolitan area network (MAN) of the infrastructure edge computing network. As an infrastructure edge data centre can act as the location where video and audio data from all sources is collated before it is sent to conference participants, the benefits of locality in terms of latency, congestion avoidance, and resiliency apply.

In other scenarios, however, where a significant proportion of the conference participants are not physically local to the infrastructure edge computing network, there is minimal if any benefit to moving the conference server and its applications from the RNDCs where it currently resides out to one or more infrastructure edge data centres. In some cases, this may even worsen the performance of the conference depending on the state of the network infrastructure in use between the infrastructure edge data centre and all the other remote conference participants.

This makes video conferencing an interesting use case for infrastructure edge computing network operators and their customers. For it to be effective, a high degree of awareness of the locations of each conference participant is required to then allow the video conference provider to determine an ideal location for that conference to be hosted, which could then be an edge data centre facility.

18.7 Content Delivery

Due to the locality of an ideal infrastructure edge computing network to its users, the capability to distribute content from these facilities by deploying elements of a CDN within infrastructure edge data centres makes sense from a network topology perspective. The closer the location of content storage is to its users, the less cumulative network resources are required to move the content to those users when they request to view or download it. In theory this results in a better utilisation of network resources for the network operator and a better user experience for the CDN and its users.

Consider the following scenario to show the cumulative use of network resources by traffic as it is moved from its original location to its destination. Every point of aggregation in the network will be accumulating traffic, and if at one or more points this causes network congestion, the operator of that network has two choices: They can either allow all of that traffic to enter the network, which will cause congestion that could impact all other users, or they can slow the rate at which traffic from those congestion points enters the network, causing a poor user experience for those users.

However, in many cases, CDNs are already deployed in distributed locations across an area such as a city and do not need to be deployed at infrastructure edge data centres in order to function. Where they do not currently have a suitable deployment location and where one does exist in the form of an infrastructure edge data centre, this facility can be a viable option, if it is financially acceptable.

Where the CDN can benefit from deployment at the infrastructure edge is when considering not just the locality of the infrastructure edge data centre facilities to the end users of the CDN's content but also the ability of the infrastructure edge data centre to facilitate interconnection between the CDN and other networks which are present in or interconnected with the infrastructure edge network.

Some elements of this equation may change over time as CDN operators look to diversify their own service offerings and densify their equipment. In this case, a CDN operator may begin to look and operate more like a public or private cloud. Where the need to support services which require moving large volumes of data between a user and the data centre or low latency between user and application is required, the infrastructure edge computing network can provide the CDN with those benefits.

Reverse streaming services which rely on user-generated content present an interesting adjustment to the traditional CDN model of distributing static content from a store of content in the network to its viewers. In these applications which include live streams of gaming or other similar content that is generated by users in real time, the CDN model of caching a single piece of content which can then be distributed out to many users from a local location does not apply, and so the use of an edge data centre facility to receive, process, and distribute these live streams can make sense if the cost of data transport or the impact of any network congestion is too high to use the closest regional data centre.

18.8   Other Use Cases

Much like any solution or technology, it is easy to assume that every use case or application will be improved by infrastructure edge computing. However, this is lazy thinking; if something is good for everything, it is typically not very good at anything, and infrastructure edge computing has its own unique set of characteristics as have been described throughout this book which make it very well suited to supporting some use cases while concurrently making it difficult to justify for other uses.

The key factors which determine whether a use case or application is a good fit for infrastructure edge computing are listed here, and they match the main factors we have often discussed in this book:

1) Need for low latency connectivity
   a) The primary performance benefit which an infrastructure edge computing data centre facility can provide over a RNDC facility is, when access or last mile network interconnection is achieved, a lower latency between a user and their application. Use cases which do not need this performance benefit are, as has been shown throughout this book, difficult to justify in many cases.

2) Movement of large volumes of data
   a) Some use cases generate large amounts of data which may be expensive or difficult to move efficiently from the access or last mile network to the nearest RNDC facility. If a lower cost of data transportation or a decreased chance of network congestion are achievable using an infrastructure edge data centre facility instead, such a use case can make financial sense at these locations.

A few examples of use cases which, by applying these factors, we can see are not a good fit for infrastructure edge computing will help to make this point clear. Consider the following use cases:

1) Standard web browsing
   a) In the early ideation of what became the infrastructure edge computing model, one of the use cases which was often discussed was web browsing. However, the level of performance improvement which this model can contribute to this use case and the value of that improvement to its users is not appealing for standard web browsing as this is a use case which operates at far greater latencies than even telephone calls.
2) Bulk cold data storage
   a) Bulk cold or even warm data storage relies on tape or mechanical disc storage which takes up significant amounts of physical space and by its very nature does not need to be accessible at very low latencies. This makes these applications a very poor fit for an infrastructure edge data centre facility which is restricted in terms of its size.
3) Online commerce applications
   a) These use cases are very similar to the standard web browsing use case in that they just do not require the performance characteristics of infrastructure edge computing in order to function, and the addition of increased performance does not make any noticeable change to their user experience or their ability to be operationally viable.

As has been mentioned previously, infrastructure edge computing is not magic, and it is not a good fit for every use case. The key to utilising it effectively, like any technology, is in understanding which use cases make effective use of its positive attributes while negating or avoiding its negative ones.

18.9 Summary

Infrastructure edge computing is applicable to many use cases across a range of different user types and industry segments. The key, as with any technology, is distinguishing those which make the best use of infrastructure edge computing from those which do not. Some use cases such as those which are explored previously in their own chapters are significant enough to function as anchor use cases for the infrastructure edge; others, such as those described in this chapter, are often able to benefit from this new tier of data centre and network infrastructure but are unlikely to be first movers to it.

In the next chapter, we will explore an example infrastructure edge project from start to finish.

19

End to End

An Infrastructure Edge Project Example

19.1 Overview

In this chapter, we will assume the role of a customer of an infrastructure edge computing network operator and follow an example project through from initial ideation to deployment and operation.

The example project described in this chapter is intended to allow a customer to determine whether their solution, incorporating infrastructure edge computing, is capable of achieving its goals by using a limited scale and careful observation before attempting a real large scale commercial deployment.

Although this example cannot cover all of the intricacies inherent in such a project, it is intended to provide a set of steps which can be built upon by the customer of an infrastructure edge computing network operator to ensure that they have given proper consideration to the challenges of such a project with the goal of defining and achieving success for the project together, without falling foul of any of the unique characteristics of infrastructure edge computing and by utilising its advantages.

19.2 Defining Requirements

Like any significant project, the deployment of equipment to one or more data centre facilities should be based on a realistic and agreed upon set of requirements which accurately represent factors and concerns across key areas such as business needs in terms of time to market and the operational cost of the resulting solution,

Understanding Infrastructure Edge Computing: Concepts, Technologies and Considerations,
First Edition. Alex Marcham.
© 2021 John Wiley & Sons Ltd. Published 2021 by John Wiley & Sons Ltd.

technical needs in terms of the network and compute performance that are required to capitalise on the identified market opportunity, and any other considerations such as market perception, company strategy, and de-risking future deployments.

One of the key requirements to define during an infrastructure edge computing-related project is the acceptable serve transit fail (STF) metric for the targeted application or user base over time. This metric, as was described in Chapter 3, provides a means for the customer and the infrastructure edge computing network operator to determine the effectiveness of the infrastructure edge computing network for any specific set of use cases and customers which are of interest. The reader is encouraged to revisit the STF metric and create their own for an example project following the structure of this chapter.

During the requirements gathering phase of the project, a decision point will be reached at which it must be decided which equipment should be deployed at which locations and why. Bearing in mind that the locations in question will often include several infrastructure edge data centres (IEDCs) as well as any regional or national scale data centres that are able to satisfy the cost and performance needs for the project, the result may be a topology for the project where resources are spread across the gradient from infrastructure edge to core data centre. As described in Chapters 10 and 11, this is a reasonable choice in many projects which is capable of making use of the best elements of each of the pieces of infrastructure along that gradient, if they are designed and operated appropriately.

19.2.1 Deciding on a Use Case

Projects that have a commercial purpose typically begin with an identified market need, which itself is driven by a use case. However, it is common for a project to be formed and pushed forward with inadequate levels of specificity, leading to the need to revisit all of the initial assumptions behind it.

There are many questions to answer when deciding on the use case for a project that will have an infrastructure edge computing component. Although it is easy to rush over these when establishing projects, the majority of project failures can be traced back to not having solid answers to these:

1) Who is the target customer?
    a) Many projects begin with a class of customer in mind. Ideally over the course of the definition process, the target customer is narrowed down to one or more specific entities whom the idea can be tested against once it is far enough along.
2) What does this solve for them?
    a) As with the previous question, the level of specificity available in this answer will determine its value. Can the resulting solution solve a key business

challenge for an end customer, such as significantly lowering costs, improving their total addressable market, or enabling new opportunities that they did not have before? These are all examples of demonstrable business value that a customer can achieve by using the solution, which makes their usage of the solution much easier to justify at all levels.

3) Can they get this solution elsewhere?

   a) The answer to this question should inform us how differentiated the solution that we are proposing to create really is in the market. Although it is not possible to be completely sure that no closely competing service exists or will be launched during the lifespan of the project, some market research will tell us whether there is any obvious competitor already in existence.

Not all projects that will utilise resources on an infrastructure edge computing network will begin with a defined commercial aim; they may start as a proof of concept (PoC) or proof of technology (PoT) deployment where an organisation wishes to test out certain things within an infrastructure edge environment to validate their assumptions or gather data they can use to make decisions at later dates on the viability of using such infrastructure for commercial projects. Even so, projects organised as PoC or PoT efforts must still answer a few key questions to be most likely to succeed:

1) What is our hypothesis?

   a) Like any test, the project must begin with a point which is trying to be proved. An example is that by deploying an application in an IEDC facility, the latency experienced by the user population will be halved compared with the same application which is deployed in a regional or national data centre.

2) How are we testing our hypothesis?

   a) Once the hypothesis to be proven has been identified, the means to prove it must be defined and agreed. To continue our previous example, the hypothesis can be proven by deploying the same application in an IEDC and a regional or national data centre and then comparing the performance of both of these application instances for end users who are within the same user population.

3) Which factors will alter our outcome?

   a) This question is designed to identify the key variables which will materially change the outcome of the project. These are factors that will directly impact whether or not the hypothesis identified previously will be proven, or whether it can be proven. For our example scenario, some of these factors include the latency of the network between the user and each type of data centre and the processing time required.

As has been mentioned throughout this book, use cases which benefit greatly from a lower latency between the user and the application operating in a data centre, and from being able to lower the total cost of data transportation, are the best examples of use cases to select for this type of project.

For this example, we will choose a computer vision use case which uses data from a large array of cameras to improve the operating efficiency of a factory production line by controlling a robotic arm. Our hypothesis is that the reduction in latency provided by the infrastructure edge computing model will make this use case practical to operate without the use of any on-premises data centre facilities.

19.2.2 Determining Deployment Locations

As much of the value of the infrastructure edge computing model is derived by the physical location of network and data centre infrastructure, the choice of which edge data centre facility to use is vital in ensuring that the project will be able to properly test its hypothesis. Although none of the physical locations used in this example are real, they serve to illustrate the location determination process.

In the example for this chapter, we will choose locations for the project in the United States; to begin, in the greater Phoenix area located in the state of Arizona. This choice is completely arbitrary and has no special purpose beyond Phoenix being home to one of the largest cities in the United States and a significant established base of traditional large scale data centre facilities. These existing facilities will force us to evaluate the benefit of our infrastructure edge computing based solution in an area where there are already competing data centre facilities which are just as suitable for many potential use cases.

To illustrate the other type of area where an infrastructure edge computing project may be needed, we will select a more rural location which does not have an existing base of data centre facilities and so imposes a different set of considerations onto the project. In this case, we will use Brownsville, Texas. This city is fairly distant from the nearest large data centre hub and is the 131st largest city in the US, so despite its lack of digital infrastructure, it maintains a reasonable size and user population.

Our use case requires the lowest possible latency for our chosen user population. This requires us to select the edge data centre facility which has the most direct interconnection to the access network which that user population connects to, and which has the closest position physically to those users. This is a simple example where the physical and logical topology match up and allow us to easily pick the appropriate edge data centre facility. In a real world deployment, however, these two factors may be dispersed across multiple edge data centre facilities, which then complicates the facility selection.

For our first deployment scenario in the Phoenix area, we can see the selected edge data centre in the diagram in Figure 19.1. In this example, our use case requires

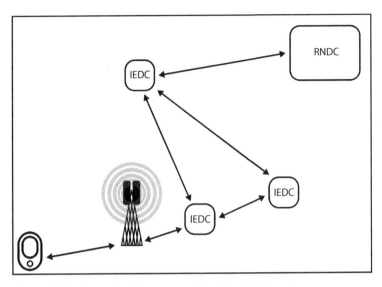

Figure 19.1 Example infrastructure locations in Phoenix.

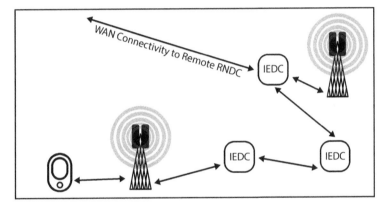

Figure 19.2 Example infrastructure locations in Brownsville.

sufficiently low latency that it makes sense to utilise the closest IEDC facility in this fashion as opposed to utilising the regional or national data centre in the area or an IEDC which is a greater distance away. As has been noted throughout this book, this is a minority of use cases, and this type of use case is being used in this section only to provide a simple example of a site selection process.

In the case of our second deployment scenario in Brownsville, we will use the same use case and a similar selection process. This selection process is even easier as there is not a large amount of data centre infrastructure within the city when compared to that of the previous deployment scenario (see Figure 19.2).

Both deployment scenarios show that, for our criteria, there is a single ideal edge data centre facility for deployment and a number of less optimal choices. If the project has a different set of needs such as the requirement to operate at the lowest possible cost of data transportation, the specific facility selected may vary. These requirements are ultimately all driven by the use case, and it is imperative that the customer has a keen understanding of the real performance and cost requirements of their application as well as of the proven capabilities of the infrastructure edge computing network itself.

19.2.3 Identifying Required Equipment

Once a specific location for your project has been established, the specific pieces of equipment or infrastructure that can be used can be identified. This is the stage at which the specifications of any server equipment to be deployed in the IEDC facility must be determined.

Although the use of the term infrastructure in this book has been focused on the physical network and data centre infrastructure, the term infrastructure can also apply to the operational software systems which are required by the resulting solution and should be considered during this phase of project planning. A project which seems to require minimal operational cost from a network and a hardware perspective may incur significant expense in terms of upfront or ongoing software costs whether for development, maintenance, or licencing purposes if any risk factors are not considered.

The ideal set of equipment for deployment to prove the project hypothesis is one which does not require unnecessary hardware or software expense; does not limit the performance of the solution to a point where it may be challenging to determine what the real cause of any performance, cost, or functionality issues with the solution may be; and which can be easily deployed without any issues.

With any project of this kind, there is a trade-off to be made in the time and expense spent preparing equipment for deployment, such as creating custom densified racks and software support for service reliability which utilises a multi-site redundancy model versus the value of the project. This will vary depending on the scale and importance of the project, but it is recommended that a minimum viable set of equipment and both hardware and software be created which is sufficient to prove the hypothesis of the project without investing additional time and expense. This allows the project to be financially justifiable while retaining its ability to prove out the core hypothesis, which is the optimal balance.

By limiting the amount of data which the machine learning (ML) models our project uses will be required to process in real time, we can control the scale of the server resources we will require for the project. In this case, we will utilise a single server with middling central processing unit (CPU) capabilities and multiple dedicated graphics processing unit (GPUs) for $5000.

19.2.4   Choosing an Infrastructure Edge Computing Network Operator

Where more than one infrastructure edge computing network is available in the selected area, the customer must then compare their options and choose the most appropriate operator to use in the same way as they do when choosing between any other set of two or more options such as between regional or national data centre operators, network providers, or any other multi-source scenario.

The number and type of access networks which interconnect with the infrastructure edge computing network of a particular operator is an important consideration when comparing multiple operators. If your use case targets a user base which utilises a particular access network for connectivity, but that access network is not interconnected at the infrastructure edge network you have chosen, it will be impossible for your solution to improve the user experience for those users until this is so.

Apart from this key factor, the choice between infrastructure edge computing network operators in an area comes down to the physical positions of their edge data centre facilities and the services and costs they are able to offer you using them. Cost comparisons are described further in this chapter.

19.2.5   Regional or National Data Centres

As has been described in previous chapters, applications are likely to utilise IEDC facilities as well as their regional or national counterparts concurrently for different parts of their application workloads, depending on the specific requirements of each workload component.

With our factory automation use case, we have split the training and inferencing functions between the regional or national data centre and the IEDC, respectively. The latter must operate as close to real time as possible, and the former needs access to large amounts of data. These factors make this functional split optimal and allow the application workload to perform well.

For our example, we will use the exact same server equipment between the IEDC and the regional data centre. Although in reality there is typically a large hardware difference between racks operating in the IEDC and the regional data centre, for the purposes of our example project, we will use the duplicate server GPUs for training and inferencing.

19.3   Success Criteria

Now that we have defined a use case and a deployment location, we can define specific success criteria to help us determine later whether or not the project hypothesis has been proved. Though success criteria can be defined earlier in the project, defining them after the hypothesis and after determining the use case, equipment, and deployment locations allows us to avoid redoing criteria once these factors have been fleshed out. For example, the use case, equipment, and deployment locations will all impact the number of users the project can realistically be expected to benefit.

Much of the work of defining success criteria builds on the definition and agreement of the project hypothesis. All of the success criteria should be specific goals which, if achieved, will prove out the validity of the project hypothesis over the duration of the project. In our example, a project duration of three months combined with three specific success criteria is sufficient to prove our hypothesis.

On metric which can be used as success criteria for the project is the STF metric, which was defined during the requirements stage.

For our example project, we will use the following three success criteria for evaluating the project:

1) STF metric
    a) For our example use case, which, as we discussed, can be tuned to account for the equipment capacity being used for the project, we will target an initial STF metric of 0.30, which we expect to grow to an STF metric of 0.50 over the project duration.
2) Application performance
    a) We expect that the inferencing application workload can be performed at the same level of speed for the same rack of equipment in the IEDC facility as it can in the regional or national data centre facility. Speed in this context refers only to the processing time, not the network latency, and can be used to show that the equipment is functioning correctly in the facility without any thermal issues.
3) Network latency
    a) We expect that network latency can be consistently at an average of 30 ms round trip from user to infrastructure edge application workload, with peaks that do not exceed 40 ms in order to support our use case. This is our most important criteria with this example project, as this latency is what enables the use case to operate.

Each of these success criteria should be tested regularly over the project duration to ensure that any exceptions are logged and understood so that the project success can be properly judged later on.

19.4 Comparing Costs

When comparing the costs of service offerings as potentially complex as network and data centre services across infrastructure edge, regional, and national locations, it is important to understand fully exactly what is being offered and how it is being priced before a relevant comparison can be made. In many cases, services may be bundled together in order to blend their true cost across a range of offerings, or individual operators may have different ideas of what constitutes the basic offering for a category such as data centre colocation services, which can then lead to an extensive and complicated comparison process between operators, which the customer must then undertake.

Consider comparing two infrastructure edge computing network operators. Both of them provide data centre and network services, but when it comes to the specifics, they may each define them differently, bundle them together in a different way, and price them differently as well. This book cannot capture how two or more infrastructure edge computing network operators may choose to price and bundle their services in enough detail to be useful, as these are evolving service offerings.

With that in mind, as in any purchasing decision, the customer is advised to communicate what they need from the infrastructure edge computing network operator as often as possible and to ensure that any translation of those needs into the terminology and product offerings of the operator does actually match what the customer is asking for. This is the only way to perform a true comparison of the service offerings from multiple operators – by abstracting as much as possible away from specific products and marketing terminology that these operators may opt to use in their product pricing.

In regard to costs, it is important to understand the reimbursement available to the customer that each operator will provide in the event of a breach of their service level agreement (SLA), as well as what constitutes such a breach. This and other potential hidden costs should be determined at a second round of pricing comparisons so that the full cost and value of the operator's services are understood. Also consider factors such as response times, equipment deployment costs, site access charges, and other fees.

Consider whether the IEDC and regional or national data centre facilities in question support any sort of project or demonstration pricing for short term use cases, which may then lead to longer term deployments. It may not be necessary to commit to an extended tenancy at full pricing with some operators, which helps to limit the cost of the project overall in comparison.

19.5 Alternative Options

In some cases, it simply does not make sense to deploy the solution at one or more IEDC facilities. This could be due to a variety of factors which will occur for many of the projects which consider utilising infrastructure edge computing as organisations get acclimated with the unique characteristics of the infrastructure edge computing model, which make it useful across a range of use cases while having the opposite effect on others. Like any technology, the infrastructure edge model can be used effectively or ineffectively by understanding its strengths and alternatives.

If the use case does not need a lower latency or a lower cost of data transportation than the existing data centre and network infrastructure are able to provide, or if an infrastructure edge computing network is not able to lower these factors to a level where they achieve a significant benefit, that specific use case in that specific area is not a good fit for the infrastructure edge and so should be deployed elsewhere. If the application workload can perform at a reduced level from a regional or national data centre, then that is an option; and if not, the workload may have to be abandoned.

Another example is if an existing on-premises data centre exists, or there is sufficient reason to build one compared to utilising an infrastructure edge computing network such as latency requirements that even a nearby IEDC facility cannot meet, then that alternative option should be utilised instead as it is the best fit for that particular use case in that particular location.

If these or any other alternative options are discovered to be preferable during the project, that is a good thing. The ultimate goal of any project of this type should be to make a solution which allows a given application workload to operate optimally in terms of cost, performance, and functionality. It is rarely a good idea to be dead set on using a particular technology that is not essential to the project as this can easily obscure the goal of an optimal application workload and lead to some poor choices.

19.6   Initial Deployment

The initial deployment of equipment and application workloads for the project will be similar to that of many other projects or commercial deployments. Depending on how the operators chosen by the customer allow equipment to be installed, the customer may have several options in this regard, and whichever one is chosen is immaterial to the project overall as long as the success criteria are not at all specific about the timeframe or method of the equipment and application workload deployment.

If any alterations to the application workload to support the infrastructure edge model were made, such as to support the functional split for our factory automation use case between inferencing that occurs at the infrastructure edge and ML model training that occurs at the regional or national data centre, the time of initial deployment may expose teething issues with the new software which can be addressed in many cases before the official start timer for the project has begun. A customer in this position should typically delay the start timer for the project, or at least for the operation part, until they can be certain that any issues are not due to their own software or hardware concerns. Where problems are being created by the infrastructure edge computing network, however, these can and should be determined, logged, and, if possible, corrected during the next operational phase.

The customer may seek to use the equipment deployment services of the operator in order to tell whether or not these services would support a wide-scale deployment of the use case should the project be a success. In this case, the customer may even wish to add the cost and speed of such services as well as other parameters such as installation proficiency to the project success criteria.

Once the equipment has been deployed and the application workload has begun operation, the project can move forward into the ongoing operation phase for the next portion of the project.

19.7 Ongoing Operation

Once the solution, which is the full combination of services from the infrastructure edge computing network and regional or national data centre operators combined with the hardware and software chosen or created by the customer, has been deployed, it can begin operation. In terms of time, this phase should be the majority of the project and given sufficient runtime to capture variations of the performance of the solution over time to expose key issues such as transient network congestion.

It is important that to truly determine its performance, the solution should be left to operate with the same level of care and feeding as it would during commercial operation as often as possible. In measuring the performance and functionality of the solution, it should be a priority to avoid the need to interfere in its operation so that the results of the project are as representative as possible of the true capabilities of the solution. If it is possible to keep the solution performing adequately only, for example, by applying constant manual effort, then the solution is unlikely to be commercially viable.

The STF metric established during the requirements phase of the project will provide an ongoing guide by which to measure the success of the project alongside the performance requirements which were defined as part of the success criteria. There are many ways to measure the latency of the infrastructure edge computing network, for example, so this section cannot elaborate on all of the possible methods. However, what is important is that these measurements are taken at a clear and consistent set of intervals which allow the performance of the solution to be accurately shown.

During the ongoing operation phase, the solution should be treated as much as possible as if it were already a commercial service. This is important so that it is judged with the right set of expectations.

19.7.1 SLA Breaches

During the ongoing operation phase of the project, one or more SLA breaches may occur. Where they do occur, it is important for the customer to highlight the failure to the infrastructure edge computing network operator, or to any other operator whom they believe is responsible for the issue, so that it can be remediated using the operator's standard processes wherever possible. Ideally the standard processes are used to provide an experience for the customer that is representative of the real commercial operation of the solution as opposed to relying on any special service exceptions.

The definition of what constitutes an SLA breach will depend on exactly what the documentation provided by the infrastructure edge computing operator and signed by the customer determines a breach to be. Note that the definition of an SLA breach is unlikely to map precisely on to any of the success criteria defined for the project by the customer. A breach of an SLA may cause one or more success criteria to fail for a period of time, but the reverse is not true in the majority of real cases.

In this example, for the sake of simplicity, we will not simulate any SLA breaches during the life span of the project. However, especially with new network and data centre infrastructure, breaches can be a fact of life, and understanding the value of any available protections will ensure that customers can properly account for the expected performance and cost of the solution on a commercial basis.

19.8 Project Conclusion

Once a sufficient amount of time has elapsed, which in our example is three months, the project can be concluded and it can be determined whether or not it was a success. At this point the project will move to a post-mortem stage, where the performance of the solution during the ongoing operation phase of the project can be analysed and then compared against the success criteria for evaluation.

Determining how long the project should run before being concluded may seem challenging. It can turn into an ongoing issue if a timescale is not defined and kept to for the project while it is in its early stages. However, if an unexpected development occurs, such as an SLA issue which sets back project progress for a month, it may be worthwhile extending the end date of the project to account for this delay. If difficult issues keep occurring, it may be challenging to attain the desired period of uninterrupted operation time, so it is sensible to have a maximum total project time in mind as well.

For this example project, we could use a desired period of uninterrupted operation time of three months combined with a total project time of six months, which includes the period of the project before initial deployment and any time to accommodate disruptive issues during ongoing operation.

It is unlikely that every success criterion will be hit for the duration of the project if the project is really seeking to prove a difficult use case can be supported effectively. Much of the point of using an emerging technology such as infrastructure edge computing is to push the limits of what is really possible and operationally viable. That being said, it is up to the customer to determine the priority of their identified success criteria and what any acceptable deviations from these criteria may be.

In this example, the project success criteria, some example results, and criteria priority are here:

1) STF metric
   a) In our example, we underestimated the amount of processing power required for a given number of cameras for our factory automation use case, which led to a lower than desired STF metric. However, we understand the issue, and it can be corrected by increasing the inferencing capability of the server in the edge data centre facility.
   b) Priority: Medium, accepting that we made a mistake in designing our server size.
2) Application performance
   a) Besides our mistake on the amount of processing power that was required in the edge data centre facility to perform inferencing, we did not encounter any examples of application performance being below par. Specifically for our success criteria, the performance of our application workload was not restricted by the edge data centre.
   b) Priority: Medium, as this is really table stakes for the use of the edge data centre.
3) Network latency
   a) Outside of a few isolated incidents of network congestion which were identified and examined by the infrastructure edge computing network operator, in our example, the network latency held to our performance requirements, which allows the use case to be supported as long as any congestion issues are avoided in the future.
   b) Priority: Highest, as acceptable network latency is what enables the use case.

If the project was a success, the exceptions to these criteria should be noted so that they can be fully understood and accounted for in the event that the solution later becomes commercially deployed. It is just as important to create an account of the successes of the project as well to serve as a point of measurement for the project as well as for any comparison with any future projects which occur.

If, however, the project was a failure, the same process should be followed where all failures and all successes are recorded and stored so that they can be reviewed at a later date. Despite any upset or disappointment, it is important that all of the information regarding the project be collected into a thorough test report so that it can be properly understood and communicated across many teams.

In our example, the project can be considered a success with the provision that for real commercial deployment, the solution must have a better understanding of the server resources that are needed at each location and that the network latency must be fully understood and controlled beforehand.

In either case, the customer may seek to move to commercial production for the solution, perform another project, or postpone or abandon the solution entirely. The success or failure of the project does not necessarily determine which of these paths are chosen, as the specific reasons for success and failure must be determined and fully analysed before any significant next step can be chosen.

Any challenging project is unlikely to be a complete success. Whether this is due to issues with parts of the solution that the customer is responsible for, whether it is due to one of more of the services which are provided by the operators, or a misunderstanding of how these may be applied, there are likely to be issues which occur during the project which require engineering effort in order to fix. It is then up to the customer to determine the value of these activities, but being aware that none of the technologies in use are likely to be perfect will help set a realistic set of expectations from the start.

19.9 Summary

This chapter explored an example customer project using an infrastructure edge computing network from start to finish. Some of the key considerations for the customer have been highlighted, such as the importance of measuring the project against a set of defined success criteria. In many ways, such a project is not considerably different from other technology and use case evaluation projects, if it is approached with an understanding of the unique characteristics of infrastructure edge computing.

In the next chapter, we will explore some key predictions about the future of infrastructure edge computing and the key factors which will affect its ability to realise its potential on a global scale.

20

The Future of Infrastructure Edge Computing

20.1 Overview

As others have said, it is difficult to make predictions, especially about the future. Despite that very notable challenge, this chapter will still attempt to predict how infrastructure edge computing will evolve over the next 10 years at a broad level based on the content of all of the previous chapters.

20.2 Today and Tomorrow

Infrastructure edge computing deployment is in its nascent stages, and over the next year or so, the industry landscape around the technology will develop as companies from across the wider internet infrastructure ecosystem formulate and continue to execute on their strategies for edge computing.

The application workloads which will utilise infrastructure edge computing to create new and unique value across the ecosystem must begin to emerge in the near future to maintain the momentum and expectations that currently exist around infrastructure edge computing. These use cases must be of sufficiently unique value that they are able to justify the excitement that currently exists around the infrastructure edge computing model. If they are not, it is likely that the technology will fall into the trap of appearing to have overpromised on its capabilities, leading to disillusionment which is likely to inflict a lot of damage on the willingness of the industry in general to maintain significant interest.

Understanding Infrastructure Edge Computing: Concepts, Technologies and Considerations,
First Edition. Alex Marcham.
© 2021 John Wiley & Sons Ltd. Published 2021 by John Wiley & Sons Ltd.

20.3 The Next Five Years

The deployment and evolution of infrastructure edge computing will take place in tandem with the worldwide deployment of fifth generation (5G) networks. During this period, it is likely that some but not all networks will utilise infrastructure edge computing for their network infrastructure as well as for new services that benefit from lower latencies. This does not mean that these networks will necessarily be reliant upon infrastructure edge computing or that their services will operate from these locations. It will be a useful proof point of the utility of the infrastructure edge computing model for this use case.

However, the need for infrastructure edge computing to have commercially proven itself will be a priority for each infrastructure edge computing network operator during this time. Especially once 5G networks are deployed, if the use cases which make optimal use of infrastructure edge resources remain nascent, the value of this entire tier of internet infrastructure will remain limited as will its deployment. This should not be surprising; a technology for technology's sake is difficult to justify a significant financial outlay to design, deploy, and operate, especially on the scale of hundreds of sites.

20.4 The Next 10 Years

If the use cases which are able to use infrastructure edge computing to create new and unique value are highly commercially viable, to the extent that they are capable of justifying the cost of the data centre and network infrastructure that is required to realise the model on a widespread basis, it is likely that infrastructure edge computing deployment will continue to proliferate across the world.

If, however, these use cases do not emerge, it is likely that the infrastructure edge computing model will see only limited deployment and will not fulfil its potential for wide-scale transformative change.

20.5 Summary

In this chapter, we have taken a brief look across three prediction timeframes for the success of the infrastructure edge computing model. The success of the model relies on its use cases, particularly those which can generate new and unique value across the ecosystem. To that end, this is the key factor which will determine whether or not the infrastructure edge computing model is a success.

21

Conclusion

Infrastructure edge computing represents a continuation of the progressive evolution of our internet infrastructure, which has continued to spread further out from its original centralised locations and has become more local to its users over time. Although it has unique characteristics and the ability to enable a range of new use cases which require lower latencies between user and application and a lower cost of data transportation, it is in many ways a very similar entity to current technologies.

However, the success of this new technology is not guaranteed. This depends on the viability and commercial success of use cases which are able to use infrastructure edge computing to generate unique value. If these use cases fail, so too will the infrastructure edge computing model insofar as creating an entirely new tier of internet infrastructure that is deployed on a global basis and which is utilised to create significant sources of new and unique value across the entire internet ecosystem.

Thank you to the reader for joining me on this journey through an exciting and promising technology which carries with it a lot of potential, as well as a lot of things to prove over the next few years of its existence as it faces widespread deployment and the need to prove its commercial value. As with all new technologies, it is easy to get caught up in all of the excitement and promises of transformative change that surround infrastructure edge computing. As an industry, let us think big and act practical.

Understanding Infrastructure Edge Computing: Concepts, Technologies and Considerations,
First Edition. Alex Marcham.
© 2021 John Wiley & Sons Ltd. Published 2021 by John Wiley & Sons Ltd.

Appendix A

Acronyms and Abbreviations

3GPP	3rd Generation Partnership Project
4G	Fourth Generation
5G	Fifth Generation
5G CN	5G Core Network
5G NR	5G New Radio
AI	Artificial Intelligence
ANN	Artificial Neural Network (see Chapter 15)
API	Application Programming Interface
AR	Augmented Reality
ARM	Advanced RISC Machine
ARP	Address Resolution Protocol
ARPANET	Advanced Research Projects Agency Network
ARQ	Automatic Repeat Query
AS	Autonomous System
ATM	Automated Teller Machine
AWS	Amazon Web Services
BBS	Bulletin Board System
BGP	Border Gateway Protocol
BGP4	Border Gateway Protocol version 4
CAPEX	Capital Expenditure
CDN	Content Delivery Network
CIO	Chief Information Officer
CISC	Complex Instruction Set Computer
CMTS	Cable Modem Termination System
CPU	Central Processing Unit

Understanding Infrastructure Edge Computing: Concepts, Technologies and Considerations,
First Edition. Alex Marcham.
© 2021 John Wiley & Sons Ltd. Published 2021 by John Wiley & Sons Ltd.

CSO	Chief Security Officer
CU	Centralised Unit
DCI	Data Centre Interconnect
DL	Deep Learning
DOCSIS	Data Over Cable Service Interface Specification
DPU	Data Processing Unit
DSL	Digital Subscriber Line
DSP	Digital Signal Processor
DU	Distributed Unit
ECC	Elliptic Curve Cryptography
EGP	Exterior Gateway Protocol
ETSI	European Telecommunications Standards Institute
EVPN	Ethernet Virtual Private Network
EX	Edge Exchange
EXP	Edge Exchange Point
FPGA	Field Programmable Gate Array
FWA	Fixed Wireless Access
Gbps	Gigabits Per Second
GPGPU	General Purpose Graphics Processing Unit
GPU	Graphics Processing Unit
HTTP	Hypertext Transfer Protocol
IaaS	Infrastructure as a Service
ICMP	Internet Control Message Protocol
IDS	Intrusion Detection System
IEDC	Infrastructure Edge Data Centre
IEEE	Institute of Electrical and Electronics Engineers
IGP	Interior Gateway Protocol
IIoT	Industrial Internet of Things
IoT	Internet of Things
IP	Internet Protocol
IPv4	Internet Protocol version 4
IPv6	Internet Protocol version 6
IPC	Instructions Per Clock
IPS	Intrusion Prevention System
IR	Infrared
IS-IS	Intermediate System to Intermediate System
ISP	Internet Service Provider
IT	Information Technology
IVA	Intelligent Video Analytics
IX	Internet Exchange
IXP	Internet Exchange Point

LAN	Local Area Network
LOA	Letter of Agreement
LOI	Letter of Intent
LOU	Letter of Understanding
LTE	Long-Term Evolution
MAC	Medium Access Control
MAN	Metropolitan Area Network
Mbps	Megabits Per Second
MEC	Multi-access Edge Computing
MED	Multi Exit Discriminator
ML	Machine Learning
MMDC	Micro Modular Data Centre
MMR	Meet Me Room
MPLS	Multiprotocol Label Switching
NAT	Network Address Translation
NFS	Network File System
NIC	Network Interface Card
NLP	Natural Language Processing
NOC	Network Operations Centre
OCP	Open Compute Project
OOB	Out of Band
OPEX	Operational Expenditure
O-RAN	Open Radio Access Network
OS	Operating System
OSI	Open Systems Interconnection
OSPF	Open Shortest Path First
PCIe	Peripheral Component Interconnect Express
PDU	Power Distribution Unit
PGW	Packet Gateway
PNG	Portable Network Graphics
PoC	Proof of Concept
PoT	Proof of Technology
PSA	Packet Session Anchor
PUE	Power Usage Effectiveness
QoE	Quality of Experience
QoS	Quality of Service
RAM	Random Access Memory
RAN	Radio Access Network
RF	Radio Frequency
RIP	Routing Information Protocol
RISC	Reduced Instruction Set Computer

RNDC	Regional or National Data Centre
RRU	Remote Radio Unit
RSA	Rivest-Shamir-Adleman
RU	Rack Unit
SaaS	Software as a Service
SAN	Storage Area Network
SASE	Secure Access Service Edge
SCTP	Stream Control Transmission Protocol
SD-WAN	Software Defined Wide Area Network
SGW	Serving Gateway
SLA	Service Level Agreement
SPF	Shortest Path First
STF	Serve Transit Fail
STP	Spanning Tree Protocol
Tbps	Terabits Per Second
TCP	Transmission Control Protocol
ToR	Top of Rack
TPU	Tensor Processing Unit
TTL	Time to Live
UAV	Unmanned Aerial Vehicle
UDP	User Datagram Protocol
UPF	User Plane Function
UPS	Uninterruptible Power Supply
V2I	Vehicle to Infrastructure
V2V	Vehicle to Vehicle
V2X	Vehicle to Everything
VLAN	Virtual Local Area Network
VM	Virtual Machine
VoIP	Voice over Internet Protocol
VRF	Virtual Routing and Forwarding
VXLAN	Virtual Extensible Local Area Network
WAN	Wide Area Network

Index

Understanding Infrastructure Edge Computing: Concepts, Technologies and Considerations,
First Edition. Alex Marcham.
© 2021 John Wiley & Sons Ltd. Published 2021 by John Wiley & Sons Ltd.